My
HTC One®

Craig James Johnston
Guy Hart-Davis

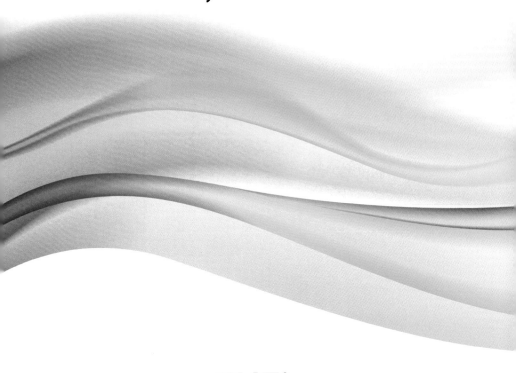

800 East 96th Street,
Indianapolis, Indiana 46240 USA

My HTC One®

Copyright © 2014 by Pearson Education, Inc.

ISBN-13: 978-0-7897-5262-8

ISBN-10: 0-7897-5262-X

Library of Congress Control Number: 2013953112

Printed in the United States of America

First Printing: December 2013

Trademarks

Warning and Disclaimer

Special Sales

For information about buying this title in bulk quantities, or for special sales opportunities (which may include electronic versions; custom cover designs; and content particular to your business, training goals, marketing focus, or branding interests), please contact our corporate sales department at corpsales@pearsoned.com or (800) 382-3419.

For governement sales inquiries, please contact governmentsales@ pearsoned.com.

For questions about sales outside the U.S., please contact international@pearsoned.com.

Editor-in-Chief
Greg Wiegand

Acquisitions Editor
Michelle Newcomb

Development Editor
Brandon Cackowski-Schnell

Managing Editor
Sandra Schroeder

Project Editor
Mandie Frank

Copy Editor
Barbara Hacha

Indexer
Erika Millen

Proofreader
Sarah Kearns

Technical Editor
Christian Kenyeres

Editorial Assistant
Cindy Teeters

Designer
Mark Shirar

Compositor
Mary Sudul

Contents at a Glance

Online Element: Tracking Your Tasks

Online Element: Use Your HTC One as a Remote Control

Table of Contents

2 Customizing Your HTC One   87

8 Phone and Instant Messaging   265

9 Audio, Video, Photos, and Movies   293

Online Element: Use Your HTC One as a Remote Control

About the Authors

Craig James Johnston has been involved with technology since his high school days at Glenwood High in Durban, South Africa, when his school was given some Apple Europluses. From that moment, technology captivated him, and he has owned, supported, evangelized, and written about it.

Craig has been involved in designing and supporting large-scale enterprise networks with integrated email and directory services since 1989. He has held many IT-related positions in his career, ranging from sales support engineer to mobile architect for a 40,000-smartphone infrastructure at a large bank.

In addition to designing and supporting mobile computing environments, Craig co-hosts the Crackberry.com podcast and guest hosts on other podcasts, including iPhone and iPad Live podcasts. You can see Craig's previously published work in his book *Professional BlackBerry*, and in many books in the *My* series, covering devices made by BlackBerry, Palm, Google, Samsung, HTC, and Motorola.

Craig also enjoys high-horsepower, high-speed vehicles and tries very hard to keep to the speed limit while driving them.

Originally from Durban, South Africa, Craig has lived in the United Kingdom, the San Francisco Bay Area, and New Jersey, where he now lives with his wife, Karen, and a couple of cats.

Craig would love to hear from you. Feel free to contact Craig about your experiences with *My HTC One* at http://www.CraigsBooks.info.

All comments, suggestions, and feedback are welcome, including positive and negative.

Guy Hart-Davis is the author of various computer books, including *My Samsung Galaxy Note II, Kindle Fire Geekery,* and *How to Do Everything: Samsung Galaxy Tab.*

Dedication

"Their eyes scaled with ignorance, bigotry and greed, the Spanish erased a previous heritage of mankind when they arrived in Mexico. In doing so they deprived the future of any detailed knowledge concerning the brilliant and remarkable civilizations which once flourished in Central America."

—*Graham Hancock*

Acknowledgments

We would like to express our deepest gratitude to the following people on the *My HTC One* team who all worked extremely hard on this book:

- Michelle Newcomb, acquisitions editor, who worked with us to give this project an edge

- Christian Kenyeres, our technical editor, who double-checked our writing to ensure the technical accuracy of this book

- Brandon Cackowski-Schnell, our developmental editor, who developed the manuscript skillfully

- Barbara Hacha, who copy edited the manuscript with a light touch

- Mandie Frank, who kept the project rolling and on schedule

- Mary Sudul, who laid out the book and made it look great

We Want to Hear from You!

As the reader of this book, *you* are our most important critic and commentator. We value your opinion and want to know what we're doing right, what we could do better, what areas you'd like to see us publish in, and any other words of wisdom you're willing to pass our way.

We welcome your comments. You can email or write to let us know what you did or didn't like about this book—as well as what we can do to make our books better.

Please note that we cannot help you with technical problems related to the topic of this book.

When you write, please be sure to include this book's title and author as well as your name and email address. We will carefully review your comments and share them with the author and editors who worked on the book.

Email: feedback@quepublishing.com

Mail: Que Publishing
           ATTN: Reader Feedback
           800 East 96th Street
           Indianapolis, IN 46240 USA

Reader Services

Visit our website and register this book at quepublishing.com/register for convenient access to any updates, downloads, or errata that might be available for this book.

In this chapter, you become familiar with the external features of the HTC One and the basics of getting started with the HTC version of the Android operating system. Topics include the following:

→ Your HTC One's external features
→ Fundamentals of Android 4.1.2 (Jelly Bean) and HTC Sense 5.0
→ First-time setup
→ Synchronization software

Getting to Know Your HTC One

Let's start by getting to know more about your HTC One by examining the external features, device features, and how Google's operating system, Android 4.1.2 (or Jelly Bean) and HTC Sense, works.

One important thing to remember about versions of the Google Android operating system is that Google releases a new version of Android and makes it available to its Nexus line of smartphones and tablets. That version of Android is then taken by different manufacturers and modified (sometimes quite extensively) to differentiate their model of Android smartphone or tablet. Your HTC One is running HTC's version of Android, which is Android 4.1.2 plus HTC Sense 5.0.

Your HTC One's External Features

Becoming familiar with the external features of your HTC One is a good place to start because you will be using them often. This chapter also covers some of the technical specifications of your HTC One, including the touchscreen and camera.

Front

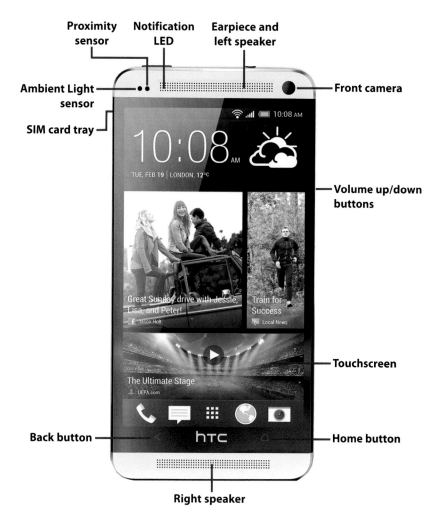

Proximity sensor

Notification LED

Earpiece and left speaker

Ambient Light sensor

SIM card tray

Front camera

Volume up/down buttons

Touchscreen

Back button

Home button

Right speaker

Ambient Light sensor—Adjusts the brightness of the screen based on the brightness of the ambient light.

Proximity sensor—Detects when you lift your HTC One to your ear to talk on a call. When it detects this, it turns off the screen and disables touch to prevent accidental actions.

SIM card tray—The SIM card tray is located on the left side of your HTC One. Use the included SIM card tray ejection tool to eject the tray and insert or replace the Micro-SIM card.

Earpiece and left speaker—Hold to your ear when on a phone call. This area also houses the left speaker when playing audio or video.

Notification LED—Positioned on the bottom row of holes, the third hole in, the Notification LED indicates that you have a pending notification (like new SMS, new email, new Facebook update) by flashing green. It also indicates when your HTC One is connected to a power source (computer or power adapter) and the battery is fully charged by showing as solid green. It flashes orange when the battery is very low, and is solid orange when the battery is being charged.

Front camera—2.1 megapixel front-facing camera with a wide angle lens that you can use for video chat, taking self-portraits, and even unlocking your HTC One using your face.

Touchscreen—The HTC One has a 4.7-inch, 1080×1920 pixel Super Liquid Crystal Display (LCD) 3 screen that incorporates capacitive multitouch and is covered by Corning Gorilla Glass 2.

Back button—Touch to go back one screen when using an application or menu. This button is touch sensitive and does not require pressure.

Home button—Touch to go to the Home screen. The application that you are using continues to run in the background. This button is touch sensitive and does not require pressure.

Right speaker—This is the right speaker that is used when playing audio or video.

Volume up/down buttons—Located on the right side of your HTC One, these buttons control the audio volume on calls and while playing audio and video.

Back

LED camera flash—Illuminates the area when taking photos or recording video. It has five levels of brightness that are automatically selected based on distance to the people or objects in the frame.

Rear camera—4-megapixel rear-facing camera with a 28mm lens and an aperture of F2.0.

Rear microphone—This microphone works in conjunction with the microphone on the bottom of your HTC One while on phone calls to cancel out any background noise. This microphone is also used when recording videos.

Top

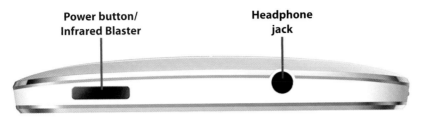

**Power button/
Infrared Blaster**

**Headphone
jack**

Headphone jack—This is a standard 3.5 mm headphone jack that can be used to plug in headphones and earbuds.

Power button/Infra Red Blaster—Press once to wake your HTC One. While it is still locked, press and hold for six seconds to restart your HTC One. When your HTC One is unlocked, pressing and holding the power button for two seconds reveals a menu of choices. The choices enable you to put your HTC One into airplane mode (all radios off), power off your HTC One, restart it, or enable Kid mode. When in Kid mode, your HTC One will allow access only to age-appropriate games and more. We cover setting up Kid Mode in Chapter 2, "Customizing Your HTC One." The power button is also an Infrared Blaster, which means that your HTC One can be used as a TV remote control. We cover more on how that works in a later chapter.

Bottom

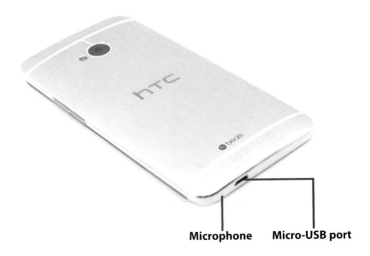

Microphone   **Micro-USB port**

Micro-USB port—The micro-USB 2.0 Port with Mobile High Definition Video Link (MHL) allows you to charge your HTC One and synchronize media and other files to your computer. It also allows you to plug your HTC One directly into a High Definition Multimedia Interface (HDMI) port on your A/V Receiver or TV to watch movies or other content. This requires a special micro-USB to HDMI cable.

Microphone—This microphone is used when you are on the phone.

Other Sensors and Radios

Your HTC One includes a Wi-Fi (WLAN) radio that supports 802.11 a/ac/b/g/n for connecting to your home or office networks or to Wi-Fi hotspots in airports, coffee shops, and even on planes. In addition, it has a Bluetooth V4.0 radio with aptX enabled for connecting Bluetooth accessories, such as headsets. The aptX technology provides a superior audio quality when playing audio using Bluetooth. Your HTC One also includes a Near Field Communications (NFC) radio for mobile payments and swapping information between other Android devices, and a Global Positioning System (GPS) radio for detecting your exact location on planet earth. On the sensor front, it has an accelerometer for detecting movement and a gyroscope for assisting with movement detection and gaming.

First-Time Setup

Before setting up your new HTC One, it is advisable (but not required) that you have a Google account. This is because your HTC One running Android is tightly integrated into Google and enables you to store your content in the Google cloud, including any books and music you buy or movies you rent. If you do not already have a Google account, head to https://accounts.google.com on your desktop computer and sign up for one.

You Need Wi-Fi or Cellular Data to Set Up Your HTC One

You need to be able to connect to a Wi-Fi network or cellular data network when you set up your HTC One.

Set Up Your HTC One Before Taking It Out of the Box

HTC allows you to pre-setup your HTC One using its website (http://start.htc-sense.com). Visit the website, and either create a new HTC account for yourself or log in to an existing HTC account. When you are logged in, click Get Started, and you will be taken through a series of steps to choose your HTC phone model. Then you can use pre-setup for many settings and features, including news feeds you want to subscribe to, apps you want to preinstall, sounds and ringtones you want to include or upload, web browser bookmarks to prepopulate, wallpapers, and lock screen configurations. You will also be able to use pre-setup to specify accounts you want on your HTC One, such as Facebook, Twitter, email, and more. After this setup is complete, it will be available to use when you reach step 8 in the following steps, or if your HTC One is already set up, the new setup or changes to the setup will be automatically sent to your HTC One to be applied.

**Click to get
started**

**Pre-setup every aspect
of your HTC One**

1. Touch and hold the Power button until you see the animation start playing.

2. Swipe the lock icon up to start the setup process.

3. Touch to change your region and language if needed.

4. Touch Start to continue with the setup.

5. Touch the Wi-Fi network you want to connect to; if you don't want to connect to a Wi-Fi network, touch Next and skip to step 8.

6. Type in the Wi-Fi network password.

7. Touch Connect.

Touch to skip Wi-Fi setup and continue using cellular data

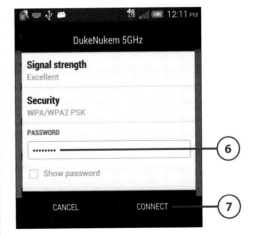

8. Touch to choose Set Up from Scratch.

9. Touch Next.

How Can I Transfer My Old Settings and Content?

If you choose to restore, transfer, or import, you will be able to transfer content and settings from either an older HTC Android smartphone, another Android smartphone running Android version 2.3 (Gingerbread) or newer, an Apple iPhone 3G or newer, a BlackBerry smartphone, and other smartphones, feature phones, and "dumb" phones made by manufacturers such as LG, Motorola, Nokia, Samsung, and Sony Ericsson. If you previously set up your HTC One using the HTC Sense UI website (http://start.htc-sense.com), you will also be able to download that setup. Finally, you will be able to restore from an HTC backup that was previously made from your old HTC Android smartphone.

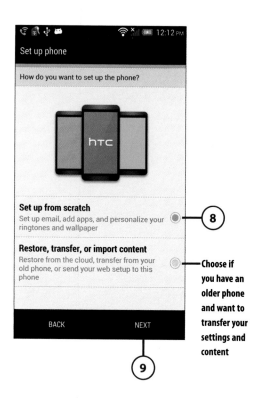

Choose if you have an older phone and want to transfer your settings and content

10. Touch Skip to continue.

Set Up Using Your Computer

If you choose to set up your HTC One using your computer, the process will be very similar to the one described in the earlier margin note titled "Set Up Your HTC One Before Taking It Out of the Box," but a code will be provided that pairs your HTC One to your HTC account.

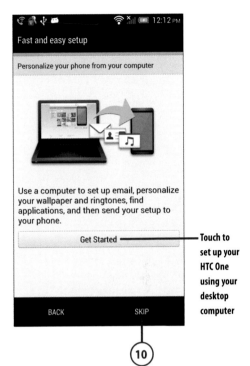

Touch to set up your HTC One using your desktop computer

11. Check the box if you want apps to be able to download data even when they are inactive.

12. Choose one or more accounts to set up on your HTC One. You can set up these accounts later if you like.

13. Touch Next.

14. Touch Sign in.

What Is Dropbox?

Dropbox is an online service that provides 2 gigabytes of free storage (this is enough to store about 600 pictures or about 500 songs) that you can use to store anything you like. If you invite a friend to Dropbox and the friend signs up, you are given an extra free 500 megabytes. Just for being an HTC customer and buying your HTC One, Dropbox gives you 25 gigabytes free for two years, which is a great deal and provides a huge online, free repository for all your pictures, music, video, HTC backups, and much more.

Touch to create a Dropbox account

Touch to skip using Dropbox

15. Touch to enable a feature that automatically saves your pictures and videos to your Dropbox account.

16. Check this box if you are okay with Google collecting information about your geographic location at any time. Although Google keeps this information safe, if you are concerned about privacy rights, you should uncheck this box.

17. Check this box if you are okay with Google using your geographic location for Google searches and other Google services such as navigation.

18. Touch to go to the next screen.

Touch to skip saving your photos and videos in Dropbox

19. Choose how you want to synchronize your Facebook friends' contact pictures, their status, and contact info from Facebook to the Contacts app on your HTC One. You can also choose not to synchronize this info.

20. Touch to go to the next screen.

21. Choose how you want to log in to your HTC account if you chose to synchronize Facebook content in the previous step. You can log in using your HTC Account or your Facebook account.

22. Touch to allow a backup of your HTC One to be saved in your Dropbox account.

23. Enter a name for your HTC One.

24. Touch to choose a method for locking your HTC One, if you want to use a locking method. You can choose from a numeric PIN, an onscreen pattern, a password, or you can use your face to unlock your phone. You can also choose to use no lock method.

25. Touch to start using your HTC One.

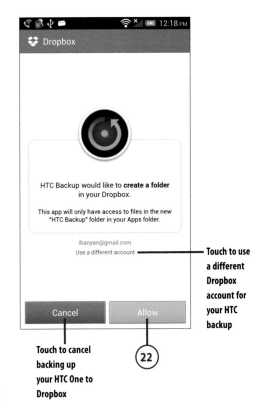

Touch to use a different Dropbox account for your HTC backup

Touch to cancel backing up your HTC One to Dropbox

22

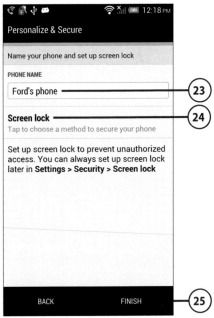

23

24

25

Fundamentals of Android 4.1.2 and HTC Sense UI

Your HTC One is run by an operating system called Android. Android was created by Google to run on any tablet or smartphone, and quite a few tablets and smartphones run on Android today. Your HTC One uses a recent version of Android, called Android 4.1.2 (or Jelly Bean), in conjunction with modifications that HTC has made to Android, which it calls HTC Sense UI. Let's go over how to use Android 4.1.2 and HTC Sense UI.

The Lock Screen

If you haven't used your HTC One for a while, the screen goes blank to conserve battery power. Here is how to interact with the Lock screen.

1. Press the Power button to wake up your HTC One.

2. Slide the padlock icon up to unlock your HTC One.

3. Slide the Phone icon up to unlock your HTC One and launch the Phone app.

4. Slide the Messages icon up to unlock your HTC One and launch the Text Messages app.

5. Slide the Globe icon up to unlock your HTC One and launch the web browser app.

6. Slide the Camera icon up to unlock your HTC One and launch the Camera app.

7. Touch to clear all notifications.

8. Touch to go to Settings on your HTC One.

Work with Notifications on the Lock Screen

With Android 4.1, you can work with notifications right on the lock screen. If you see notifications in the Notification bar, pull down the Notification bar to view and clear them. Touching a notification takes you straight to the app that created it. Read more about the Notification bar later in this chapter.

BlinkFeed

BlinkFeed is a feature of your HTC One and provides quick access to the information you are interested in. When you unlock your HTC One, you are taken directly to the BlinkFeed screen.

1. Scroll up to see all feeds in your BlinkFeed.

2. Touch a story to read more about it.

3. Swipe to the right to go to your HTC One's Home screen.

4. Touch the Phone icon to launch the Phone app.

5. Touch the Messages icon to launch the Text Messaging app.

6. Touch the Launcher icon to go to a list of all apps installed on your HTC One.

7. Touch the Web Browser icon to launch the Web browser.

8. Touch the Camera icon to launch the Camera app.

Configuring BlinkFeed

1. Pull down the feed slightly until you see the menu appear.

2. Touch the Menu button to reveal the menu choices.

3. Touch Topics and Services.

4. Check the box next to all services you want to see featured headlines from.

5. Swipe left to choose which services and apps to add to your BlinkFeed.

6. Swipe right to choose the categories you are interested in for your feeds.

7. Touch to return to BlinkFeed.

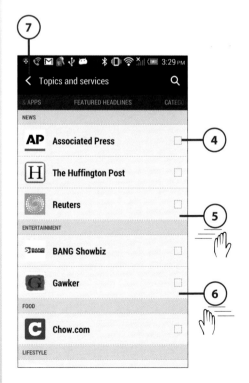

It's Not All Good

CANNOT ADD TO BLINKFEED

As of the writing of this book, it is not possible to add new content to BlinkFeed. Although you can select and unselect the existing news services and feeds, you cannot add new ones. You are also not able to add apps like Instagram or Vine to BlinkFeed. You can use only Facebook, Twitter, Flickr, and LinkedIn.

The Home Screen(s)

After you unlock your HTC One and swipe to the right on the BlinkFeed, you are presented with the main Home screen. Your HTC One has two Home screens (you can add more). The Home screens contain application shortcuts, a Launcher icon, Notification bar, Shortcuts, Favorites tray, and widgets.

Notification bar—The Notification bar shows information about Bluetooth, Near Field Communications (NFC), Wi-Fi, and cellular coverage, as well as your Sound Profile, the battery level, and time. The Notification bar also serves as a place where apps can alert or notify you using notification icons.

Notification icons—Notification icons appear in the Notification bar when an app needs to alert or notify you of something. For example, the Phone app can show the missed call icon, indicating that you missed a call.

Working with Notifications

To interact with notifications that appear in the Notification bar, place your finger above the top of the screen and drag it down to reveal the notifications. Swipe each individual notification off the screen to the left or right to clear them one by one. Using two fingers, drag down on a notification to expand it.

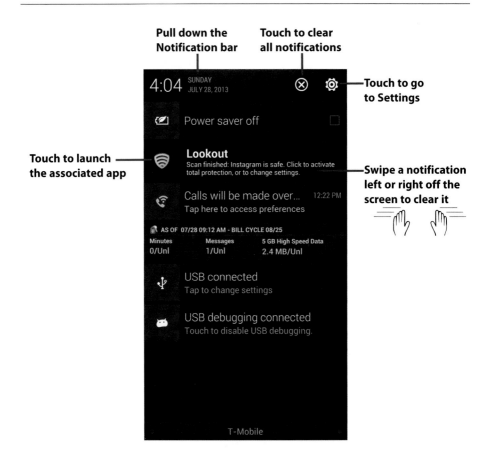

Pull down the Notification bar

Touch to clear all notifications

Touch to go to Settings

Touch to launch the associated app

Swipe a notification left or right off the screen to clear it

Widgets—Widgets are applications that run right on the Home screens. They are specially designed to provide functionality and real-time information. An example of a widget is one that shows the current weather or provides search capabilities. You can move and resize widgets.

App shortcut—Touching an app shortcut launches the associated app.

Creating App Shortcuts

Touch the Launcher icon to see all your apps. Touch and hold on the app you want to make a shortcut for. Drag it up to the word Shortcut on the top left of the screen. Keep holding the icon when the Home screen appears. Drag the app shortcut to where you want it on the Home screen, drag it to an App folder to add it to the folder, or drag it left or right off the screen to move it between Home screens. If you change your mind, just drag the icon to the word Cancel and release it. After you have found a home for your App Shortcut, release the icon.

Drag the icon up to Shortcut

Touch and hold an app icon

Drag to CANCEL
if you change
your mind

Drag right to place
it on the second
Home screen

Drag to where
you want it
and release it

App Folders—App Folders are groups of apps that you can use to organize apps and declutter your screen.

Creating App Folders

To create a new App Folder, drag one app shortcut onto another one. An App Folder is created automatically. To name your new App Folder, touch the folder to open it and touch the word Folder to enter your own name.

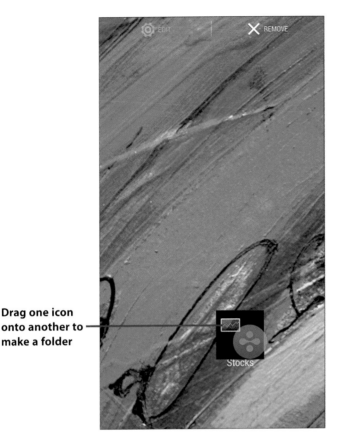

Drag one icon onto another to make a folder

Launcher bar—The Launcher bar is visible on all Home screens and when you touch the Launcher icon. You can drag apps to the Launcher bar so that they are available no matter which Home screen you are looking at. You can rearrange and move apps in the Launcher bar.

Managing the Launcher Bar

The Launcher bar is one of those things that is different from the regular version of Android. The regular version of Android calls this area the Favorites tray, and you can drag apps to it and off it while on the Home screen. However, on your HTC One, you can only drag apps to the Launcher bar and drag apps off it after you first touch the Launcher icon to see all apps.

Launcher icon—Touch to show application icons for all applications that you have installed on your HTC One.

Touch to name your App Folder

Using Your Touchscreen

Interacting with your HTC One is done mostly by touching the screen—what's known as making gestures on the screen. You can touch, swipe, pinch, double-tap, and type.

Touch—To start an application, touch its icon. Touch a menu item to select it. Touch the letters of the onscreen keyboard to type.

Touch and hold—Touch and hold to interact with an object. For example, if you touch and hold a blank area of the Home screen, a menu pops up. If you touch and hold an icon, you can reposition it with your finger.

Drag—Dragging always starts with a touch and hold. For example, if you touch the Notification bar, you can drag it down to read all the notification messages.

Swipe or slide—Swipe or slide the screen to scroll quickly. To swipe or slide, move your finger across the screen quickly. Be careful not to touch and hold before you swipe, or you will reposition something. You can also swipe to clear notifications or close apps when viewing the recent apps.

Double-tap—Double-tapping is like double-clicking a mouse on a desktop computer. Tap the screen twice in quick succession. For example, you can double-tap a web page to zoom in to part of that page.

Pinch—To zoom in and out of images and pages, place your thumb and forefinger on the screen. Pinch them together to zoom out or spread them apart (unpinch) to zoom in. Applications such as Browser, Gallery, and Maps support pinching.

Rotate the screen—If you rotate your HTC One from an upright position to being on its left or right side, the screen switches from portrait view to landscape view. Most applications honor the screen orientation. The Home screens and Launcher do not.

Where Is the Menu Button?

If you are familiar with previous versions of Android, you know there used to be a Menu button. This Menu button provided contextual actions for the app you were using. In Android 4.0 (Ice Cream Sandwich) and Android 4.1 (Jelly Bean), the Menu button has been moved and is mostly found in the upper right of the screen when it is needed within an app. It can also sometimes be found in the bottom right or elsewhere on the screen as is needed by the app. The Menu button is now three vertical dots.

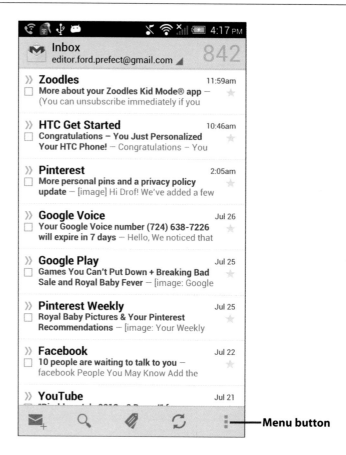

Menu button

Using Your Keyboard

Your HTC One has a virtual (onscreen) keyboard for those times when you need to enter text. You might be a little wary of a keyboard that has no physical keys, but you will be pleasantly surprised at how well it works.

Some applications automatically show the keyboard when you need to enter text. If the keyboard does not appear, touch the area where you want to type and the keyboard slides up ready for use.

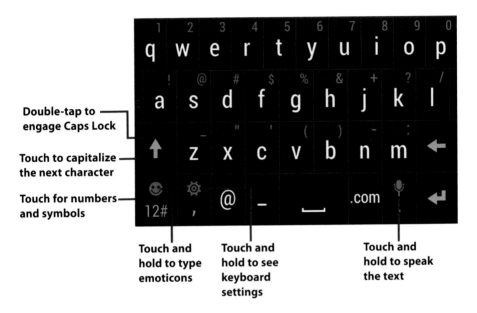

Double-tap to engage Caps Lock

Touch to capitalize the next character

Touch for numbers and symbols

Touch and hold to type emoticons

Touch and hold to see keyboard settings

Touch and hold to speak the text

Keyboard Quick Tips

If you are typing an email address or a website address, the keyboard shows a button labeled .COM. If you touch it, you type .COM, but if you touch and hold it, you can choose between .EDU, .GOV, .ORG, and .NET. If you touch and hold the Return key, the cursor jumps to the next field. This is useful if you are filling out forms on a website or moving between fields in an app. If you touch and hold the microphone key, you can use dictation instead of typing.

Using the virtual keyboard as you type, your HTC One makes word suggestions. Think of this as similar to the spell checker you would see in a word processor. Your HTC One uses a dictionary of words to guess what you are typing. If the word you were going to type is highlighted, touch space or period to select it. If you can see the word in the list but it is not highlighted, touch the word to select it.

List of suggested words

Touch to select an alternative suggested word

Touch space to accept the highlighted word

Add Your Word

If you type a word that you know is correct, you can add it to your personal dictionary so that next time you type it, your HTC One won't try to correct it. To do this, after you have typed the word (in this case, we typed "StreetTalk"), you see it as the highlighted word. Touch the word once. Your word is now added to your Personal Dictionary and will be used in the future as you type.

Touch to add your word to the dictionary

To make the next letter you type a capital letter, touch the Shift key. To make all letters capitals (or Caps), double-tap the Shift key to engage Caps Lock. Touch Shift again to disengage Caps Lock.

To type numbers or symbols, touch the Symbols key.

When on the Numbers and Symbols screen, touch the Symbols key to see extra symbols. Touch the ABC key to return to the regular keyboard.

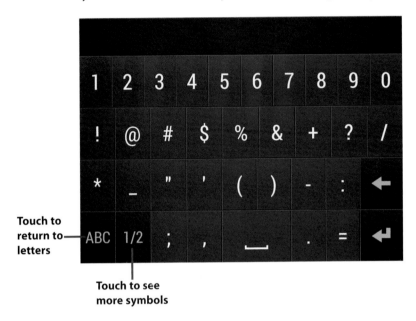

Touch to return to letters

Touch to see more symbols

To enter an accented character, touch and hold any vowel or the C, N, or S keys. A small window opens, enabling you to select an accented or alternative character. Slide your finger over the accented character and lift your finger to type it.

Touch and hold for accented characters

To reveal other alternative characters, touch and hold any other letter, number, or symbol.

Want a Larger Keyboard?
Turn your HTC One sideways to switch to a landscape keyboard. The landscape keyboard has larger keys and is easier to type on.

Landscape keyboard

Swipe to Type

Instead of typing on the keyboard in the traditional way by touching each letter individually, you can swipe over the letters in one continuous movement. This is called Continuous Input. It is enabled by default so to use it just start swiping your finger over the letters of the word you want to type. Lift your finger after each word. No need to worry about spaces because your HTC One will add them for you. To type a double letter (like in the word hello), loop around that letter on the keyboard. As you swipe over the letters, a yellow trail will follow.

Dictation: Speak Instead of Typing

Your HTC One can turn your voice into text. It uses Google's speech recognition service, which means that you must have a connection to the cellular network or a Wi-Fi network to use it.

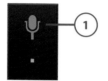

1. Touch and hold the microphone key, releasing it when you see the microphone icon appear.

2. Wait until you see Speak Now and then start saying what you want to be typed. You can speak the punctuation by saying "comma," "question mark," "exclamation mark," or "exclamation point."

3. Touch to return to the regular keyboard after you have stopped speaking for a few seconds.

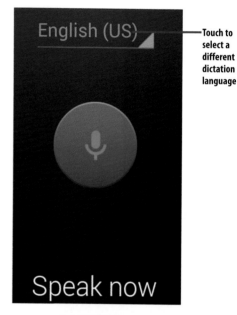

Touch to select a different dictation language

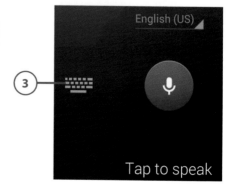

Editing Text

After you enter text, you can edit it by cutting, copying, or pasting the text. Here is how to select and copy text and then paste over a word with the copied text.

1. While you are typing, touch and hold a word you want to copy.

2. If you want to select more text, slide the blue end markers until you have selected all of the text you want to copy.

3. Touch to copy the text.

4. Touch and hold the word you want to paste over.

5. Touch Paste.

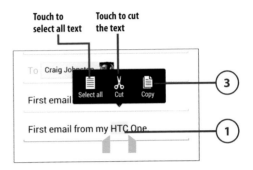

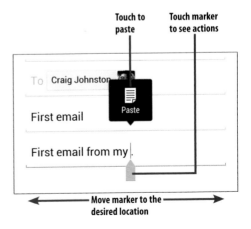

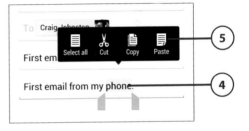

Simpler Copy/Paste

You might want to copy some text and paste it somewhere else, instead of pasting it over a word. To do this, after you have copied the text, touch once in the text area, and then move the single blue marker to where you want to paste the text. Touch the blue marker again and touch Paste.

Menus

Your HTC One has two types of menus: Regular menus and Context menus. Let's go over what each one does.

Most applications have a Menu button (menu). This enables you to make changes or take actions within that application. The Menu button should always appear in the top right of an app; however, it can sometimes appear in the bottom right, or elsewhere in the app.

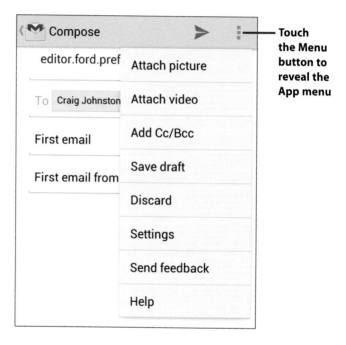

Touch the Menu button to reveal the App menu

A Context menu applies to an item on the screen. If you touch and hold something on the screen (in this example, a web link in an email), a Context menu appears. The items on the Context menu differ based on the type of object you touched.

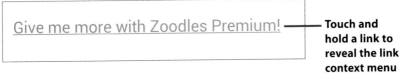

Touch and
hold a link to
reveal the link
context menu

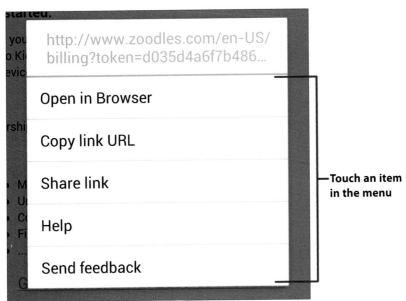

Touch an item
in the menu

Switching Between Apps

Unlike other Android devices, your
HTC One does not have a Recent
Apps button; however, you can still
access the Recent Apps list where
you can switch between apps, close
apps, and force them to quit if they
have stopped responding. Here is
how:

1. Double-tap the Home button.

2. Touch an app to switch to it.

3. Swipe an app up off the screen to
   close it.

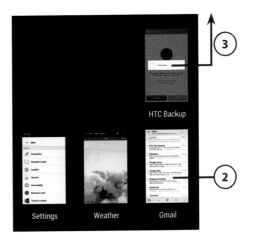

Installing Synchronization Software

Because your HTC One is tightly integrated with Google and its services, all media that you purchase on your tablet is stored in the Google cloud and accessible anywhere and anytime. However, you might have a lot of music on your computer already that you need to copy to your Google cloud. If so, you need to install the Google Music Manager software.

HTC Sync Manager

Although Google does provide its free cloud service so you can keep all of your music, music, and pictures in Google's cloud, you may not want to use it, or it may not be available in your country. As an alternative, you can install HTC Sync Manager on your computer, which will allow you to synchronize content between your computer and your HTC One without needing to use the Google cloud. HTC Sync Manager also allows you to move information from your old phone to your HTC One. To download and install HTC Sync Manager, visit www.htc.com/www/software/htc-sync-manager/ on your computer.

Installing Google Music Manager (Apple Mac)

Don't install Google Music Manager unless you plan to upload files from your computer to the Google Music cloud.

1. Visit https://play.google.com/music/listen#manager_pl from your desktop web browser and log in to your Google account if prompted.

2. Click to download Music Manager.

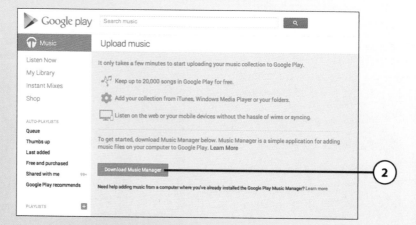

3. Click the downloads icon to reveal your downloaded files.

4. Double-click the musicmanager.dmg in your Safari Downloads.

5. Drag the Music Manager icon to the Applications shortcut to install the app.

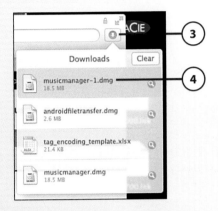

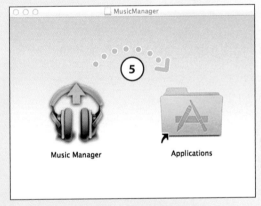

6. Double-click the Music Manager icon in the Applications folder.

7. Skip to the "Configuring Music Manager" section later in the chapter to complete the installation.

Installing Google Music Manager (Windows)

Don't install Google Music Manager unless you plan to upload files from your computer to the Google Music cloud.

1. Visit https://music.google.com/music/listen#manager_pl from your desktop web browser and log in to your Google account if prompted.

2. Click to download Music Manager.

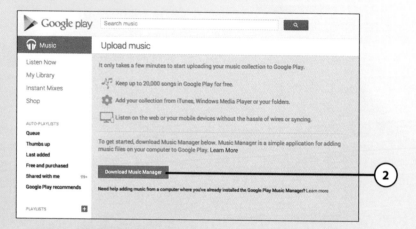

3. Double-click the musicmanagerinstaller app in your Downloads folder.

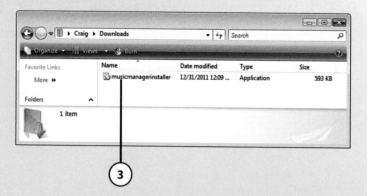

4. See the "Configuring Music Manager" section later in the chapter to complete the installation.

Configuring Music Manager (Windows and Apple Mac)

1. Click Continue.

2. Enter your Google (Gmail) email address.

3. Enter your Google (Gmail) password.

4. Click Continue.

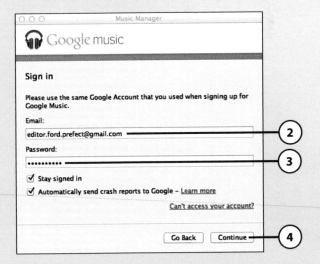

5. Choose where you keep your music.

6. Click Continue.

7. Choose whether to upload all your music or just some of your playlists. Remember that you can upload only 20,000 songs for free. Skip to step 12 if you choose to upload all music.

8. Check if you want to also upload podcasts.

9. Click Continue.

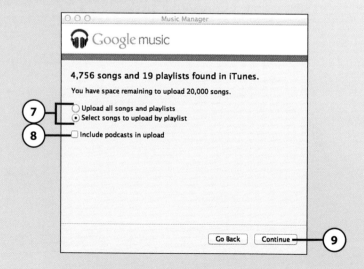

10. Select one or more playlists of music.

11. Click Continue.

12. Choose whether you want to automatically upload any new music that is added to your computer.

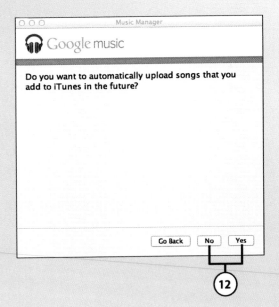

13. Click Continue.

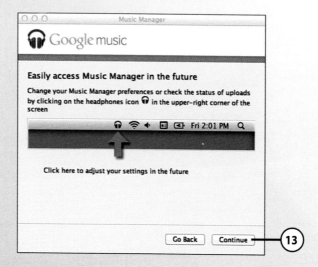

14. Click Close.

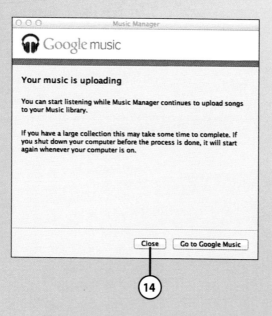

Touch to turn Wi-Fi on and off

Control NFC, hot spot, and Wi-Fi Calling

In this chapter, you learn about your HTC One's connectivity capabilities, including Bluetooth, Wi-Fi, VPN, and NFC. Topics include the following:

- → Pairing with Bluetooth devices
- → Connecting to Wi-Fi networks
- → Virtual Private Networks (VPN)
- → Using your HTC One as a Wi-Fi Hotspot
- → Using Near Field Communications (NFC) and Beaming
- → Wi-Fi Calling (some models)

Connecting to Bluetooth, Wi-Fi, and VPNs

Your HTC One can connect to Bluetooth devices such as headsets, computers, and car in-dash systems, as well as to Wi-Fi networks, and 2G, 3G, and 4G cellular networks. It has all the connectivity you should expect on a great smartphone. Your HTC One can also connect to virtual private networks (VPN) for access to secure networks. Your HTC One can even share its cellular data connection with other devices over Wi-Fi, and depending on your cellular provider, make calls over Wi-Fi.

Connecting to Bluetooth Devices

Bluetooth is a great personal area network (PAN) technology that allows for short distance wireless access to all sorts of devices such as headsets, SmartWatches, computers, and even car in-dash systems for hands-free calling. The following tasks walk you through pairing your HTC One to your device and configuring options.

Pairing with a New Bluetooth Device

Before you can take advantage of Bluetooth, you need to connect your HTC One with that device, a process called *pairing*. After you pair your HTC One with a Bluetooth device, they can connect to each other automatically in the future.

Put the Bluetooth Device into Pairing Mode First

Before you pair a Bluetooth device to your HTC One, you must first put it into Pairing mode. If you are pairing with a Bluetooth headset, this normally involves holding the button on the headset for a certain period of time. Please consult your Bluetooth device's manual on how to put that device into Pairing mode.

1. Pull down the Notification bar and touch the Settings icon.

2. Touch Bluetooth under the Wireless & Networks section.

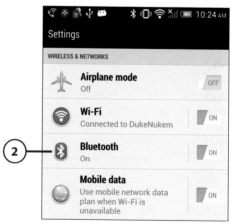

3. Touch Scan for Devices if you don't see the device you want to connect to in the list of discovered devices.

4. Touch the Bluetooth device you want to connect to. In this case, we are going to connect to the Metawatch.

5. Touch Device Name to change the name that your HTC One uses when it broadcasts on the Bluetooth network. In this example, we will be pairing with a MetaWatch SmartWatch.

6. If all went well, your HTC One should now be paired with the new Bluetooth device.

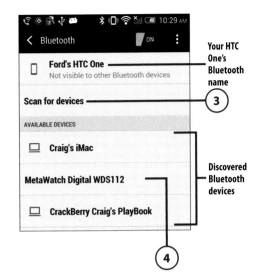

Your HTC One's Bluetooth name

Discovered Bluetooth devices

Bluetooth Passkey

If you are pairing with a device that requires a passkey, such as a car in-dash system or a computer, the screen shows a passkey. Make sure the passkey is the same on your HTC One and on the device you are pairing with. Touch Pair on your HTC One, and confirm the passkey on the device you are pairing with.

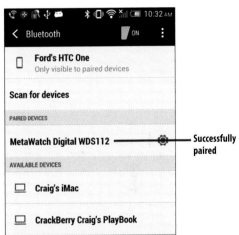

Successfully paired

All Zeros

If you are pairing with an older Bluetooth headset, you might be prompted to enter the passkey. Try using four zeros as the passkey. It usually works. If the zeros don't work, refer to the headset's manual.

Touch to confirm the passkey and pair

Reverse Pairing

The steps in this section describe how to pair your HTC One with a Bluetooth device that is in Pairing mode, listening for an incoming pairing command. You can pair Bluetooth the other way, where you put your HTC One in Discovery mode. To do this, touch the Bluetooth name of your HTC One on the screen. Your HTC One will go into Pairing mode for two minutes.

Touch to make your HTC One visible for pairing

Changing Bluetooth Settings

You can change the name your HTC One uses when pairing over Bluetooth, and change the amount of time it remains visible when pairing. Here is how.

1. Touch the Menu button.

2. Touch to rename your HTC One phone. Change it from the obscure HTC model number to something more friendly like "Craig's HTC One."

3. Touch to enable or disable Bluetooth FTP Server (when people want to send you files over Bluetooth) and Message access (aka Messaging Access Protocol, which allows access by car in-dash Bluetooth systems).

4. Touch to change how long your HTC One stays visible when pairing.

5. Touch to see any files people have sent you over the Bluetooth net-work.

Changing Bluetooth Device Options

After a Bluetooth device is paired, you can change a few options for some of them. The number of options depends on the Bluetooth device you are connecting to. Some have more features than others.

1. Touch the Settings icon to the right of the Bluetooth device.

2. Touch to rename the Bluetooth device to something more friendly.

3. Touch to disconnect and unpair from the Bluetooth device. If you do this, you won't be able to use the device until you redo the pairing as described in the previous task.

Bluetooth Profiles

Each Bluetooth device can have one or more Bluetooth profiles. Each Bluetooth profile describes certain features of the device. This tells your HTC One what it can do when connected to it. A Bluetooth headset normally has only one profile, such as Phone Audio. This tells your HTC One that it can use the device only for phone call audio. Some devices might have this profile, but provide other features such as Phone Book Access profile, which would allow it to synchronize your HTC One's address book. The latter is typical for car in-dash Bluetooth. For an explanation of all Bluetooth profiles, visit this URL: http://en.wikipedia.org/wiki/Bluetooth_profile.

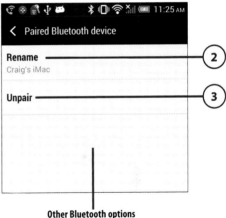

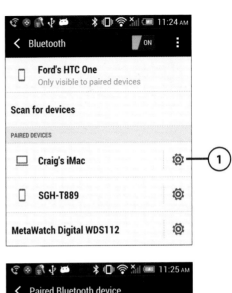

Other Bluetooth options appear here, if available

It's Not All Good

BLUETOOTH FTP BUGGY

Although sending files to your HTC One via Bluetooth might be a feature, we were never able to get it to work. There seems to be some issues with the support for it on the HTC One, so look for future updates to fix this.

Wi-Fi

Wi-Fi (Wireless Fidelity) networks are wireless networks that run within free radio bands around the world. Your local coffee shop probably has free Wi-Fi, and so do many other places, such as airports, train stations, malls, and other public areas. Your HTC One can connect to any Wi-Fi network and provide you with higher Internet access speeds than the cellular network.

Connecting to Wi-Fi

The following steps explain how to find and connect to Wi-Fi networks. After you have connected your HTC One to a Wi-Fi network, you automatically are connected to it the next time you are in range of that network.

1. Pull down the Notification bar and touch the Settings icon.

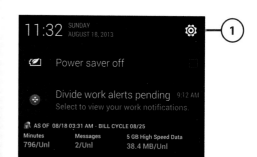

2. Touch Wi-Fi under the Wireless & Networks section.

3. Touch to turn Wi-Fi On if the slider is in the Off position.

4. Touch the name of the Wi-Fi network you want to connect to. If the network does not use any security, you can skip to step 7.

5. Enter the Wi-Fi network password.

6. Touch to connect to the Wi-Fi network.

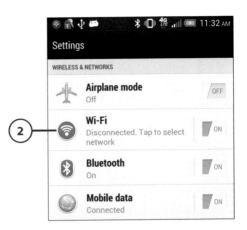

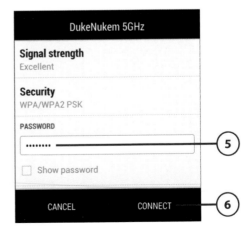

Adding a Hidden Network

If the network you want to connect to is not listed on the screen,
it may be purposely hidden. If it is
hidden, it does not broadcast its
name, which is also known as its
SSID. You will need to touch the
Menu icon, Add Network, then
type in the SSID and choose the
type of security that the network
uses. You should get this information from the network administrator ahead of time.

7. If all goes well, you see the Wi-Fi
network in the list with the word
Connected under it.

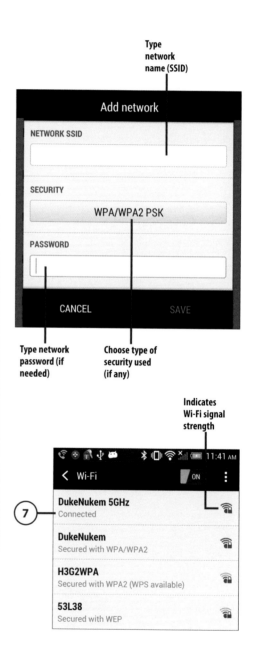

Type
network
name (SSID)

Type network
password (if
needed)

Choose type of
security used
(if any)

Indicates
Wi-Fi signal
strength

Wi-Fi Network Options

1. Touch a Wi-Fi network to reveal a pop-up that shows information about your connection to that network.

2. Touch Disconnect to tell your HTC One to not connect to this network in the future.

3. Touch and hold on a Wi-Fi network to reveal two actions.

4. Touch to forget the Wi-Fi network, its connection settings, and no longer connect to it. This is the same as the previous step 2.

5. Touch to change the Wi-Fi network password or encryption key that your HTC One uses to connect to the network.

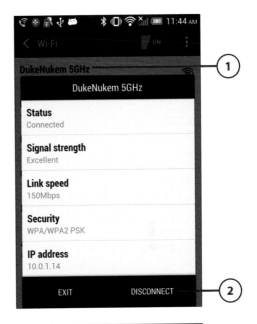

Advanced Wi-Fi Options

Your HTC One allows you to configure a few advanced Wi-Fi settings
that can help preserve your battery
life.

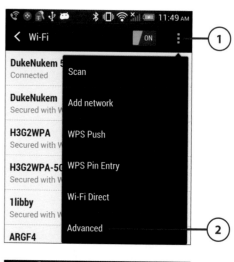

1. Touch the Menu button.

2. Touch Advanced.

3. Touch to enable or disable the
   capability for your HTC One to
   automatically notify you when it
   detects a new Wi-Fi network.

4. Touch to manage which open
   Wi-Fi networks you have previously blocked.

5. Touch to change the Wi-Fi sleep
   policy. This allows you to choose
   whether your HTC One should
   keep its connection to Wi-Fi when
   it goes to sleep.

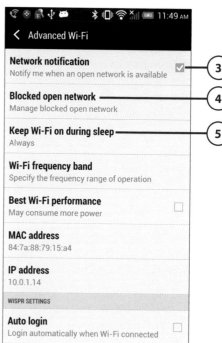

Should You Keep Wi-Fi on During Sleep?

In step 5, you can choose how
your HTC One handles its connection to Wi-Fi when it goes
to sleep. Because Wi-Fi is much
faster, more efficient than 3G or
4G, and is free, you should keep
this set to Always. However, battery usage can be impacted by
keeping the Wi-Fi connection
always connected; you may want
to set this to Only When Plugged
In, which means that if your HTC
One is not charging, and it goes
to sleep, it will switch to the cellular network for data, but when it
is charging and it goes to sleep, it
will stay connected to Wi-Fi. If you

set this setting to Never, it means that when your HTC One goes to sleep, it will switch to using the cellular network for all data. This can lead to more data being used out of your cellular data bundle, which may cost you extra, so be careful.

---

6. Touch to choose which Wi-Fi frequency bands your HTC One should use. You can leave it on Auto or manually choose between 5GHz and 2.4GHz.

7. Touch to enable or disable Best Wi-Fi Performance. When disabled, the Wi-Fi performance is not very good in some environments, so if you are having Wi-Fi coverage issues, try enabling this.

8. Scroll down for more options.

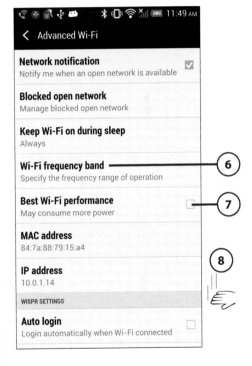

9. Check to set your HTC One to automatically log in using your Wireless Internet Service Provider roaming (WISPr) credentials when it connects to a WISPr-enabled Wi-Fi hotspot.

What Is WISPr?

Wireless Internet Service Provider roaming (WISPr), pronounced "whisper," is a protocol that allows devices to roam between Wi-Fi Internet service providers. For example, you may have an account on Boingo, which provides Wi-Fi coverage at airports in the United States. While you are in another country, a Wi-Fi Internet service provider there may have a roaming agreement with Boingo, and if your HTC One is set up correctly, it will automatically log in to the Wi-Fi login page, allowing you to gain Internet access seamlessly.

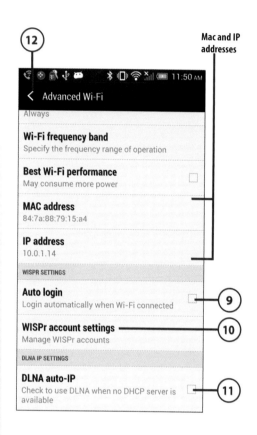

Mac and IP addresses

10. Touch to manage your WISPr accounts.

11. Touch to use Digital Living Network Alliance (DLNA) to pick your own IP address on a network where Dynamic Host Configuration Protocol (DHCP) is not being used (very uncommon).

12. Touch to save your settings and return to the previous screen.

WHAT ARE IP AND MAC ADDRESSES?

A Media Access Control (MAC) address is a number burned into your HTC One that identifies its Wi-Fi adapter. This is called the physical layer because it is a physical adapter. An Internet Protocol (IP) address is a secondary way to identify your HTC One. Unlike a Physical Layer address or MAC address, the IP address can be changed anytime. Modern networks use the IP address when they need to deliver data to you. Normally when you connect to a network, a device on the network that uses the Dynamic Host Configuration Protocol (DHCP) assigns you a new IP address. On home networks, this is typically your Wi-Fi router.

Some network administrators use a security feature to limit who can connect to their Wi-Fi network. They set up their network to only allow connections from Wi-Fi devices with specific MAC addresses. If you are trying to connect to such a network, you will have to give the network administrator your MAC address, and he or she will add it to the allowed list.

What Is DLNA?

DLNA, or Digital Living Network Alliance, is a protocol that allows devices on a network to connect to and play each other's media content. This is an attempt to provide an alternative to Apple's very successful AirPlay protocol. DLNA is not standard on Android devices; however, on some HTC Android devices like your HTC One, it has been added as a standard feature. DLNA allows any device that supports the DLNA protocol to play content from other DLNA devices, and allows content to be played from it. On networks that do not use DHCP, DLNA can use its own internal mechanism to choose an IP address for your device (see the previous step 11).

What Is WISPr?

Wireless Internet Service Provider roaming (WISPr), pronounced "whisper," is a protocol that allows devices to roam between Wi-Fi Internet service providers. For example, you may have an account on Boingo, which provides Wi-Fi coverage at airports in the United States. While you are in another country, a Wi-Fi Internet service provider there may have a roaming agreement with Boingo, and if your HTC One is set up correctly, it will automatically log in to the Wi-Fi login page, allowing you to gain Internet access seamlessly.

CONNECT TO WI-FI WITH A PUSH OF A BUTTON

Most new Wi-Fi routers have a button labeled WPS, which stands for Wi-Fi Protected Setup. This allows the Wi-Fi router and a device that supports WPS to work together to set up a secure Wi-Fi connection automatically without your having to know or type in any information. Sometimes you may choose to use a numeric PIN to make the connection. Your HTC One provides a way to use both the WPS and the WPS PIN method of connecting. From the main Wi-Fi settings screen, touch the Menu button and touch WPS Push or WPS Pin Entry.

Touch Menu

Choose your WPS method

Wi-Fi Direct

Wi-Fi Direct is a feature that allows two Android devices running version 4.1 (Jelly Bean) or later to connect to each other using Wi-Fi and exchange files. Because Wi-Fi is much faster than Bluetooth, if you are sending large files, using Wi-Fi Direct makes sense. Although Wi-Fi Direct is built in to Jelly Bean Android devices, because of some bugs, it does not currently work on the HTC One. This means that any apps that attempt to use Wi-Fi Direct will fail. Next, we cover how Wi-Fi Direct should work in the event that HTC fixes the bugs. We are using a Samsung Galaxy Note II for the screenshots.

Setting Up Wi-Fi Direct

In this section, we cover how to use Wi-Fi Direct. As we said earlier, Wi-Fi Direct doesn't work right now, but if this is corrected in the future, these steps should be followed to set it up.

1. Pull down the Notification bar and touch the Settings icon.

2. Touch Wi-Fi under the Wireless & Networks section.

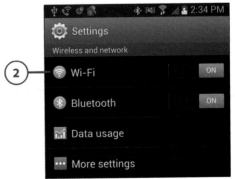

3. Touch Wi-Fi Direct.

4. Touch the Menu button.

5. Touch Rename Device to rename your HTC One from its generic name (in this example, Android_d592) to something more meaningful.

6. Type a new name for your HTC One as it will appear to others using Wi-Fi Direct.

7. Touch OK.

Using Wi-Fi Direct (the Official Way)

These are the steps that must be followed to connect two Android devices running version 4.1 (Jelly Bean) or later via Wi-Fi Direct. After they are connected, you should theoretically be able to send files between them, but as of the writing of this book, it does not work.

1. Ask the other person to enable Wi-Fi Direct on his or her Android device, and it should appear on your screen under Available Devices.

2. Touch the device to invite it to connect with your HTC One via Wi-Fi Direct.

3. On the device you are inviting, touch Accept.

4. The device will show as Connected.

After You Are Connected, Then What?

After you are connected with another device via Wi-Fi Direct, theoretically you should be able to open a picture, video, or music file, touch the Share icon, and share it via Wi-Fi Direct. When you touch to share it via Wi-Fi Direct, you will see a list of devices connected via Wi-Fi Direct. Touch to choose the device you want to share it with. This, however, does not work at all (or at least it didn't during the writing of this book).

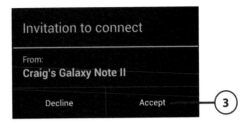

Touch to share via Wi-Fi Direct

Choose the device to share with

Wi-Fi Direct (Using the WiFi Shoot App)

Because the official method of using Wi-Fi Direct doesn't work, you can download an app called WiFi Shoot from Google Play (see Chapter 11, "Working with Android Applications," for more on how to use Google Play). WiFi Shoot, although not perfect, should allow you to send files via Wi-Fi Direct. To use WiFi Shoot, you and the person you want to share files with must both install and open WiFi Shoot.

1. Ask the other person to run WiFi Shoot on his or her Android device before you start.

2. Find a picture, music file, or video file you want to share, and touch the Share icon.

3. Touch WiFi Shoot.

4. Touch the device you want to send the file to.

5. The user of the other device must accept the connection.

6. Touch Shoot and the file will be sent.

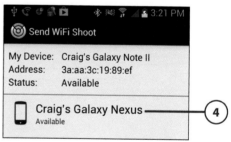

Near Field Communications (NFC)

Your HTC One has the capability to swap data via its Near Field Communications (NFC) radio with other phones that use NFC, or read data that is
stored on NFC tags. NFC can also be used for paying for items you have
purchased or by apps to inject information. Android Beam uses NFC to
send files between Android devices by setting up the sending process
automatically via NFC and continuing it via Bluetooth or Wi-Fi Direct.

Enabling NFC and Android Beam

To get the full benefit from NFC, you
need to enable the NFC radio, and
we should enable Android Beam.

1. Pull down the Notification bar
   and touch the Settings icon.

2. Touch More.

3. Touch to enable NFC.

4. Touch to save your changes.

Using Android Beam

All Android devices running version 4.0 (Ice Cream Sandwich) or later have a feature called Android Beam. This feature sends small bits of data via NFC (such as links to YouTube videos or links to apps in Google Play), which allows you to effectively share content, but also automates sending actual files between devices, such as pictures and videos via Bluetooth.

Using Android Beam to Send Links to Content

Android Beam can be used to send links to content such as apps, music, and video in the Google Play store and website links. Android Beam will work only between devices running Android 4.0 (Ice Cream Sandwich) or later.

1. Open a website that you'd like to share the link to.

2. Put the back of your HTC One about one inch from the back of another NFC-enabled phone. You will know if the two devices have successfully connected when the web page zooms out.

3. Touch the web page after it zooms out.

4. The other device will open its web browser and go straight to that link.

Beam Google Play Content and YouTube Videos

If you like a song, movie, book, or app that is in the Google Play store, you can beam it to someone. Open the song, movie, book, or app in Google Play, touch your devices together, and touch to beam. To beam a YouTube video, open the video in the YouTube app, touch the devices together, and touch to beam. The other device will open YouTube and jump directly to the video.

Using Android Beam to Send Real Files

Android Beam can also be used to send real content, such as pictures, music, and video stored on your HTC One. Sending real files using Android Beam will work only between devices running Android 4.1 (Jelly Bean) or later. In this example, we beam a picture.

1. Open the picture you want to beam. Note that the picture must

reside on your HTC One and not in the Google cloud.

2. Put the back of your HTC One about one inch from the back of another NFC-enabled phone. You will know if the two devices have successfully connected when the picture zooms out.

3. Touch the picture after it zooms out.

4. Your HTC One sends the picture to the other device. The file is sent using Bluetooth in the background.

5. Touch to open the beamed file on the other device after it completes receiving it.

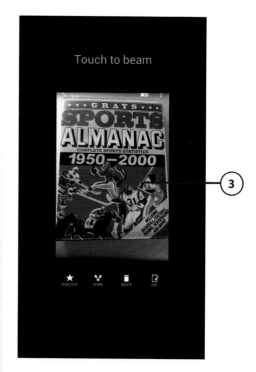

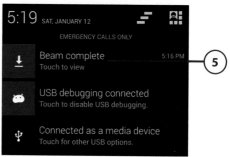

Cellular Networks and Wi-Fi Calling

Your HTC One can connect to many different cellular networks around the world. The exact networks that it can connect to are determined by the varient of your HTC One because not all carriers use the same technology, and to complicate it further, many use different frequencies from one another. Some carriers provide Wi-Fi Calling, which allows Wi-Fi to augment the cellular data coverage and provide free calling.

Changing Mobile Settings

Your HTC One has a few options when it comes to how it connects to cellular (or mobile) networks.

1. Pull down the Notification bar and touch the Settings icon.

2. Touch to enable or disable cellular data. If this is set to off, your HTC One will be able to use only a Wi-Fi network for data.

3. Touch Mobile data to change more mobile data settings.

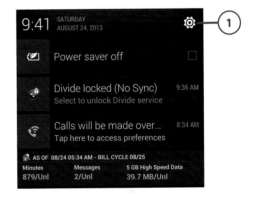

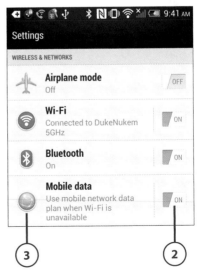

4. Touch to enable or disable cellular data roaming. If this is unchecked, your HTC One will not attempt to use data while you roam away from your home cellular network.

5. Touch to enable or disable playing a sound to alert you when you connect to a roaming network.

What Is an APN?

APN stands for Access Point Name. You normally don't have to make changes to APNs, but sometimes you need to enter them manually to access certain features. For example, if you need to use tethering, which is where you connect your laptop to your HTC One and your HTC One provides Internet connectivity for your laptop, you might be asked by your carrier to use a specific APN. Think of an APN as a gateway to a service.

6. Touch to view, edit, and add APNs. It is unlikely that you will need to make any APN changes.

7. Touch to change the network mode. This setting allows you to choose to force your phone to connect to a slower 2G network (GSM) to save battery, or always to a faster 3G (WCDMA) or 4G (LTE) network for the best speed, or to leave it set to Auto mode and let your phone choose for you.

8. Touch to view and choose mobile operators to use manually.

9. Touch to save any changes and return to the previous screen.

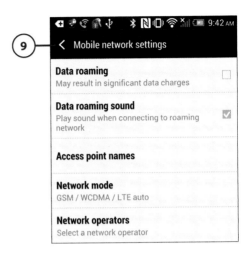

Why Select Operators Manually?

When you are roaming in your home country, your HTC One automatically selects your home cellular provider. When you are roaming outside your home country, your HTC One will register on a cellular provider based on its name and how it scores alphabetically. The lowest score will always win. For example, a carrier whose name starts with a number will always be chosen over carriers whose names start with letters. A carrier whose name starts with the letter "A" will be chosen over a carrier whose name starts with the letter "B", and so on. As you roam, your home carrier may not have a good roaming relationship with a carrier that your HTC One has chosen based on its name, so you should choose the carrier manually to ensure the best roaming rates—and many times, just basic connectivity. You will notice that sometimes carrier names will not be displayed, but rather their operator code (or PLNM). For example, 53024 is actually 2Degrees in New Zealand, and 53005 is Telecom New Zealand.

Changing Wi-Fi Calling Settings

Wi-Fi Calling is a feature provided by some carriers around the world. It is sometimes known by its technical name, Universal Mobile Access (UMA). On your HTC One, you can enable or disable Wi-Fi Calling, or set its connection preferences.

1. Pull down the Notification bar and touch the Settings icon.

2. Touch More.

3. Touch to enable or disable Wi-Fi Calling.

4. Touch to change Wi-Fi Calling connection preferences.

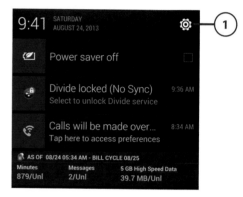

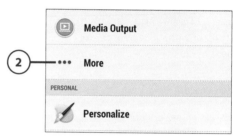

5. Touch Connection Preferences.

6. Choose how you would prefer Wi-Fi Calling to work.

7. Touch to save your changes and return to the previous screen.

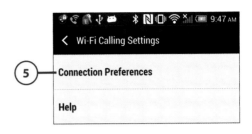

What Is Wi-Fi Calling?

Wi-Fi Calling, also known as Universal Mobile Access (UMA), is provided by some cellular carriers to both augment their coverage and to provide free calls over Wi-Fi. This is not Voice over IP (VoIP) calling but a regular GSM voice call, routed via a Wi-Fi hotspot, over the Internet, to your carrier. Because the call is not using the cellular network infra-structure, the calls are free, and because of the speeds at which Wi-Fi networks operate, the call quality is much higher because much less compression is needed. To read more about UMA, try this online article: http://crackberry.com/saving-call-charges-recession-your-blackberry.

Virtual Private Networks (VPN)

Your HTC One can connect to virtual private networks (VPNs), which are normally used by companies to provide a secure connection to their inside networks or intranets.

Adding a VPN Profile

Before you add a VPN, you must first have all the information needed to set it up on your HTC One. Speak to your network administrator and get this information ahead of time to save frustration. This information includes the type of VPN protocol used, the type of encryption used, and the name of the host to which you are connecting.

1. Pull down the Notification bar and touch the Settings icon.

2. Touch More.

3. Touch VPN.

4. Touch OK to set up a Lock screen PIN, pattern, or password. If you already have a Lock screen PIN or password, you won't be prompted at this point and you can proceed to step 6.

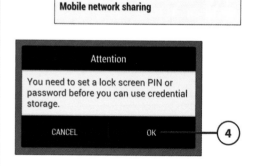

Why Do You Need to Set a PIN or Password?

If you don't already have a screen unlock PIN, password, or pattern set up before you create your first VPN connection, you are prompted to create one. This is a security measure that ensures your HTC One must first be unlocked before anyone can access a stored VPN connection. Because VPN connections are usually used to access company data, this is a good idea.

5. Choose either Pattern, PIN, or Password to unlock your HTC One, and follow the steps to create it.

6. Touch Add VPN Profile.

7. Enter a name for your VPN network. You can call it anything you like; for example, "Work VPN" or the name of the provider, such as "Public VPN."

8. Touch to choose the type of security the VPN network uses.

9. Enter the remaining parameters that your network administrator has provided.

10. Touch Save.

Touch to set advanced options such as DNS and forwarding

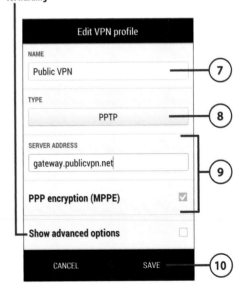

Connecting to a VPN

After you have created one or more VPN connections, you can connect to them when the need arises.

1. Pull down the Notification bar and touch the Settings icon.

2. Touch More under the Wireless & Networks section.

3. Touch VPN.

4. Touch a preconfigured VPN connection.

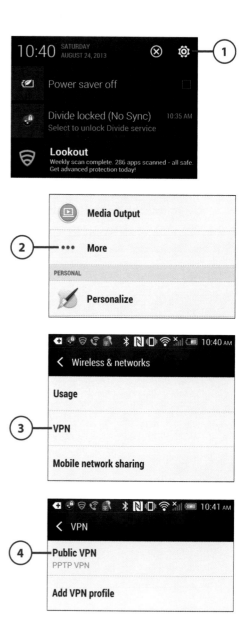

5. Enter the VPN username.

6. Enter the VPN password.

7. Touch Connect. After you're connected to the VPN, you can use your HTC One's web browser and other applications normally, but you now have access to resources at the other end of the VPN tunnel, such as company web servers or your company email.

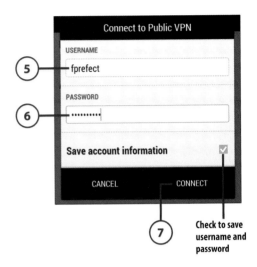

Check to save username and password

>>>Go Further

HOW CAN YOU TELL IF YOU ARE CONNECTED?

After your HTC One successfully connects to a VPN network, you will see a Key icon in the Notification bar. This indicates that you are connected. If you pull down the Notification bar, you can touch the icon to see information about the connection and to disconnect from the VPN.

Connected to VPN

Disconnect, Edit, or Delete a VPN

You can edit an existing VPN or delete it by touching and holding the name of the VPN. A window will pop up with a list of options. To disconnect a VPN connection, touch the VPN Profile name once.

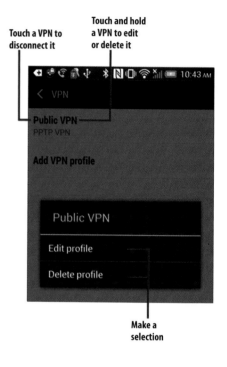

Touch a VPN to disconnect it

Touch and hold a VPN to edit or delete it

Make a selection

A MUCH QUICKER WAY TO START A VPN CONNECTION

You can create a shortcut on your Home screen to take you straight to the VPN screen, which cuts down on the steps required to start a VPN. To do this, touch and hold on the Home screen in a free area where there are currently no widgets or shortcuts. Touch the selector and choose Shortcuts. Find the Settings Shortcut widget and touch it. Scroll down and select VPN. Now each time you touch the VPN shortcut on your Home screen, you will be taken directly to the VPN screen where you can launch your VPN connection.

Choose Shortcuts

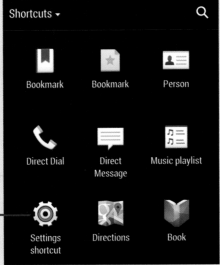

Touch Settings Shortcut

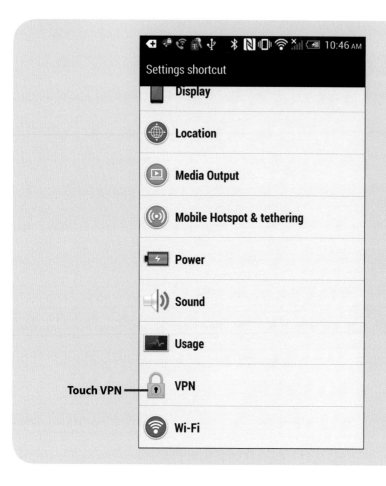

Mobile Wi-Fi Hotspot

Your HTC One has the capability to share its cellular data connection with up to five devices over Wi-Fi. Before you use this feature, you usually need to sign up for a tethering or hotspot plan with your cellular provider, which is typically an extra monthly cost.

Starting Your Mobile Wi-Fi Hotspot

1. Pull down the Notification bar and touch the Settings icon.

2. Touch More.

3. Touch Mobile Network Sharing.

4. Touch Mobile Hotspot Settings.

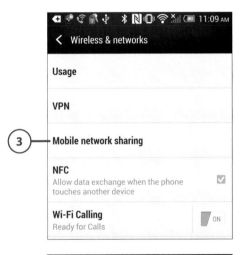

5. Choose a Network name for your mobile hotspot. You can leave it set to the autogenerated name or change it to something more friendly. This is also known as the SSID, or Service Set Identifier.

6. Touch to choose the type of security to use for your mobile hotspot, or choose None to use no security.

7. Enter a password that people connecting must use if you chose to use a security method in step 6.

8. Touch the Menu icon.

9. Touch Advanced.

10. Touch to enable or disable hiding your Wi-Fi network name (or SSID).

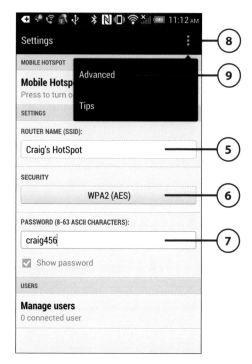

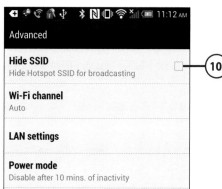

WHY HIDE YOUR SSID?

If you choose to hide your SSID, it means that your Wi-Fi hotspot will not be visible when people look for Wi-Fi hotspots. You may want to do this if you don't want people trying to connect to your hotspot when you are using it. In general, it is better to use security to limit who can connect.

11. Touch to change the Wi-Fi channel that your hotspot will use, or leave it to Auto and let your HTC One choose the best one.

12. Touch to make more advanced changes to the way in which your hotspot hands out network addresses to devices that connect, and the network address range that your hotspot uses.

13. Touch to set your hotspot to always remain on, no matter if there are periods of inactivity, or set it to turn itself off after either 5 or 10 minutes of inactivity.

14. Touch the Back button to return to the previous screen.

15. Touch to turn on your hotspot and let people connect.

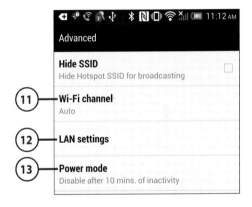

Limiting Who Can Connect

People can connect to your hotspot only after you give them the connection information. However, you can further limit who can connect to your Mobile Hotspot by allowing only certain devices. The steps that follow must be performed before you turn on your hotspot.

1. Touch Manage Users.

2. Touch to check the box next to Allowed Users Only.

3. Touch Done.

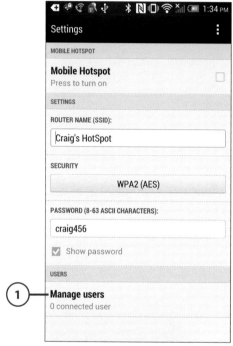

Touch to change the maximum number of users who can connect

4. Touch to start your hotspot and wait for connection requests.

5. Touch the Connection Requests Received alert.

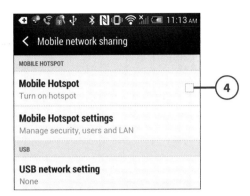

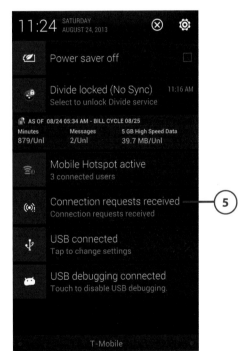

6. Select to Allow or Block the requesting devices.

7. Touch Done.

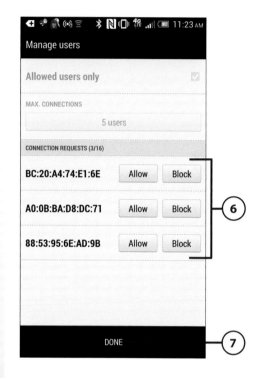

HOW DOES ALLOWED USERS WORK?

If you choose to use the Allowed Users feature, your HTC One's hotspot uses connecting devices' Media Access Control (MAC) address to allow or deny them access to your hotspot. The MAC address is hard-coded onto each device's Wi-Fi adapter. Before using this feature, make sure you know the MAC addresses of the devices you want to allow. If you take too long to allow a connection request, the person's device that is requesting to connect may time out. Devices requesting to connect to your hotspot will be temporarily blocked until you touch Allow.

Choose a widget

In this chapter, you learn how to customize your HTC One to suit your needs and lifestyle. Topics include the following:

→ Wallpapers and live wallpapers
→ Replacing the keyboard
→ Sound and display settings
→ Setting region and language
→ Kid Mode

Customizing Your HTC One

Your HTC One arrives preconfigured to appeal to most buyers; however, you might want to change the way some of the features work, or even personalize it to fit your mood or lifestyle. Luckily, your HTC One is customizable.

Change Your Wallpaper

Your HTC One comes preloaded with a cool wallpaper. You can install other wallpapers, use live wallpapers that animate, and even use pictures in the Gallery application as your wallpaper.

1. Pull down the Notification bar and touch the Settings icon.

2. Touch Personalize.

3. Touch Wallpaper.

4. Touch the type of wallpaper you want to use. Use the steps in one of the following three sections to select your wallpaper.

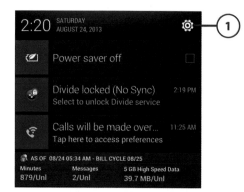

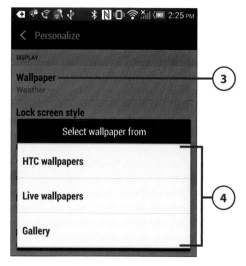

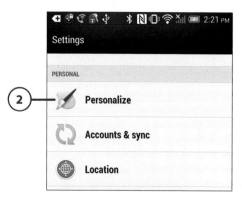

Wallpaper from Gallery Pictures

You can use any picture in your Gallery as a wallpaper.

1. Select the photo you want to use as your wallpaper.

2. Move the crop box to the part of the photo you want to use.

3. Adjust the size of the crop box to include the part of the photo you want.

4. Touch Done to use the cropped portion of the photo as your wallpaper.

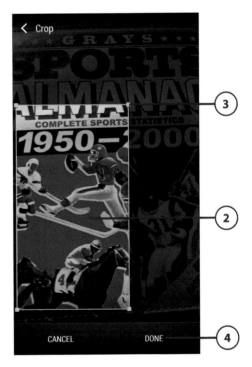

Live Wallpaper

Live wallpaper is wallpaper with some intelligence behind it. It can be a cool animation, an animation that keys off things such as the music you are playing on your HTC One, or it can be something simple, such as the time. There are some very cool live wallpapers in Google Play that you can install and use.

1. Touch the live wallpaper you want to use. In this example, we will use the ST: Red Alert Live Wallpaper.

2. Touch to see and change the live wallpaper settings, if it has settings to change.

3. Touch Set Wallpaper to use the live wallpaper.

Find More Wallpaper

You can find wallpaper or live wallpaper in Google Play. Open Google Play and search for "wallpaper" or "live wallpaper." Read more on how to use Google Play in Chapter 11, "Working with Android Applications."

Swipe left and right to see more

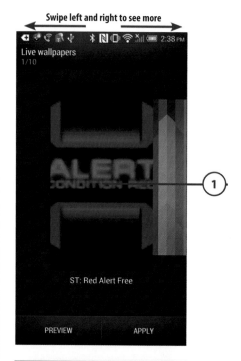

HTC Wallpaper

Choose a static wallpaper.

1. Swipe left and right to see all the wallpapers.

2. Touch a wallpaper to preview it.

3. Touch Apply to use the wallpaper.

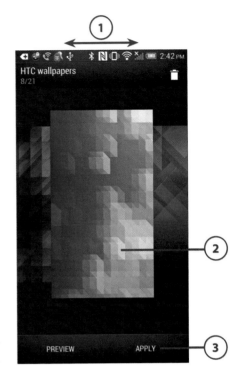

Changing Your Keyboard

If you find it hard to type on the standard HTC One keyboard, or you just want to make it look better, you can install replacement keyboards. You can download free keyboards or purchase replacement ones from Google Play. Make sure you install a keyboard before following these steps.

1. Touch Settings.

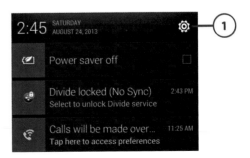

2. Touch Language & Keyboard.

3. Touch to flip the switch to On next to the keyboard you have previously installed from the Google Play store (in this example, we used GO Keyboard) to make that keyboard available for use.

4. Touch the name of the keyboard to start the keyboard's custom installation process.

Do Your Research

When you choose a different keyboard in step 3, the HTC One does not warn you that nonstandard keyboards have the potential for capturing everything you type, but the truth is that they do. Do your research on any keyboards before you download and install them.

5. Touch Step2:switch to GO Keyboard.

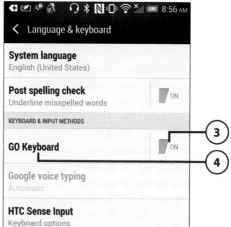

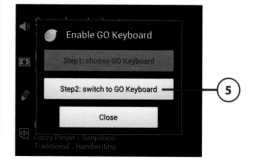

6. Touch the name of your new keyboard to select it.

What Can You Do with Your New Keyboard

Keyboards you buy in Google Play can do many things. They can change the key layout, change the color and style of the keys, offer different methods of text input, and even enable you to use an old T9 predictive input keyboard that you may have become used to when using an old "dumb phone" that only had a numeric keypad.

It's Not All Good

NO BUILT-IN WAY TO CHANGE YOUR KEYBOARD

On the standard version of Android, and in many other versions, there is a way to manually change your keyboard. A menu option right in the Language & Input settings screen brings up the keyboard chooser dialog you see in step 6. However, on your HTC One, the only way to access the keyboard chooser dialog is by running the keyboard custom installation.

Adding Widgets to Your Home Screens

Some applications that you install come with widgets that you can place on your Home screens. These widgets normally display real-time information, such as stocks, weather, time, and Facebook feeds. Your HTC One also comes preinstalled with some widgets. Here is how to add and manage widgets.

Adding a Widget

Your HTC One should come pre-installed with some widgets, but you might also have some extra ones that have been added when you installed other applications. Here is how to add those widgets to your Home screens.

1. Touch and hold in an open area on your Home screen.

2. Touch the drop-down menu and choose Widgets.

3. Touch and hold a widget to select it. Keep holding the widget as you move to step 4. In this example, we are using the Calendar widget.

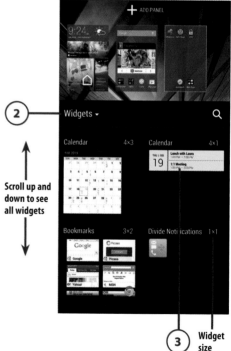

Scroll up and down to see all widgets

Widget size

4. Drag the widget to the Home screen panel you want to place it on.

5. Drag the widget to where you want to position it on the Home screen panel.

6. Release your finger to place the widget. Some widgets ask you a few questions after they are positioned.

How Many Widgets Can I Fit?

Each part of the Home screen is divided into four blocks across and four blocks down. When you see the list of widgets, you'll notice that each one shows its size in blocks across and down. From that, you can prejudge if a widget will fit on the screen you want it to be on, but it also helps you position it in step 4.

Red indicates that there is not enough space for the widget

Faint preview of how much space it will require

Resizing Widgets

Some widgets can be resized. To resize a widget, touch and hold the widget until you see an outline, and then release it. If the widget can be resized, you will see the resizing borders. Drag them to resize the widget. Touch anywhere on the screen to stop resizing.

Drag to resize the widget

Edit or Move a Widget

Sometimes you want to remove a widget or edit its configuration. Here is how:

1. Touch and hold the widget until you see a blue shadow, but continue to hold the widget.

2. Drag the widget to the word Remove to remove it.

3. Drag the widget to the word Edit to change the widget's settings.

4. Release the widget.

System Language

If you move to another country or want to change the language used by your HTC One, you can do so with a few touches.

1. Pull down the Notification bar and touch Settings.

2. Touch Language & Keyboard.

3. Touch System Language.

4. Touch the language you want to switch to.

What Obeys the Language Setting?

When you switch your HTC One to use a different language, you immediately notice that all standard applications and the HTC One menus switch to the new language. Even some third-party applications honor the language switch. However, many third-party applications ignore the language setting on the HTC One. So, you might open a third-party application and find that all of its menus are still in English.

Accessibility Settings

Your HTC One includes built-in settings to assist people who might otherwise have difficulty using some features of the device. The HTC One has the capability to provide alternative feedback, such as vibration, sound, and even the speaking of menus.

1. Pull down the Notification bar and touch Settings.

2. Touch Accessibility.

3. Touch to enable or disable TalkBack. When enabled, TalkBack speaks everything, including menus.

4. Touch to set the font size used on your HTC One. You can choose sizes ranging from tiny to huge.

5. Touch to choose whether to use the power button to end calls.

6. Touch to enable automatic screen rotation. When disabled, the screen will not rotate between portrait and landscape modes.

7. Touch to enable or disable the feature where your HTC One speaks your passwords as you type them.

8. Touch to enable or disable showing the magnifier when selecting text.

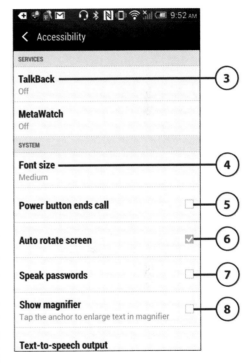

How Does the Magnifier Work?

When you enable the Show Magnifier option, anytime you select text on the screen, and you move the blue markers (known as anchors) to select more or less text, the text around the marker you are moving will be magnified to make it easier to see what text you are selecting.

9. Scroll down for more settings.

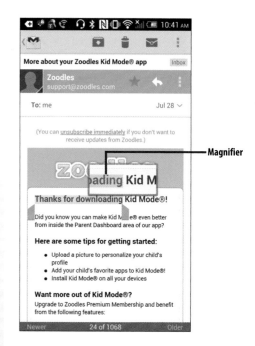

Magnifier

10. Touch to choose which text-to-speech service to use (Google or ones you have installed from the Google Play store), and rate of the speech.

11. Touch to set the touch and hold delay, which is the amount of time your HTC One will wait between when you touch something on the screen and the time it decides you are trying to perform a touch-and-hold gesture.

12. Touch to allow or disallow websites from installing scripts on your HTC One to make accessing their website more accessible.

13. Touch to save your settings and return to the previous screen.

More About Text-to-Speech

By default, your HTC One uses the Google Text-to-Speech service to speak any text that you need to read. You can install other text-to-speech software by searching for them in the Google Play store. After they are installed, they will show as a choice in step 10.

Sound Settings

You can change the volume for games, ringtones, and alarms, change the default ringtone and notification sound, and you can control what system sounds are used.

1. Pull down the Notification bar and touch Settings.

2. Touch to enable or disable Beats Audio.

What Is Beats Audio and Can I Control the EQ?

Beats Audio is functionality built in to your HTC One that has preset Equalizer (EQ) settings to make audio sound great on the front-facing BoomSound speakers. Your only option is to turn Beats Audio on or off, and you have no way to change many EQ settings to fine-tune the sound to your taste. If you want to go beyond how Beats Audio sets the EQ settings, try downloading an app like Equalizer (https://play.google.com/store/apps/details?id=com.smartandroidapps.equalizer) from Google Play. It provides access to the built-in Android settings that go beyond what Beats Audio offers. Or if you like the way your audio sounds out of the box, leave Beats Audio enabled.

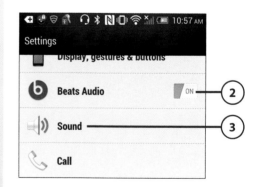

3. Touch Sound.

4. Touch to choose the Sound Profile to use. You can choose between Normal, Vibrate, and Silent.

5. Touch to change the volume levels for games and media, such as videos and music, ringtones and notifications, and alarms.

6. Touch to choose whether your HTC One must vibrate when a phone call you have made connects.

7. Touch to choose the default notification ringtone or add new ones.

8. Touch to choose if the volume of the ringtone should get softer when it detects you picking up your HTC One.

9. Touch to choose if you want the ringtone volume to be increased if your HTC One detects it is in your pocket or in a bag.

10. Touch to change the sound that plays when you receive a new notification.

11. Scroll down for more settings.

12. Touch to choose what sounds play when the alarm is triggered.

13. Touch to choose whether touch tone sounds are used when using the phone dial pad.

14. Touch to choose whether a sound is played when you touch items on the screen.

15. Touch to choose whether a sound is played when you lock and unlock your HTC One.

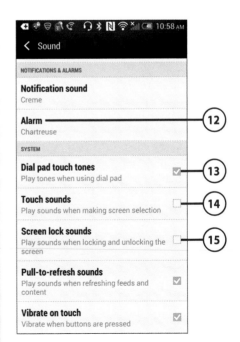

16. Touch to choose whether a sound is played when you receive updated content, like news feeds.

17. Touch to choose whether your HTC One provides a short vibration when you successfully touch a virtual button on the screen.

18. Touch to save your changes and return to the previous screen.

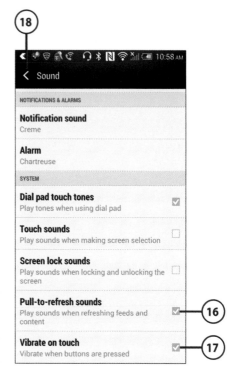

Display, Gestures, and Buttons Settings

1. Pull down the Notification bar and touch Settings.

2. Touch Display, Gestures & Buttons.

3. Touch to enable or disable autorotate, which is when your HTC One uses the acceleromoter to detect its orientation and rotate the screen to match it.

4. Touch to choose the font size of all text. Choices range from Small to Extra Large.

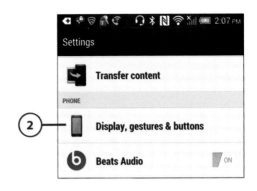

5. Touch to change the screen brightness manually or set it to automatic. When on automatic, your HTC One uses the built-in light sensor to adjust the brightness based on the light levels in the room.

6. Touch to choose a sleep timeout or use Auto.

How Does Sleep Timeout Work?

In step 6, you can choose the sleep timeout or leave it set to Auto. This means that you can choose a period of time to elapse of no usage before your HTC One turns the screen off and goes to sleep. If you set it to Auto, your HTC One uses its internal sensors to detect if you are holding it in your hand. If it detects that you are holding it in your hand, it waits for one minute of no activity before putting itself to sleep. If it detects that it is lying on a desk, it puts itself to sleep after only 15 seconds.

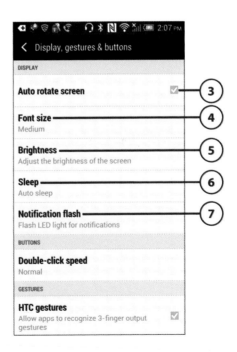

7. Touch to choose which notifications the LED will flash for.

8. Touch to set the double-click speed for the Home and Back buttons. This really should read "double-tap speed" because it refers to the period in-between taps when you want to double-tap the Home or Back buttons. Refer to the Prologue to read why you would want to double-tap these buttons.

9. Touch to choose whether you want to allow apps to recognize the special HTC three-finger gestures. Disable if you have games or other apps that use three or more finger gestures or controls.

What Is the Three-Finger Gesture?

Actually there is only one three-finger gesture, and it is for sharing media content with speakers and other devices using DLNA. If you want to send media to another device that is using DLNA, swipe up on the screen with three fingers. The only issue with enabling this gesture is that it interferes or overrides the regular gesture recognition mechanism, which means that if you use apps or games that use three or more fingers for gestures or controls, they will not work. You will need to turn off the HTC gestures to regain use of those apps or games.

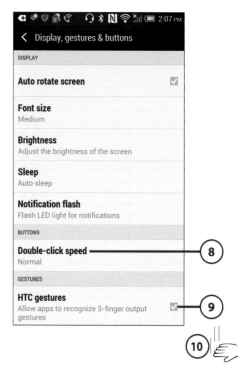

10. Scroll down to calibrate the G-Sensor.

What Is the G-Sensor?

The G-Sensor is the Gyroscope. It detects spatial movement, and it is the primary way your HTC One detects whether you are holding your device vertically or horizontally. If it detects a switch, it rotates the screen to match. If you are finding that the screen rotation is not working properly or not at all, you can calibrate the Gyroscope, or G-Sensor.

11. Touch to calibrate the G-Sensor.

12. Touch to save your changes and return to the previous screen.

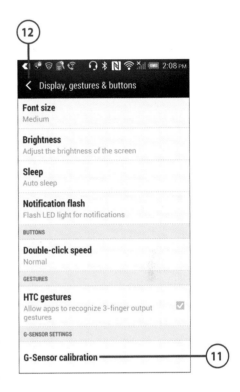

Kid Mode

Your HTC One has a built-in feature that allows you to put it into Kid Mode. While in Kid Mode, your HTC One will not allow visits to non-age-appropriate websites and allows access only to the games and apps that you have set up for them.

First-Time Setup

1. Touch the Kid Mode icon.

2. Touch Get Started.

3. Enter your email address.

4. Type a password that you want to use when setting up and configuring Kid Mode.

5. Touch Save.

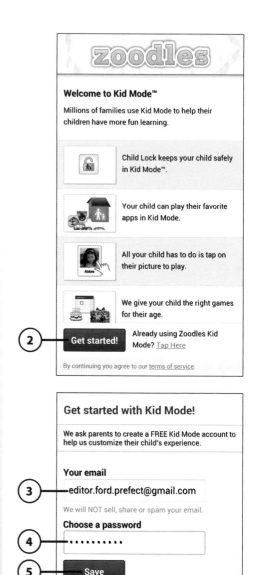

6. Type the name of your child.

7. Choose your child's birth month and year.

8. Touch to add a picture of your child if you want to.

9. Touch Done.

10. Touch to edit the list of apps your child has access to.

11. Touch to turn on Child Lock (or enable Kid Mode).

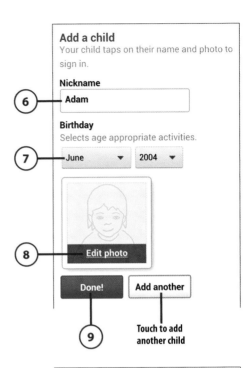

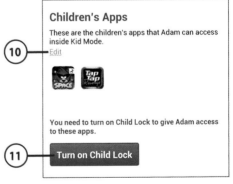

12. Touch Begin to start enabling Kid Mode.

13. Select Kid Mode.

14. Touch Always to complete the enablement of Kid Mode.

15. Your child will touch on his or her picture to open content specific to them.

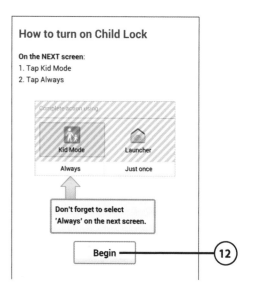

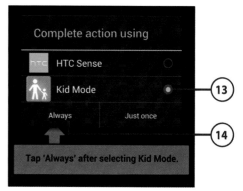

How Do I Start Kid Mode in the Future?

Each time you run Kid Mode, you will need to perform only steps 12 to 15. Steps 12 to 15 tell your HTC One that the Kid Mode app should take over control of your phone and even control what happens when you touch the Home button.

Give Control Back to HTC Sense

When you exit Kid Mode, you are again prompted to choose which app should now take over control of your HTC One. You must always choose HTC Sense and touch Always, unless you have been told otherwise. In this example, I have installed Divide, which I use for my work email. Divide is one of those apps that must be in control of your device, so I would choose Divide and touch Always.

Touch Always

Always choose HTC Sense

Further Kid Mode Configuration

You can use your desktop computer to browse to http://Zoodles.com to log in to your Zoodles account and manage Zoodle. You can also use the Parent Dashboard app to set up many of the features right from your HTC One.

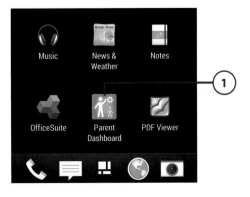

1. Touch Parent Dashboard.

2. Choose one of the basic features to configure.

3. Choose one of the premium features to configure.

4. Touch to exit the Parent Dashboard.

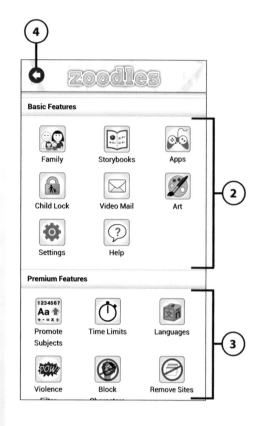

Browse without leaving traces using the Incognito feature

In this chapter, you discover how to browse the World Wide Web using the Chrome browser app that comes with your HTC One. Topics include the following:

→ Bookmarking websites
→ Using tricks to browse quickly
→ Keeping track of websites you have visited
→ Configuring Chrome to work your way

Browsing the Web

Your HTC One includes the fully featured Chrome web browser app that enables you to take full advantage of its large, sharp screen. You can bookmark sites you want to revisit, hold your HTC One in landscape orientation so you can see more on the screen, and even share your GPS location with sites.

Navigating with Chrome

The Chrome browser app enables you to access sites quickly, bookmark them for future use, and return instantly to the sites you visit most frequently. You can even sync your open Chrome tabs among your HTC One, your other portable devices, and your computer, giving yourself a seamless browsing experience no matter which device you're using.

1. Touch the Chrome icon on the Home screen.

2. Touch the omnibox—a combined address box and search box—to type in a new web address. If the website has moved the previous page up so that the omnibox is hidden, drag the web page down so that the omnibox appears again.

3. Touch to navigate among your tabs. Read more about tabs later in this chapter.

4. Touch a thumbnail to go to one of your Most Visited sites, shown in this figure.

5. Touch to display one of the pages you have closed most recently. You might need to scroll down to reach the button for the page you want.

6. Touch to display the list of Most Visited sites.

7. Touch to display your bookmarks.

8. Touch to display your Other Devices list, which shows the tabs open on your other phones, tablets, and computers that use Chrome, and sign into your Google account.

9. Touch the Menu button to display more options for working with Chrome and web pages.

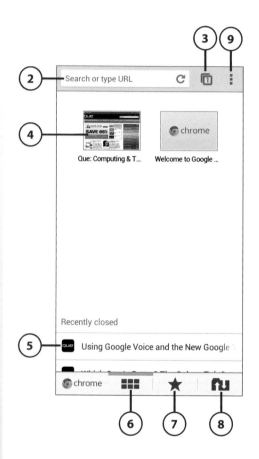

Web Page Options

While a web page is open, you have a number of options, such as creating a bookmark for the page or finding text on the page.

1. Touch the Menu button to display the menu.

2. Touch to go back to the previous web page you visited on this tab.

3. Touch to go forward to the last web page from which you went back on this tab. This button is unavailable until you go back from a page.

4. Touch to add a bookmark for this page.

5. Touch to open a new tab.

6. Touch to open a new Incognito tab for private browsing. Incognito tabs are covered later in this chapter.

7. Touch to display your bookmarks.

8. Touch to display your Other Devices list.

9. Touch to share this web page with other people using apps such as Email, Gmail, Facebook, Messaging, or Twitter. The Share via dialog shows all the apps you can use to share the web page.

10. Touch to search this page for specific text you type.

11. Touch to enable or disable forcing websites to show the regular view of a web page designed for full-size screens instead of a mobile view designed for small screens.

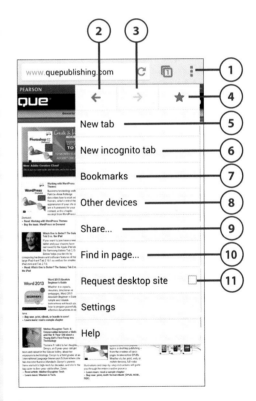

12. Touch to change the settings for Chrome. You learn about the most important settings later in this chapter.

13. Touch to get help on using Chrome to browse the Internet.

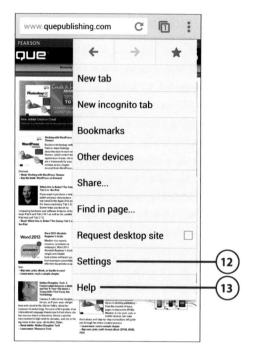

Browser Tricks

Chrome has some neat tricks to help you browse regular websites comfortably on your HTC One's screen.

Portrait

1. Rotate your HTC One so that its long edge is sideways. This puts the screen into *landscape orientation*. Your HTC One automatically switches the screen to landscape mode.

2. Double-tap the screen to zoom in and out.

Pinch to Zoom

When you need to zoom in further, or zoom in to exactly the degree you want, use the alternative way to zoom. Place your thumb and forefinger on the screen and spread them apart to zoom in. Move them back together to zoom out.

Zoomed out

Landscape

Zoomed in

Browsing with Bookmarks and Other Devices

The Chrome app enables you to bookmark your favorite websites for quick access. You can create folders and subfolders to keep your bookmarks well organized and easy to find. The app also syncs your open tabs among your devices that run Chrome and sign in to the same Google account, so you can quickly pick up browsing on your HTC One exactly where you left it on your desktop computer, laptop, or tablet—or vice versa.

Browse with Bookmarks

1. Touch the Menu button.

2. Touch Bookmarks. The Bookmarks folder opens.

3. Touch the bookmarks folder you want to open. This example uses the Mobile Bookmarks folder.

4. Touch to return to the main Bookmarks folder. From there, you can touch another bookmarks folder to open it.

5. Touch a bookmark to display the web page it marks.

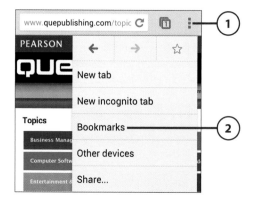

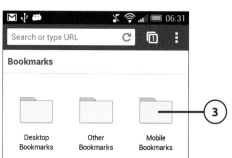

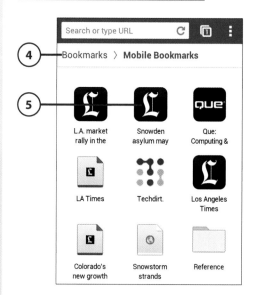

6. Touch and hold a bookmark to display a menu containing the Open in Incognito tab command. Touch this command to open the bookmarked page in an Incognito tab.

Create a Bookmark

1. Navigate to the page you want to bookmark.

2. Touch the Menu button to open the menu.

3. Touch to start creating a new bookmark.

4. Change the bookmark name if you want to. The default is the web page's title; you might prefer a shorter name.

5. Edit the address if necessary. If you went to the right page in step 1, you do not need to change the address.

6. If the In box does not show the folder in which you want to save the bookmark, touch the folder shown.

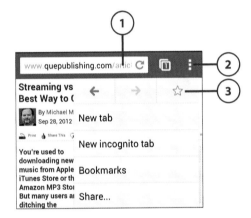

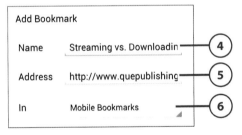

7. On the Choose a Folder screen, touch the folder to put the bookmark in. If necessary, you can create a new folder, as described in the next section.

8. Touch OK.

9. On the Add Bookmark screen, touch Save to save the bookmark.

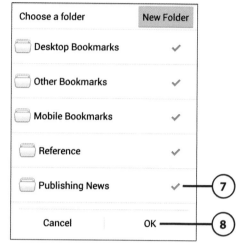

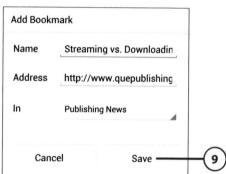

Create a New Bookmarks Folder

When creating a new bookmark, you can create one or more new bookmark folders to keep your bookmarks organized.

1. On the Choose a Folder screen, touch New Folder.

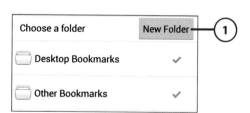

2. Type the name for the new folder.

3. If the In box does not show the folder in which you want to create the new folder, touch the folder shown. On the Choose a Folder screen, touch the folder to use, and then touch OK.

4. Touch Save to save the new folder. The Choose a Folder screen appears with the new folder selected, and you can finish creating the new bookmark.

Add Folder

Name   Computing Tips ——————— ②

In   Mobile Bookmarks ——— ③

Cancel   Save —— ④

Browse with the Most Visited Sites List

The Chrome app's Most Visited sites list enables you to quickly return to sites you visit frequently but that you have not necessarily bookmarked.

1. Touch the Menu button.

2. Touch Bookmarks to display the Bookmarks screen.

3. Touch to display the Most Visited screen.

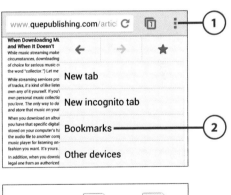

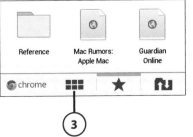

4. Touch to open one of the pages in the current tab.

5. Touch and hold to display further options.

6. Touch to open in a new tab.

7. Touch to open in an Incognito tab.

8. Touch to remove the web page from the Most Visited list.

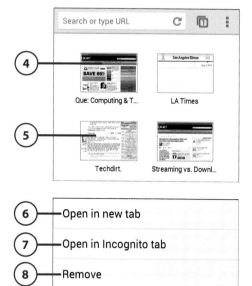

Browse with the Other Devices List

The Other Devices list gives you instant access to the tabs open in Chrome on your other devices, such as your tablet and your PC or Mac.

1. Touch the Menu button.

2. Touch Other Devices.

3. Touch a heading to expand or collapse the list of pages on a device.

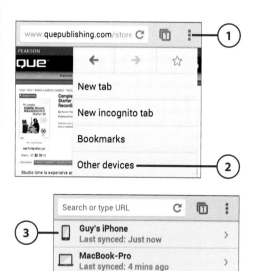

4. Touch a page to open it.

Managing Multiple Tabs

The Chrome app can have multiple web pages open at the same time, each in a different tab. This enables you to open multiple web pages at once and switch between them.

1. Touch the tab icon in the Chrome app.

2. Touch to open a new tab.

3. Touch to close an existing tab.

4. Touch a tab to switch to it.

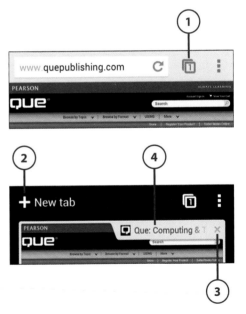

Browsing in Secret

If you want to visit a website in secret, you can. Visiting a website in secret means that the site you visit does not appear in your browser history or search history and does not otherwise leave a trace of itself on your HTC One. To browse secretly, create a new Incognito browser tab by touching the Menu button and then touching New Incognito tab. Inside that browser tab, all sites you visit are in secret.

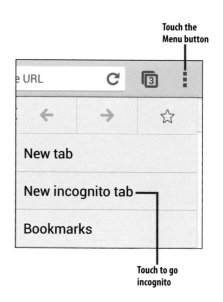

Touch the Menu button

Touch to go incognito

Customizing Browser Settings

You can customize Chrome to make it behave the way you want. Here are the various settings you can change.

1. Touch the Menu button.

2. Touch Settings.

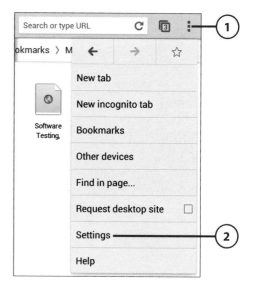

3. Touch your Google account name.

4. Touch to turn sync on or off. If you turn sync on, you can choose which items to sync: bookmarks, omnibox history, open tabs, or everything.

5. Touch to enable or disable sending web pages from your computer to the Chrome app on your HTC One.

6. Touch to enable or disable automatically signing in to Google sites. Signing in automatically saves you time and typing but decreases your privacy.

7. Touch to return to the Settings screen.

8. Touch to choose your search engine. Your choices vary depending on your location, but Google, Yahoo!, and Bing are typical.

9. Touch to enable or disable the Autofill Forms feature. This feature lets you add profile information—your name, address, and so on—and credit card information for the Chrome app to fill in automatically on web forms. This means you can complete web forms and spend your money with even less effort.

10. Touch to enable or disable the Chrome app's capability to save your passwords so it can enter them for you.

11. Touch Privacy.

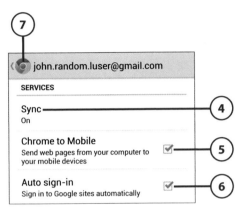

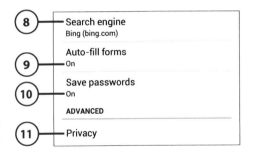

12. Touch to enable or disable seeing suggestions for web addresses that you enter incorrectly or that Chrome cannot locate.

13. Touch to enable or disable seeing related queries and popular websites similar to those you type in the omnibox.

14. Touch to enable or disable the Network Action Predictions feature. See the nearby sidebar for details.

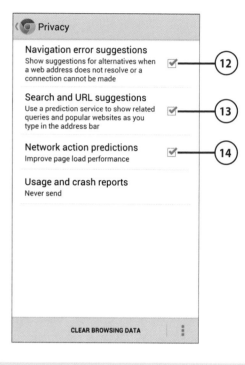

Privacy

Navigation error suggestions
Show suggestions for alternatives when a web address does not resolve or a connection cannot be made — 12

Search and URL suggestions
Use a prediction service to show related queries and popular websites as you type in the address bar — 13

Network action predictions
Improve page load performance — 14

Usage and crash reports
Never send

CLEAR BROWSING DATA

>>>Go Further

WHAT ARE NETWORK ACTION PREDICTIONS?

Network Action Predictions is a feature that allows the Chrome app to pre-load web pages you are likely to want to load. The app does this in two ways. First, when you start typing an address in the omnibox, the Chrome app preloads a matching web page if it has high confidence that you will want it—for example, because you have visited that page before. Second, when you are on a particular web page, the app might preload the pages whose links you are most likely to click—for example, the top few search results.

If Chrome has predicted correctly and loaded the correct pages into memory, when you touch a link, that page renders straight from your HTC One's memory instead of first loading over the network. Although this can be a time-saver, it means that your HTC One might preload pages that you will not look at, which can lead to wasted data usage. When you enable Network Action Predictions, you can choose Only on Wi-Fi on the Bandwidth Management screen to allow the Chrome app to preload pages only when your HTC One is connected to Wi-Fi, not when it's connected via a cellular data connection.

15. Touch to choose whether to send usage and crash reports to Google. Your choices are Always Send, Only Send on Wi-Fi, and Never Send. If you are happy to provide this data, choosing Only Send on Wi-Fi is usually the best choice, because it prevents the reports from consuming your cellular data allowance.

16. Touch to display the Clear Browsing Data dialog.

17. Touch to enable or disable clearing your browsing history. This clears the history of websites you have visited using the Chrome app on your HTC One.

18. Touch to enable or disable clearing the cache, data that Chrome stores so that it can redisplay web pages more quickly when you visit them again.

19. Touch to enable or disable clearing your cookies and website data. Browser cookies are used by websites to personalize your visit by storing information specific to you in the cookies.

20. Touch to enable or disable clearing your saved passwords.

21. Touch to enable or disable clearing your Autofill data.

22. Touch to clear the items whose boxes you checked in the Clear Browsing Data dialog.

23. Touch to return to the Settings screen.

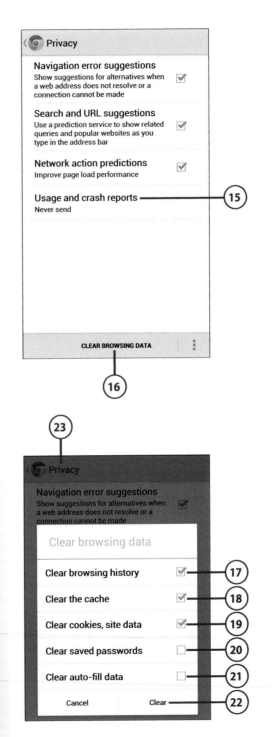

24. Touch Accessibility.

25. Drag to make the text in the Preview box appear at a comfortable size for reading. This is the minimum size to which the Chrome app zooms the text when you double-tap a paragraph.

What Is Text Scaling?

When you use text scaling, you instruct your HTC One to always increase or decrease the font sizes used on a web page by a specific percentage. For example, you can automatically make all text 150% larger than was originally intended.

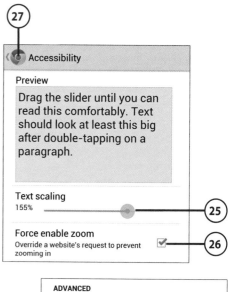

26. Touch to turn on or off Chrome's capability to zoom in on a website that prevents zooming. Some websites turn off zooming because their creators rate design higher than readability. Turning on this feature enables you to zoom anyway on such sites.

27. Touch to return to the Settings screen.

28. Touch Content Settings.

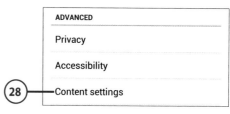

29. Touch to enable or disable accepting cookies. Browser cookies are used by websites to personalize your visit by storing information specific to you in the cookies.

30. Touch to enable or disable JavaScript. JavaScript is used on many web pages for formatting and other functions, so you might want to leave this enabled.

31. Touch to block pop-up windows. Pop-up windows are almost always advertisements, so keeping this enabled is a good idea; however, some websites might not work correctly if pop-up blocking is on. Chrome displays a message indicating that it has blocked a pop-up.

32. Touch to display the Google apps Location Settings screen.

33. Touch this switch to control whether Google apps can access your location.

34. Touch to go back to the Content settings screen.

35. Touch to view the list of websites that are storing data on your HTC One. You can then clear the data for a specific website if necessary.

36. Touch to go back to the Settings screen.

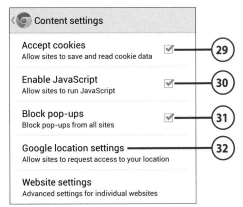

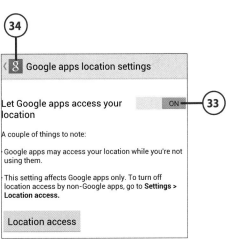

37. Touch Bandwidth Management.

38. Touch Preload Web Pages to open the Preload Web Pages dialog. (Refer to the "What Are Network Action Predictions" sidebar for more information about preloading web pages.)

39. Touch to preload pages over both Wi-Fi and cellular connections.

40. Touch to preload pages over Wi-Fi only.

41. Touch to turn off preloading. You would normally do this only if you need to minimize data use on your Wi-Fi connection.

42. Touch to return to the Settings screen.

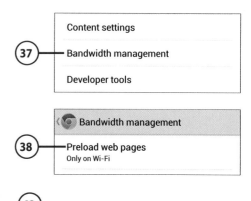

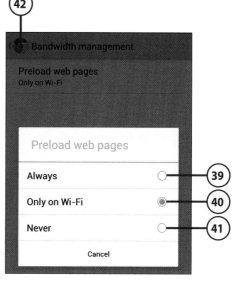

What Are the Developer Tools in Chrome Settings?

The Chrome app'sDeveloper Tools screen offers two features intended for people developing apps for Android, but one of the features is useful for nondevelopers as well. The Enable Tilt Scrolling feature enables you to scroll through your open tabs in Chrome by tilting your HTC One backward and forward. The Enable USB Web Debugging option lets developers use Chrome on a PC or Mac to hunt down bugs in Chrome on Android.

Touch to turn on tilt scrolling for tabs

‹ Developer tools

Enable Tilt Scrolling
Allow scrolling of the stack view by
flinging the device. Changes won't take
effect until Chrome has been restarted.

Enable USB Web debugging
Debug web pages from Chrome Desktop
via USB

Learn more about using USB Web debugging

Touch to open
Gmail email only

Touch to
open email

In this chapter, you learn about your HTC One's email applications for Gmail and other email accounts, such as POP3, IMAP, and even work email. Topics include the following:

→ Sending and receiving email
→ Working with attachments
→ Working with Gmail labels
→ Changing settings

Email

Your HTC One has two email programs: the Gmail app, which works only with Google's web-based Gmail service, and the Email app that works with POP3, IMAP, and work email accounts.

Gmail

When you first set up your HTC One, you set up a Gmail account. The Gmail application enables you to have multiple Gmail accounts, which is useful if you have a business account and a personal account.

Adding a Google Account

When you first set up your HTC One, you added your first Google (Gmail) account. The following steps describe how to add a second account.

1. Touch to open the Gmail app.

2. Touch the Menu button.

3. Touch Settings.

4. Touch Add Account.

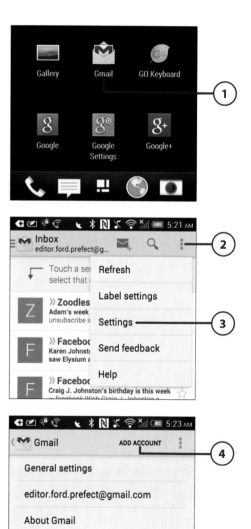

5. Touch Existing.

6. Enter your existing Google account name. This is your Gmail address.

What If I Don't Have a Second Google Account?

If you don't already have a second Google account but want to set one up, in step 5, touch Get a Google Account. Your HTC One walks you through the steps of choosing a new Google account.

7. Enter your existing Google password.

8. Touch the right arrow to continue.

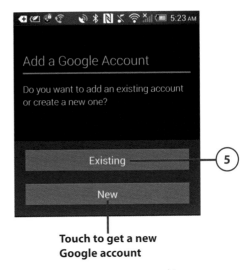

Touch to get a new Google account

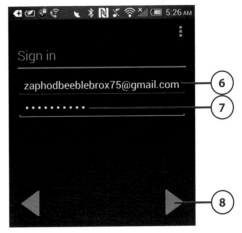

9. Select what components of your Google account you want to synchronize with your HTC One.

10. Touch to finish the Google account setup.

Why Multiple Google Accounts?

You are probably wondering why you would want multiple Google accounts. Isn't one good enough? It is not that uncommon to have multiple Google accounts. It can be a way to compartmentalize your life between work and play. You might run a small business using the one account, but email only friends with another. Your HTC One supports multiple accounts but still enables you to interact with them in one place.

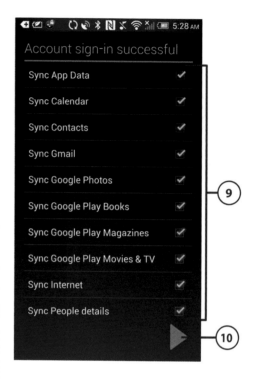

Navigating the Gmail App

Let's take a quick look at the Gmail app and learn how to navigate the main screen.

1. Touch the Gmail icon.

2. Touch to switch between Gmail accounts (if you use more than one) or switch from the Inbox label to one of your other labels.

3. Touch to compose a new email.

4. Touch to search the current label for an email.

5. Swipe down to manually refresh the current view.

6. Touch one or more email icons to mark the emails as read or unread, move them to a different label, or archive them.

7. Touch the star to add the email to the Starred label.

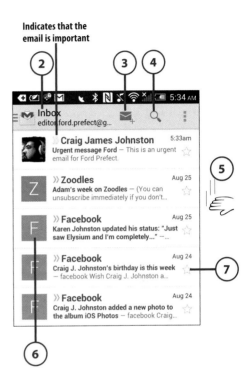

Indicates that the email is important

Stars and Labels

Gmail allows you to use stars and labels to help organize your email. In most email clients, you can create folders in your mailbox to help you organize your emails. For example, you might create a folder called "emails from the boss" and move any emails you receive to that folder. Gmail doesn't use the term *folders*; it uses the term *labels* instead. You can create labels in Gmail and choose an email to label. When you do this, it moves it to a folder with that label, but to you, the email has a label distinguishing it from other emails. And email that you mark with a star is just getting a label called *starred*. But when viewing your Gmail, you see the yellow star next to an email. People normally add a star to an email as a reminder of something important.

Composing Gmail Email

1. Touch the compose icon.

2. Touch to change the Gmail account from which the message is being sent (if you have multiple Gmail accounts).

3. Type names in the To field. If the name matches someone in your Contacts, the name is displayed, and you can touch it to select it.

Can You Carbon Copy (CC) and Blind Carbon Copy (BCC)?

While you are composing your email, you can add recipients to the To field as shown in step 3, but no Carbon Copy (CC) and Blind Carbon Copy (BCC) fields are shown. However, you can add these fields by touching the Menu button and touching Add CC/BCC. After you do that, the CC and BCC fields are displayed.

---

4. Type a subject for your email.

5. Type the body of the email.

6. Touch to send the email.

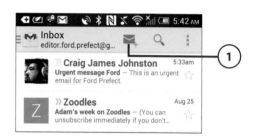

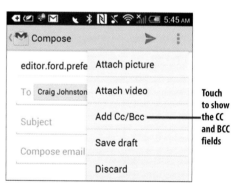

Touch to show the CC and BCC fields

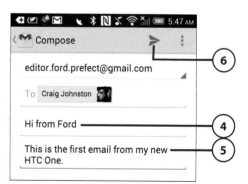

Add Attachments

Before sending an email, you can add one or more attachments. You can attach pictures or videos, but if you use Dropbox, you can attach any file that is in your Dropbox folders. If you use Office Suite for your Microsoft Office documents, you can attach files from there, too.

1. Touch the Menu button.

2. Touch Attach Picture or Attach Video (they do the same thing).

3. Touch Gallery.

4. Navigate the Gallery App to find the picture you want to attach.

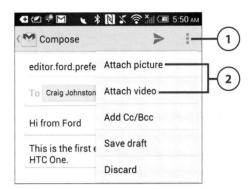

Touch to attach any file
type stored in your Dropbox

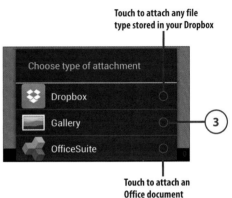

Touch to attach an
Office document
stored in Office Suite

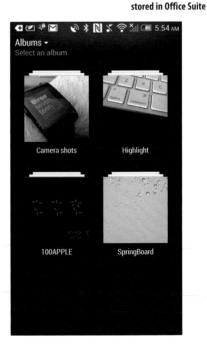

5. Attachments are listed below the body of the email.

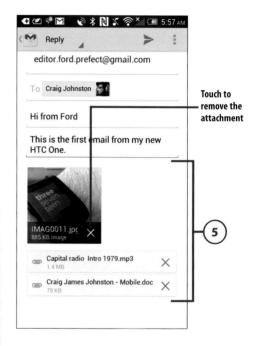

Touch to remove the attachment

Reading Gmail Email

1. Touch an email to open it.

Indicates attachments

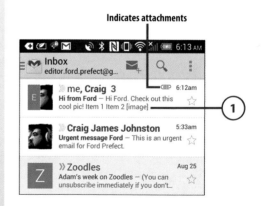

2. Touch to expand the original email, if the email you are reading is a reply.

3. Touch to reply to the sender of the email. This does not reply to anyone in the CC field.

4. Touch the Menu bar to do a Reply All (reply to all recipients) or Forward the email.

5. Touch to expand the email header to see all recipients and all other email header information.

6. Touch to "star" the email, which adds it to the star label. See more about labels in the previous section.

7. Indicates whether the sender of the email is online using Google Talk (GTalk) if that person is in your GTalk buddy list.

8. Touch to move the email to the Gmail Archive folder.

9. Touch to change the label of the email. See more about labels in the previous section.

10. Touch to mark the message as unread and return to the message list.

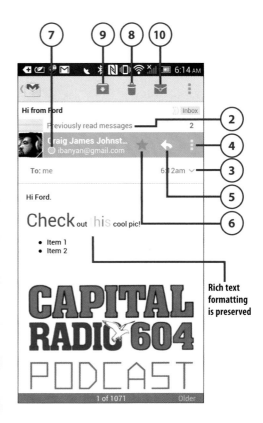

More Email Actions

1. Touch the Menu button.

2. Touch to report the email as spam.

3. Touch to mute the email conversation. When it is muted, you will no longer see emails in the conversation.

4. Touch to report the email as a phishing scam.

5. Touch to mark the message as not important or important.

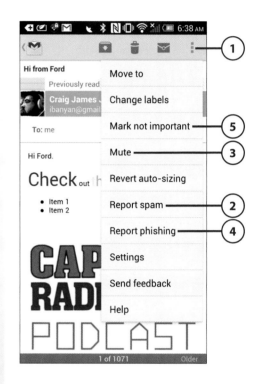

What Is Important?

Gmail tries to automatically figure out which of the emails you receive are important. As it learns, it may get it wrong. If an email is marked as important but it is not important, you can manually change the status to not important, as you see in step 5. Important emails have a yellow arrow, whereas emails that are not important have a clear arrow.

What Are Conversations?

Conversations are Gmail's version of email threads. When you look at the main view of the Gmail app, you are seeing a list of email conversations. The conversation might have only one email in it, but to Gmail that's a conversation. As you and others reply to that original email, Gmail groups those emails in a thread, or conversation.

What Happens to Your Spam and Phishing Emails?

When you mark an email in Gmail as spam or a phishing scam, two things happen. First, it gets a label called Spam. Second, a copy of that email is sent to Gmail's spam servers so they are now aware of a possible new spam or phishing scam email that is circulating around the Internet. Based on what the servers see for all Gmail users, they block that spam or phishing email from reaching other Gmail users. So the bottom line is, always mark spam emails as spam and phishing emails as phishing because it helps all of us.

Gmail Settings

You can customize the way Gmail accounts work on your HTC One, including changing the email signature and choosing which labels synchronize.

1. Touch the Menu button.

2. Touch Settings.

Email Signature

An email signature is a bit of text that is automatically added to the bottom of any emails you send from your HTC One. It is added when you compose a new email, reply to an email, or forward an email. A typical use for a signature is to automatically add your name and some contact information at the end of your emails. Email signatures are sometimes referred to as email footers.

3. Touch General Settings.

4. Touch to choose whether you want the Gmail app to show archive, delete, or both archive and delete actions on the screen.

5. Touch to choose whether you want to be able to swipe a conversation to archive it.

6. Touch to choose whether you want to see the email sender's image.

7. Touch to choose whether to make Reply All the default action when replying to emails. Normally only Reply is used. Reply All replies to the sender and all recipients.

8. Touch to enable or disable Auto-fit. When enabled, Auto-fit shrinks all emails so that they fit on the screen, but you can still use the pinch gesture to zoom in.

9. Touch Auto-advance to select which screen your HTC One must show after you delete or archive and email. Your choices are Newer Conversation, Older Conversation, and Conversation List.

10. Touch to change the behavior of the blue message actions bar as you scroll through a message. Your choices are to keep it at the top of the screen as you scroll, keep it at the top of the screen only when in portrait mode, or let it scroll up with the message as you scroll.

11. Touch to choose whether you want to be asked to confirm when you delete an email.

12. Scroll down for more options.

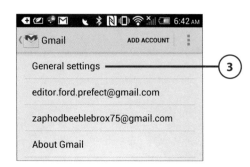

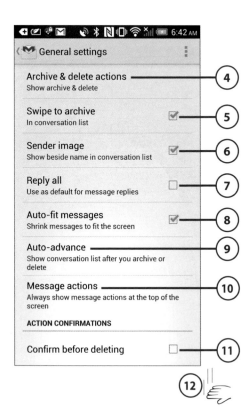

13. Touch to choose whether you want to be asked to confirm when you archive an email.

14. Touch to choose whether you want to be asked to confirm when you send an email.

15. Touch to return to the main Settings screen.

16. Touch one of your Gmail accounts to change settings specific to that account.

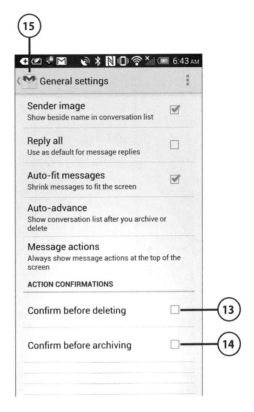

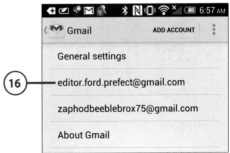

17. Touch to choose whether you want to show your Priority Inbox instead of your regular (or Default) Inbox when opening the Gmail app.

18. Touch to choose whether you want to be notified when new email arrives for this Gmail account.

19. Touch to select how to get notified when new email arrives for this account.

20. Touch to enter a signature that will appear at the end of all emails composed using this account.

21. Touch to choose whether this Gmail account is synchronized to your HTC One.

22. Touch to select how many days of mail from this Gmail account to synchronize with your HTC One.

23. Touch to manage labels. See more about managing labels in the next section.

24. Touch to choose whether to download attachments while connected to a Wi-Fi network.

25. Touch to save your changes and return to the main Settings screen.

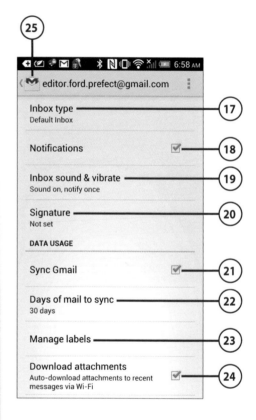

Managing Gmail Labels

Gmail labels are Google's name for email folders. You can manage how each of them synchronize and alert you. Use these steps if you want to manage labels in the previous step 23.

1. Touch a label to manage it. In this example, we have chosen the Inbox label.

2. Touch to enable synchronization of this label to your HTC One, and whether to synchronize 30 days of email or all email. When synchronization is enabled, the rest of the settings on this screen become available.

3. Touch to enable or disable being notified when new email arrives in this label.

4. Touch to select the ringtone that plays when you are notified of new email in this label.

5. Touch to choose whether to also vibrate when new email arrives in this label.

6. Touch to enable or disable notifying you once when multiple emails arrive in this label, rather than notifying for each one.

7. Touch to return to the list of labels.

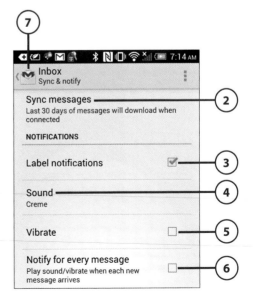

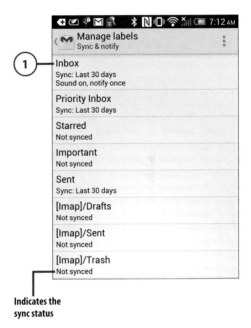

Email Application

The Email application supports all email accounts with the exception of Gmail. This includes any corporate email accounts that use Microsoft Exchange, or corporate emails systems like Lotus Domino/Notes that have an ActiveSync gateway—for example, Notes Traveler. In addition to corporate emails accounts, the Email application also supports POP3 and IMAP accounts. These are typically hosted by your Internet service provider, but also by places like Yahoo! or Hotmail.

Adding a Work Email Account

Your HTC One can synchronize your contacts from your work email account as long as your company uses Microsoft Exchange or an email gateway that supports Microsoft ActiveSync (such as Lotus Traveler for Lotus Domino/Notes email systems). It might be useful to be able to keep your work and personal contacts on one mobile device instead of carrying two phones around all day.

1. Pull down the Notification bar and touch Settings.

2. Touch Accounts & Sync.

3. Touch the plus symbol to add a new account.

4. Touch Exchange ActiveSync.

5. Enter your full corporate email address.

6. Enter your corporate network password.

7. Touch Next.

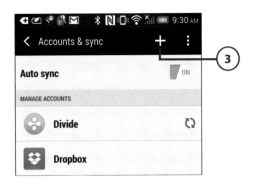

Error Adding Account? Guess the Server

Your HTC One tries to work out some information about your company's ActiveSync setup. If it can't, you are prompted to enter the ActiveSync server name manually. If you don't know what it is, you can try guessing it. If, for example, your email address is dsimons@allhitradio.com, the ActiveSync server is most probably webmail.allhitradio.com or autodiscover.allhitradio.com. If this doesn't work, ask your email administrator.

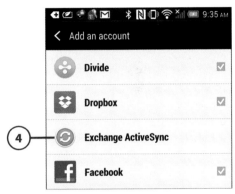

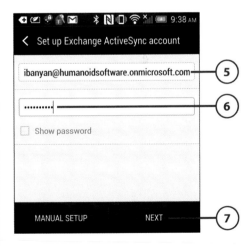

8. Enter your company's mail server name.

9. Touch to use secure connections, which encrypts your email, calendar, and contacts between your HTC One and your company's mail server. It is highly recommended that you leave this selected.

10. Touch Next.

11. Choose what you want to synchronize to your HTC One from your work account.

12. Scroll down to see all the Update Schedule options.

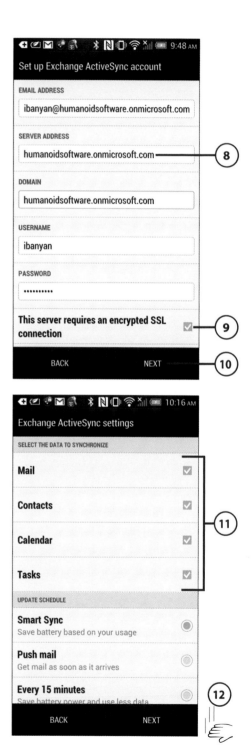

13. Touch to choose how often your corporate email is delivered to your HTC One. Push means that as it arrives in your Inbox at work, it will be delivered to your phone. You can set it to Manual, which means that your work email will be delivered only when you open the Email app on your phone. You can also set the delivery frequency to every 15 minutes. SmartSync continually adjusts the sync interval based on how often you open the Mail app.

14. Touch Next to continue.

15. Enter a friendly name for this email account.

16. Touch Finish Setup.

Remove an Account

To remove an account, from the Settings screen, touch the type of account (for example, Exchange ActiveSync), and touch the account to be removed. Touch the Menu button and touch Remove.

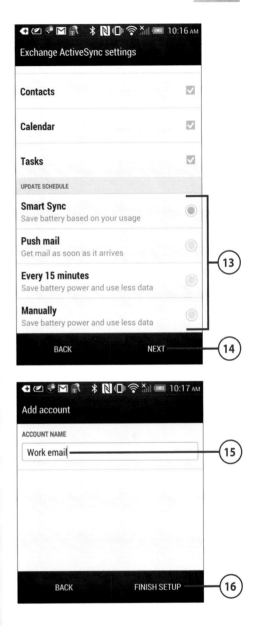

CAN YOU TRULY KEEP WORK AND PRIVATE DATA SEPARATE?

>>>Go Further

More and more companies are adopting a Bring Your Own Device (BYOD) policy, which means that they expect you to use your personal phone to get access to company emails, contacts, calendar, and internal apps. As we have seen, your HTC One fully supports accessing your company's email system, but when you activate, you have to agree to allow your administrator control over your phone. This is not ideal, because the administrator can see what apps you have installed and can send a self-destruct command to your HTC One, which means you lose all your private data and apps. Dual Persona is fast becoming the way for you to truly keep your private date private and not allow your company to wipe your phone or see what you have installed. A few companies today provide this service, including Enterproid (the product is called DIVIDE), and Good Technology (the product is called GOOD). The idea is that your HTC One has two personalities: a work persona or profile and a private persona or profile. All work data is kept in its own separate area on your phone, and your administrators have no control over the rest of your phone. Follow these links to learn more: http://divide.com http://good.com.

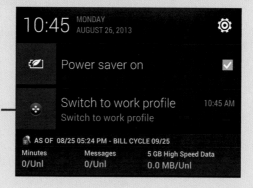

Touch to switch to the work profile

Adding a New POP3 or IMAP Account

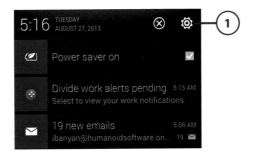

1. Pull down the Notification bar and touch the Settings icon.

2. Touch Accounts & Sync.

3. Touch the plus sign to add an account.

4. Touch Mail.

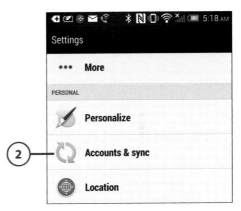

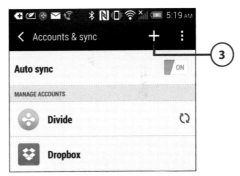

5. Enter your email address.

6. Enter your password.

7. Touch Next.

Why Manual Setup?

Your HTC One tries to figure out the settings to set up your email account. This works most of the time when you are using common email providers such as Yahoo! or Hotmail and others. It also works with large ISPs, such as Comcast, Road Runner, Optimum Online, and so on. It might not work for smaller ISPs, or in smaller countries, or if you have created your own website and set up your own email. In these cases, you need to set up your email manually.

8. Touch to choose POP3 or IMAP. IMAP has more intelligence to it, so select that where possible.

9. Ensure that the information on this screen is accurate for the incoming server and related settings.

10. Touch Next.

Where Can I Find This Information?

In steps 9 and 11, you need to make sure that items such as the IMAP server, SMTP server, security type, and username are correct. Always check your ISP's or email service provider's website, and look for instructions on how to set up your email on a computer or smartphone. This is normally under the support section of the website.

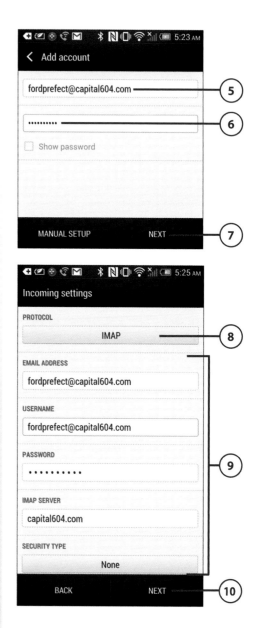

Username and Password

On the Incoming Server and Outgoing Server screens, your username and password should already be filled out because you typed them in earlier. If not, enter them.

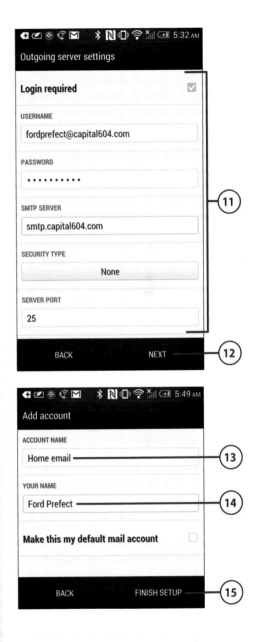

11. Ensure that the information on this screen is accurate for the outgoing server and related settings.

12. Touch Next.

13. Enter a friendly name for this account, like "Home Email."

14. Enter your full name or the name you want to be displayed when people receive emails sent from this account.

15. Touch Finish Setup to save the settings for this account and return to the Add Accounts screen.

Be Secure if You Can

If your mail provider supports email security such as SSL or TLS, you should strongly consider using it. If you don't, emails you send and receive go over the Internet in plain readable text. Using SSL or TLS encrypts the emails as they travel across the Internet, so nobody can read them. Set this under the Advanced settings for the Incoming and Outgoing Servers.

Working with the Mail App

Now that you have added two new accounts, you can start using the Mail application. Everything you do in the Mail application is the same for every email account. The Mail app allows you to work with email accounts either separately or in a combined view.

Navigating the Mail Application

Before you learn how to compose or read emails, you should become familiar with the Mail application.

1. Touch to launch the Mail app.

2. Touch to switch between email accounts or select the All Accounts view, which shows all emails from all accounts.

3. Indicates the number of unread emails in the current folder or view.

4. Touch the flag to mark an email as flagged for follow up. You can flag messages for follow up only on accounts that support that feature. In this example, only the Exchange ActiveSync (orange) account supports it.

5. Each color represents a specific email account. In this example, the IMPA account is green and the Exchange ActiveSync is orange. The presence of the color also indicates that the email is unread.

6. Check boxes next to emails to select more than one. Then you can take actions against multiple emails at once, such as Mark as Read, Delete, or Move to a new folder.

7. Touch to compose a new email.

Working with Multiple Emails at Once

When you select multiple emails by checking the boxes next to them, you can take action on all the selected messages at once. You can mark the messages as unread or read, and delete them.

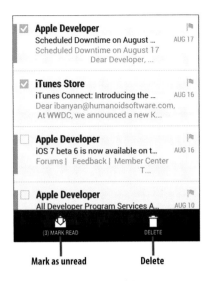

Mark as unread   Delete

Composing Email

1. Touch to compose a new email.

2. Enter one or more recipients. As you type, your HTC One tries to guess who you want to address the message to. If you see the correct name, touch it to select it. This includes names stored on your HTC One and in your company's corporate address book if you are using Exchange ActiveSync.

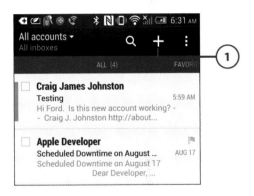

Touch to change which account you want to send the email from

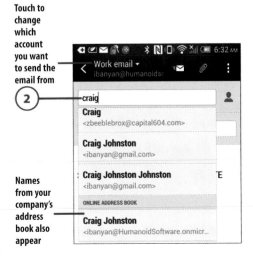

Names from your company's address book also appear

3. Enter a subject.

4. Enter the body of the message.

5. Touch to change the message priority to Low, Normal, or High Priority.

6. Touch to add one or more attachments.

7. Touch to send the message.

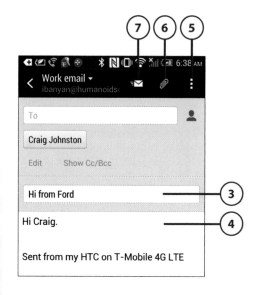

Add Attachments

Before you send your message, you might want to add one or more attachments. You can attach any type of file, including pictures, video, audio, contacts, and location.

1. Touch the attachment icon.

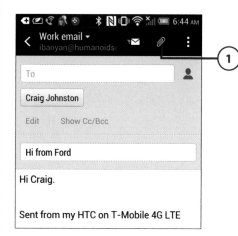

2. Choose the type of attachment. Depending on the type of attachment you choose, the screens to navigate to that file will differ.

3. Touch an attachment to either open or remove it.

4. Touch to hide the list of attachments so there is more onscreen room for you to type.

5. Touch to send the email.

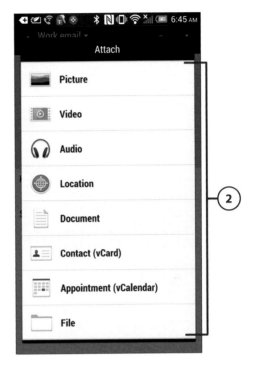

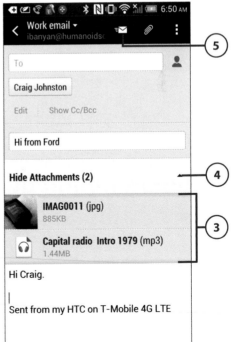

Reading Email

Reading messages in the email application is the same, regardless of which account the email has come to.

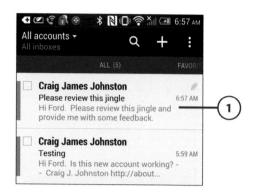

1. Touch an email to open it.

2. Touch to reply to the sender of the email. This does not reply to anyone in the CC field.

3. Touch to forward the email.

4. Touch to expand the email header to see all recipients and all other email header information.

5. Touch to reply to the sender and anyone in the CC field.

6. Touch to delete the message.

7. Touch an attachment to open it.

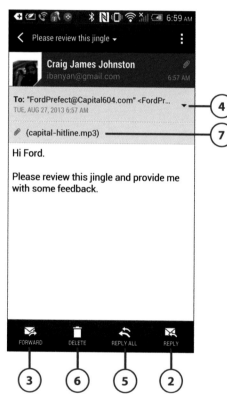

Search Google

See your
local weather

In this chapter, you learn how to use Google Maps, Navigation, and Google Now. Topics include the following:

→ Google Maps
→ Navigation
→ Google Now
→ Using Google Maps with no data coverage

Google Now and Navigation

Your HTC One can be used as a GPS navigation device while you are walking or driving around. It also includes a new app called Google Now that offers to provide you all the information you need when you need it.

Google Now

Google Now can be accessed from any screen (except the Lock screen) and allows you to search the Internet, but it also provides information such as how long it will take to drive to work and the scores for your favorite teams.

1. Touch and hold the Home button to access Google Now from any screen or any app.

2. Cards automatically appear based on your settings, such as sports teams you follow, upcoming meetings, weather where you work, and traffic on the way to work.

3. Touch and speak a request or search. You can also just say "Google" and then speak your request.

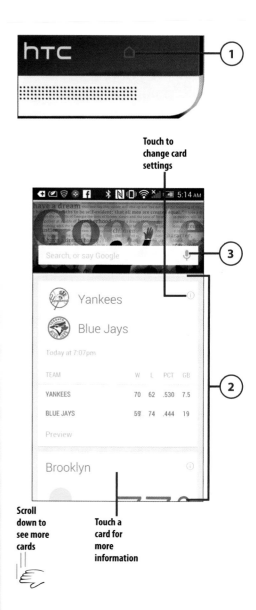

Touch to change card settings

Scroll down to see more cards

Touch a card for more information

4. Cards relevant to your search or request appear.

What Else Can Google Now Do?

When you speak to Google Now, you can ask it questions, but you can also ask Google Now to perform tasks for you. For example, you can ask Google to call a company, get directions, send a text message for you, set reminders, schedule a meeting, play music or movies, set alarms, and even launch your apps.

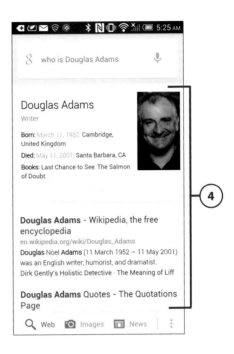

Setting Up Google Now

For Google Now to work for you, you should set it up correctly. This means not only setting up Google Now, but also setting up Google Maps, which is used heavily by Google Now.

1. Touch the Menu button.

2. Touch Settings.

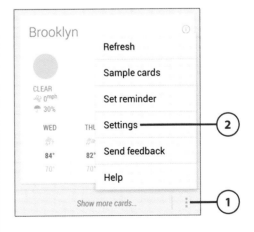

3. Touch Google Now.

4. Touch the switch to the right of each Google Now card to enable or disable it.

What Do All These Cards Do?

Google Now has many cards that it can automatically display for you. For example, the Activity Summary card shows how active you have been each day. Many cards are time and place sensitive, such as cards that show how long your commute home is—which appears only when its nearing time to go home—or cards that show your flight status as you get close to catching your flight, and even cards that show nearby restaurants and rental car kiosks as you travel. To get a full list of cards, visit http://en.wikipedia.org/wiki/Google_Now.

5. Touch to save your changes and return to the main settings screen.

Touch to turn Google Now on and off

Scroll down for more cards

6. Touch Voice.

7. Touch to choose the language that Google Now uses.

8. Touch to choose when Google Now speaks: always, only when the information it needs to convey is informative, or anytime you are using a hands-free device.

9. Touch to block or allow offensive words.

10. Touch to enable or disable Hotword detection. When enabled, while Google Now is running, it is always listening for you to say the word Google and it then launches voice search.

11. Touch to download speech recognition software so you can do voice searches even when not connected to the Internet. You can download multiple languages.

12. Touch to enable or disable personalized voice recognition. When enabled, Google tries to better understand your accent to make for more accurate searches.

13. Touch to see your Google dashboard, which shows you all your Google account info, including data collected about your devices.

14. Touch to choose whether to allow Google Now to listen for your voice via your Bluetooth headset.

15. Touch to save your changes and return to the main settings screen.

16. Touch to choose if Google Now should alert you for things like public alerts, heavy traffic tickets, and the like.

17. Touch to set up your specific information, such as where you live and work, your sports teams, and what stocks you want to follow, so that Google Now can show that information to you.

18. Touch to choose which apps installed on your HTC One are searched when you do a search in Google Now.

19. Touch Privacy & Accounts.

20. Touch to choose which Google account you want to use for Google Now.

21. Touch to choose whether Google can access your HTC One's location anytime you have it turned on and have the capability to track your location and keep a history of it.

22. Touch to enable or disable Web History.

23. Touch to manage your Web History, including the ability to delete it.

24. Touch to choose whether you want to use Personal Results, which is a feature that allows Google to provide more personal search results based on what your friends are posting on Google+ and things you search for on Google.

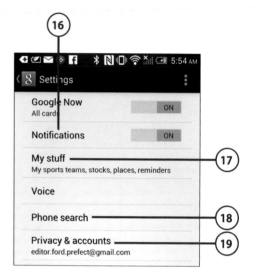

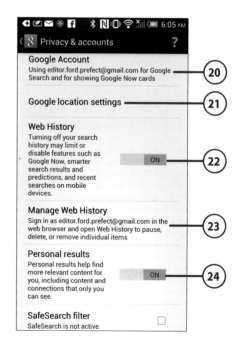

25. Touch to enable the SafeSearch filter, which lets Google filter out innapropriate content from your searches.

26. Touch to save your changes and return to the previous screen.

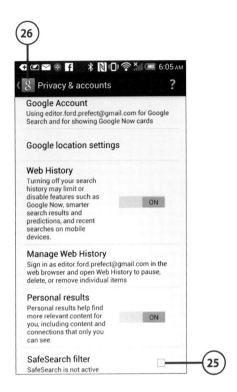

Do I Really Want Google Tracking Me?

Google Now is at its most effective when it has access to where you are, where you have been, and where you are likely to go in the future. For Google Now to be this effective, however, you have to agree to let Google track your phone all the time and keep a history of where you have been. Of course, Google does promise to keep this information private and use it only to enhance your experience; however, you will need to make a personal decision about whether you are comfortable with this.

Google Maps

Google Maps enables you to see where you are on a map, finds points of interest close to you, gives you driving or walking directions, and provides extra layers of information, such as a satellite view and traffic.

1. Touch to launch Google Maps.

2. Touch to search for a destination based on key words and the actual name of the place.

3. Touch to get walking or driving directions from one location to another. You can also choose to use public transit or biking paths to get to your destination.

4. Touch to see all your activity while using the Maps app and any reviews you've written. You will also be able to see special offers in the area.

5. Touch to add layers to the Map view, such as traffic, a satellite view, transit lines, and biking paths. You can also change the settings for the Maps app.

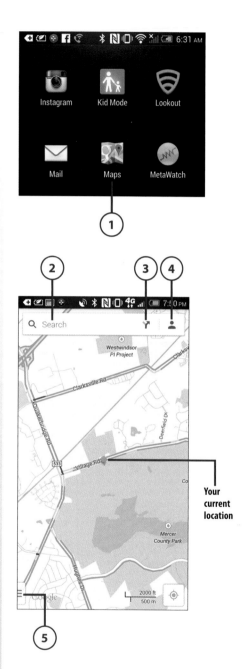

Your current location

Get Directions

Most people use Google Maps to get directions to where they want to go. Here is how:

1. Touch the Directions icon.

2. Touch to set the starting point or leave it as My Location (which is where you are now).

3. Touch to choose a location from your Contacts, My Places, a point on the map, or type it in.

4. Touch to choose between driving directions, taking public transport, cycling directions, and walking directions.

5. Touch to choose to avoid highways and/or avoid toll roads.

6. Touch to choose one of the available routes. The best route is shown on the top of the list.

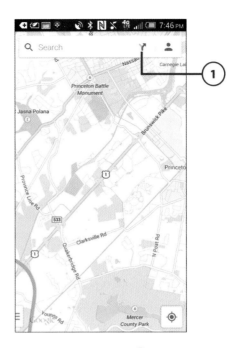

Public Transportation

If you choose to use public transportation to get to your destination, you can use two extra options. You can choose the type of public transportation, including Bus, Subway, Train, or Tram/Light Rail. You can also choose the best route, including Fewer Transfers and Less Walking.

7. Touch to start the turn-by-turn directions.

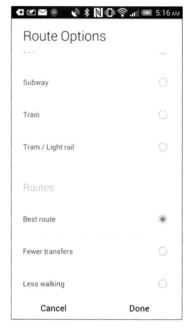

8. Touch the Menu button to see the route preview, show each step in the list of directions, mute the voice guidence, and turn on the satellite view.

9. Start driving, walking, or cycling and follow the onscreen prompts and visual guidance, or listen to the turn-by-turn spoken directions.

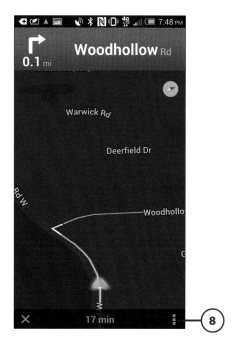

Google Maps Settings

1. Touch to slide out the menu.

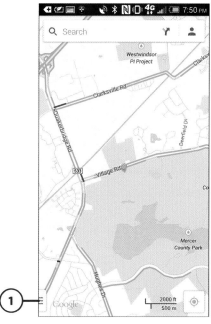

2. Touch Settings.

3. Touch to switch to another Google account to use Google Maps.

4. Touch to edit your home or work addresses.

5. Touch to let Maps improve its accuracy on your location.

6. Touch to view your Maps History and delete the items in that history.

7. Touch to change the distance units to kilometers, miles, or leave it set to automatic and let Maps decide based on what country you are in.

8. Touch to choose whether you want to be able to shake your HTC One to send feedback to Google about its Maps app.

9. Touch to change Google's location settings.

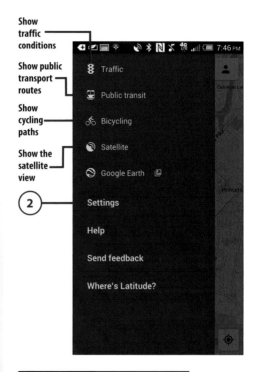

Show traffic conditions

Show public transport routes

Show cycling paths

Show the satellite view

10. Touch to choose whether Google apps (such as Google Now) have access to your location. Allowing this improves quality of the information those apps can provide you.

11. Touch to enable or disable reporting your location from your Note HTC One.

12. Touch to enable location history where Google Maps keeps track of where you have been. Having this enabled makes Google Now much better.

13. Touch to save your changes and return to the previous screen.

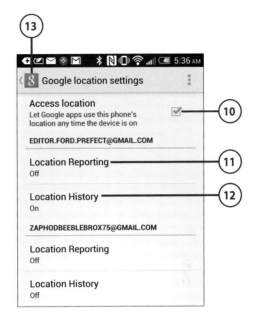

Google Maps Offers

Google Maps has a feature that allows you to see offers from local businesses, shops, and restaurants. If there are coupons to use, you can use them right from your HTC One.

1. Touch to see offers.

2. Touch any available offers.

3. Touch an offer to view it.

4. Follow the on-screen instructions. The offers can either be used via bar code, QR code, or Near Field Communications (NFC).

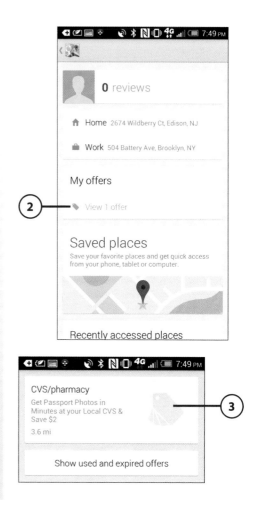

Navigation with the Car App

When you are driving, you may choose to use the Car app. The Car app also automatically launches when you insert your HTC One into a car dock. We briefly cover the navigation features of the Car app:

1. Touch to launch the Car app.

2. Touch Navigation.

3. Touch Google Maps Navigation and go directly to the Destination screen.

4. Touch choose options such as Gas Stations, your previous destinations, or restaurants to launch Google Maps and display those items on the map.

5. Touch a red dot on the map that indicates an item you chose to display. In this example, we chose restaurants. When you touch the red dot, it expands to a red pin, and details of the location are displayed at the bottom of the screen.

6. Touch to go to the directions screen.

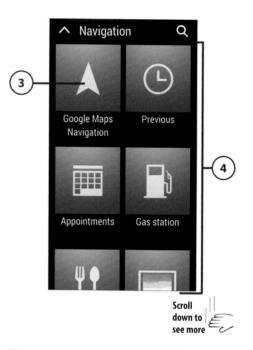

Scroll down to see more

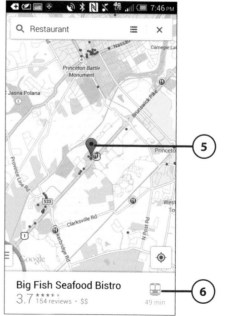

Use the World
Clock feature to
track the time in
multiple locations

In this chapter, you find out how to set the time, use the Clock app, and use the Calendar app. Topics include the following:

→ Working with the Clock app
→ Setting alarms
→ Working with the Calendar app
→ Tracking your tasks

Working with Date, Time, and Calendar

Your HTC One has a Clock app that you can use as a bedside alarm. The Calendar app synchronizes to your Google or Microsoft Exchange calendars and enables you to create meetings while on the road and to always know where your next meeting is. The Tasks app syncs your tasks lists from your Google account and your Exchange ActiveSync account and presents them together with the lists stored on the HTC One itself.

Setting the Date and Time

Before you start working with the Clock and Calendar apps, you need to make sure that your HTC One has the correct date and time.

1. Touch the Settings icon on the Apps screen to open the Settings app.

2. Touch Date & Time.

3. Touch Automatic Date & Time to enable or disable synchronizing time and date with the wireless carrier. It is best to leave this setting enabled because it automatically sets date and time based on where you are traveling.

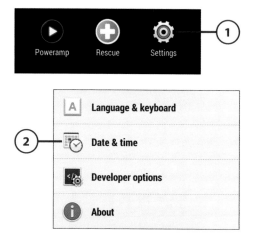

Does Network Time Sync Always Work?

In some countries, on some carriers, time synchronization does not work effectively. This means that when you get off the plane and turn off Airplane mode (see the Prologue, "Getting to Know Your HTC One," for information on Airplane mode), after a reasonable amount of time, the HTC One's settings for time, date, and time zone will still be incorrect. When this happens, disable automatic date and time and set the time, date, and time zone manually; then try it on automatic in the next country you visit or when you return to your home country.

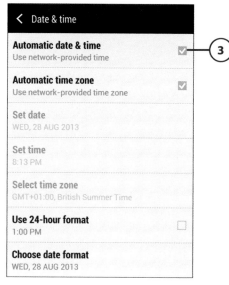

4. Touch to enable or disable synchronizing the time zone with the wireless carrier. It is best to leave this enabled because it automatically sets the time zone based on where you are traveling.

5. Touch to set the date if you choose to disable network synchronization.

6. Touch to set the time if you choose to disable network synchronization.

7. Touch to set the time zone manually if you choose to disable network synchronization.

8. Touch to enable or disable the use of 24-hour format. This format makes your HTC One represent time without a.m. or p.m. For example, 1:00 p.m. appears as 13:00 in 24-hour format.

9. Touch to change the way your HTC One shows the date. For example, people in the United States normally write the date with the month first (12/31/2013). You can make your HTC One display the date with the day first (31/12/2013), with the year first (2013/12/31), or in several other ways.

10. In the Choose Date Format dialog, touch the date format you want to use.

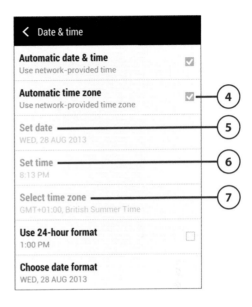

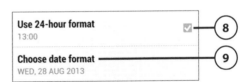

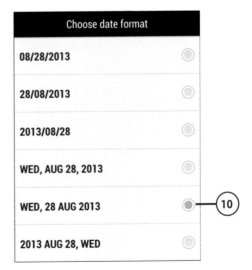

Using the Clock App

The Clock app comes installed on your HTC One and provides a World Clock, alarms, a stopwatch, and a timer.

Navigate the Clock App

1. Touch the Clock icon.

2. Touch the current tab to display the navigation list.

3. Touch the entry for the tab you want to display.

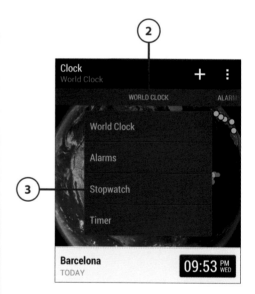

Other Ways of Navigating Among the Clock Tabs

You can also swipe left or right to navigate from one tab of the Clock app to another. If you can see the tab button for the tab you want to display, touch the tab button to display the tab.

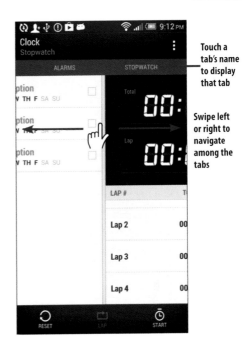

Touch a tab's name to display that tab

Swipe left or right to navigate among the tabs

Set and Manage Alarms

The Clock app enables you to set multiple alarms. These can be one-time alarms or recurring alarms. Even if you exit the Clock app, the alarms you have set will still trigger.

The Clock app comes with several sample alarms set. You can modify these alarms, delete them, or leave them in place.

Create a New Alarm

1. Touch the + icon to start creating a new alarm.

2. Spin the dials to set the alarm time.

3. Type a description of the alarm so you can easily identify it on the Alarms screen.

4. Touch to display the Alarms screen, on which you can choose the alarm sound.

5. Touch to listen to a particular alarm sound to determine if it is suitable for waking or alerting you.

6. Touch Apply.

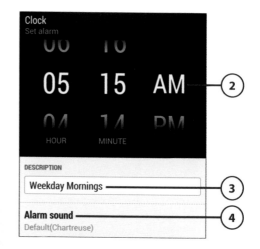

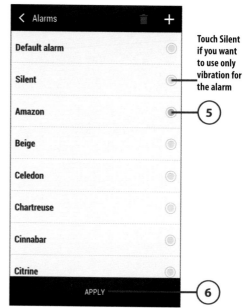

Touch Silent if you want to use only vibration for the alarm

7. Touch Repeat if you want to set up a pattern of repeating for the alarm. By default, a new alarm does not repeat. If you do not need the alarm to repeat, skip ahead to step 10.

8. Touch each day of the week when you want the alarm to trigger.

9. Touch OK to close the Repeat dialog.

10. Touch to enable or disable vibration for the alarm.

11. Touch Done to finish creating the alarm. The alarm appears on the Alarms screen.

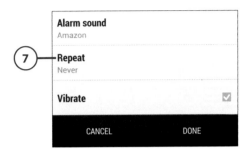

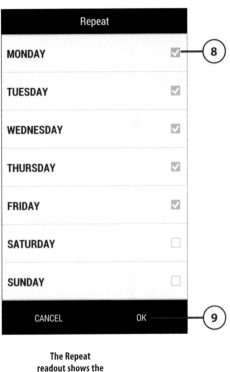

The Repeat readout shows the days you chose

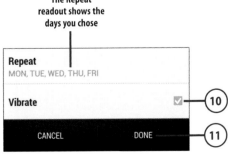

12. Touch to enable or disable the alarm.

Why Do Some Alarms Have Black Clock Faces and Others White Clock Faces?

A black clock face indicates the alarm is between 6:00 p.m. and 5:59 a.m. A white clock face indicates the alarm is between 6:00 a.m. and 5:59 p.m.

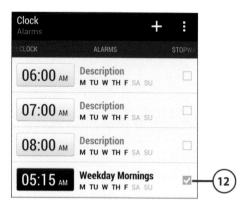

Edit an Alarm

From the Alarms screen, you can quickly edit your existing alarms.

To edit an alarm, touch it on the Alarms screen. The Set Alarm screen appears, and you can choose settings as explained in the previous section.

Delete Alarms

To delete one or more alarms, follow these steps:

1. Touch the Menu button.

2. Touch Delete to display the Delete Alarms screen.

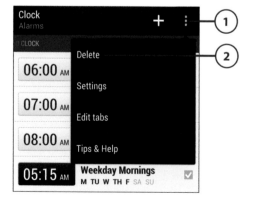

3. Touch to put an x in the check box for each alarm you want to delete.

4. Touch Delete. The Delete button shows the number of alarms you are deleting—for example, Delete (3).

Choose Settings for Alarms

You can control how your alarms behave by choosing settings for them on the Settings screen in the Clock app.

1. Touch the Menu button.

2. Touch Settings to display the Settings screen.

3. Touch to enable or disable playing the alarm when your HTC One is in Silent mode.

4. Touch to display the Alarm Volume dialog, in which you can drag the slider to set the alarm volume.

5. Touch to display the Snooze Duration dialog.

6. Touch to set the snooze period before the alarm rings again.

7. Touch Side Button Behavior to display the Side Button Behavior dialog.

8. Touch None to disable the HTC One's side buttons while the alarm is ringing. Touch Snooze to make the side buttons snooze the alarm. Touch Dismiss to make these buttons dismiss the alarm.

9. On the Settings screen, touch the Back button to return to the Alarms screen.

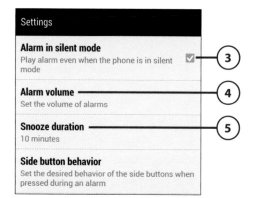

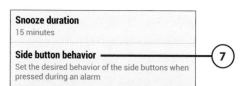

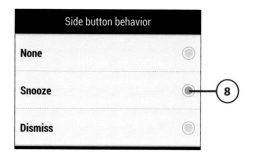

Use the World Clock

The World Clock enables you to keep track of time in multiple cities around the world.

Display the World Clock

1. Touch the current tab to display the navigation list.

2. Touch World Clock.

3. Touch the city whose information you want to display.

4. Touch the map to hide the display of the city list.

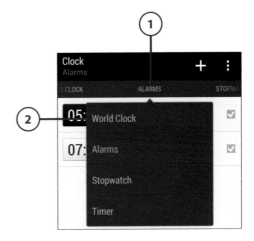

The map displays the city's current time and weather

5. Pinch outward to zoom the map in.

6. Touch to display a pop-up menu of cities, then touch the city you want to view.

7. Touch the map to display the city list again.

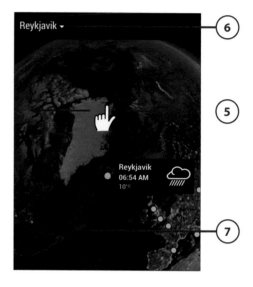

Set Your Home City

You can set your home city to make sure it always appears in the World Clock. Follow these steps:

1. Touch the Menu button.

2. Touch Home Settings.

3. Start typing the name of your home city.

4. Touch the city's name in the list of matches.

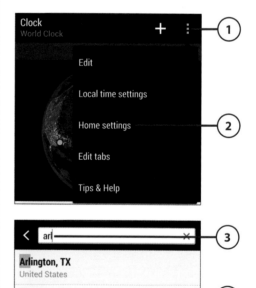

Add Cities, Remove Cities, and Choose Their Order

You can add cities to the World Clock, remove cities you do not want, and rearrange the resulting list of cities into your preferred order. Follow these steps:

1. On the World Clock screen, touch the + button.

2. Start typing the name of the city you want to add.

3. Touch the city's name in the list of matches. The city appears on the World Clock screen.

4. Touch the Menu button.

5. Touch Edit to display the Drag to Rearrange screen.

6. Touch a handle and drag a city up or down the list as needed.

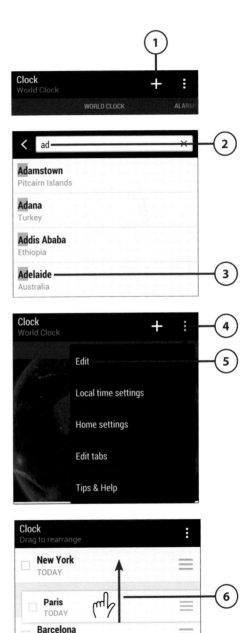

7. Touch to put an x in the check box for each city you want to remove from the list.

8. Touch Delete. The Delete button shows the number of cities you are deleting—for example, Delete (2).

The World Clock screen appears again, showing the updated list of cities.

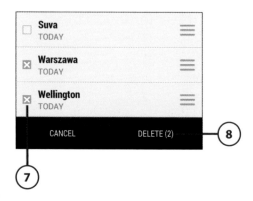

Using the Calendar App

The Calendar app enables you to synchronize all the Google Calendars under your primary Google account to your HTC One. You can accept appointments and create and modify appointments right on your phone. Any changes you make are automatically synchronized wirelessly back to your Google Calendar.

Navigate the Calendar Main Screen

The main screen of the Calendar app can show your events as one-day, one-week, or one-month views. It can also display your upcoming events as a list in Agenda view and can display a list of the invitations you have received.

1. Touch the Calendar icon.

2. Swipe right to display earlier dates.

3. Swipe left to display later dates.

4. Touch to show today's date in the current view. For example, in Month view, touching this button displays the current month with the current day's rectangle selected.

5. Touch the + button to start creating a new event.

6. Touch a date to display that date in Day view.

7. Touch to display the pop-up menu of calendar views.

8. Touch the calendar view that you want to switch to.

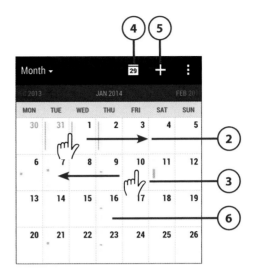

Event Colors

The Calendar app can display one calendar or multiple calendars at the same time. If you choose to display multiple calendars, events from each calendar are color coded so you can easily see which events belong to which calendar.

When you use Google Calendar on the Web, you can assign a color to an event to make it easier to identify. But when you view that same Google Calendar in the Calendar app on your HTC One, each event appears in the same color—the color the Calendar app has assigned to that calendar.

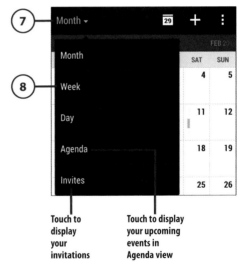

Touch to display your invitations

Touch to display your upcoming events in Agenda view

Choose Which Calendars and Task Lists to Display

If you have set up multiple accounts, each of which might have multiple calendars or task lists, you can choose which calendars and task lists the Calendar app displays at any given time.

1. Touch the Menu button.

2. Touch Accounts. This menu item's name summarizes the calendars that the Calendar app is displaying. For example, when Calendar is displaying all your calendars, the menu item is named Accounts (All Calendars).

3. On the View Accounts screen, touch to enable or disable the display of each account.

4. Touch the ellipsis (…) button at the right side of an account that has multiple calendars or task lists. This example uses Google.

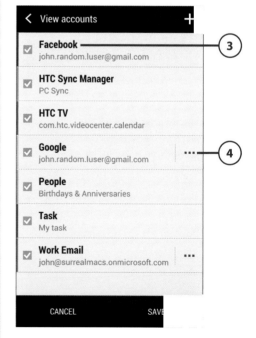

5. Touch to enable or disable the display of a calendar or task list.

6. Touch Save to save the changes you have made. The View Accounts screen appears again.

7. Touch Save to save your changes. The Calendar app displays the calendar again, now showing the calendars you just chose.

Change Calendar Settings

1. Touch the Menu button.

2. Touch Settings.

3. Touch to add an account to the Calendar app.

4. Touch to set the first day of your week. You can choose Saturday, Sunday, or Monday. Alternatively, you can choose Locale Default, which sets the first day of the week to the default day for the time zone you are in.

5. Touch to edit the four built-in Quick Responses for replying to invitations. Read more about Quick Responses later in this chapter.

6. Touch to enable or disable playing a notification sound for reminders of calendar events.

7. Touch to display the Notifications dialog, in which you can choose the notification you want the HTC One to play.

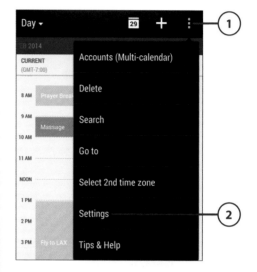

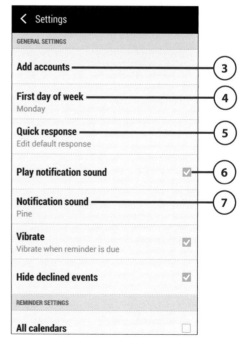

Get a Silent Notification for Calendar Events

If you want to receive a silent notification for calendar events, touch the Silent option in the Notifications dialog and touch Apply. Then, back on the Settings screen for the Calendar app, touch to place a check mark in the Vibrate check box.

8. Touch to enable or disable vibration for reminders.

9. Touch to control whether the Calendar app hides events you have declined or displays them along with the events you have accepted.

Why Display Declined Events?

Usually, it is easiest to have the Calendar app display only the events you have accepted—in fact, Calendar's default setting is to hide events you have declined. But if you have a busy social life, business life, or both, you may find it useful to be able to see the details of the events you intend to miss as well as those you mean to attend. So if the party you chose to attend turns out to be a wasteland, Calendar will show your options for finding something more fun.

10. Scroll down to reach more settings.

11. Touch to enable or disable receiving reminders for all calendars.

12. Touch to choose the calendar to which these settings apply.

13. Touch to display the Alerts & Notifications dialog, in which you choose which alerts and notifications to receive. Your choices are Alert, Status Bar Notification, or None.

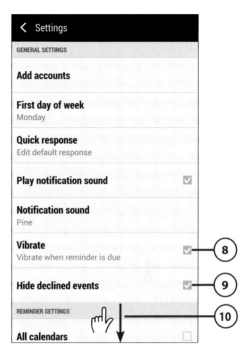

14. Touch to set the default reminder time for events. Your options include None, On Time, and intervals running from 1 Minute and 5 Minutes all the way up to 2 Weeks.

15. Touch to select your second time zone. Setting the second time zone can be helpful if you frequently travel to one other time zone—for example, if you travel from the Pacific time zone to the Eastern time zone. If you travel to various time zones, do not set the second time zone, and the HTC One automatically uses the time zone you are currently in if it is different from your home time zone.

16. Touch to open the Display Weather dialog; then touch the city for the weather you want the Calendar app to display. The cities listed are those you have set in World Clock, as discussed earlier in this chapter.

17. Touch to save your changes and return to the calendar.

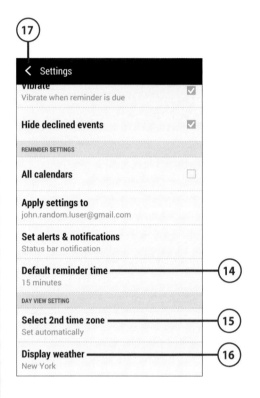

Add a New Event

While you're on the road, you can add a new appointment or event— and even invite people to it. Events you add synchronize to your Google and corporate calendars in real-time.

1. Touch the + button to start adding a new event.

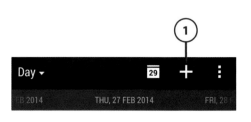

A Quicker Way to Add an Event

You can quickly add a new event by touching and holding the day you want to create the event, then touching New Event. This move works best in Day view or Week view, in which you can touch and hold the time at which you want the event to start. You can also use this move in Month view, but you will usually have to set the time manually.

Touch and hold the day and time for the new event

Touch New Event in the dialog that opens

2. Touch to select the calendar in which you want to store the event.

3. Touch to invite one or more people from your Contacts list to the event. If you don't want to invite anybody, skip to step 6.

Enter a Recipient Using Type-Down Addressing

You can also start typing a name or an email address into the To box, and then touch the contact on the pop-up menu of matches that appears. This method is handy when you want to invite a single contact.

Start typing the recipient's name or address

Touch the match on the Contacts menu

4. On the People screen, touch each recipient, putting a check mark in the check box.

5. Touch Done to add the contacts to the new event. The contacts appear as buttons below the To box.

6. Touch and type the title for the event.

7. Touch to set the time zone for the event.

8. Touch to set the start date for the event.

9. Touch to set the start time for the event.

10. Touch to set the end date for the event.

11. Touch to set the end time for the event.

12. Scroll down to display further settings for the event.

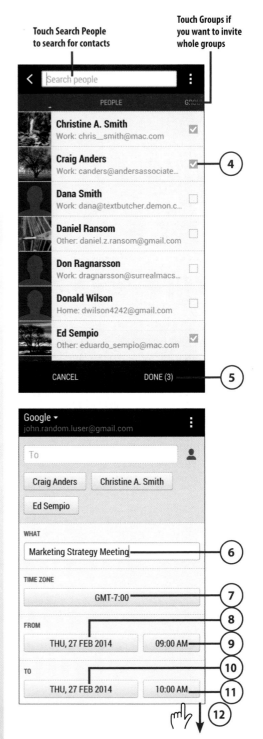

Touch Search People to search for contacts

Touch Groups if you want to invite whole groups

13. Touch to mark the event as an all-day event.

14. Touch to check your calendar to make sure the time is available.

15. Look at the Meeting Conflict readout.

16. If there is a conflict, or if you want to change the event time based on the other events you see, touch and hold the event, then drag it to change the time. You can also drag the upper blue square to change the beginning time or the lower blue square to change the end time.

17. Touch Done to return from the Meeting Conflict screen to the screen for creating the event.

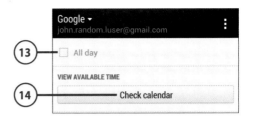

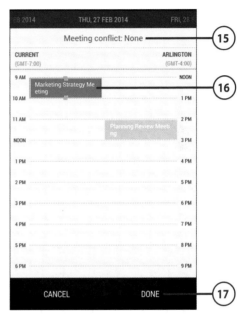

18. Touch to set the location for the event using Maps.

19. Touch to set your current location as the event's location.

20. Optionally, touch here and type a description for the event.

21. Touch to display the Status dialog, in which you can toggle the status of the event's time between Busy and Free.

22. Touch to set how long before the event the Calendar app should display a reminder. Choose None if you don't want a reminder.

23. Touch to display the Reminder Type dialog, in which you can toggle the reminder type between Notification and Email.

24. Touch to set this as a recurring event. You can make it repeat daily, weekly, or monthly on the same date each month, or set up a custom repeat. For example, you can set an event to repeat on the last Thursday of each month, no matter which date that Thursday falls on. When you set up a recurring event, you can touch the Ends On button and use the resulting dialog to set an end date for the series of events.

25. Touch to set the Privacy status for the event. Your choices are Default, Private, and Public.

26. For an event with invitees, touch Send to save the event and send invitations to the invitees. For an event without invitees, touch Save to save the event. Either way, the event appears in your calendar.

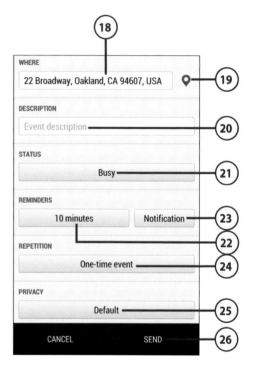

Editing and Deleting an Event

To edit or delete a calendar event, touch the event to display the Event Details screen. From here, you can touch Edit to edit the event, touch Create Note to add a note to it, or touch the Menu button and then touch Delete Event to delete it.

When you delete an event, the Calendar app sends an event decline notice to the event organizer. This helpful automatic arrangement means you don't need to decline the event before deleting it.

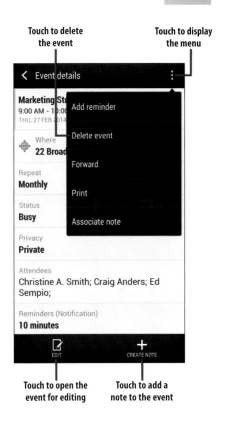

Touch to delete the event

Touch to display the menu

Touch to open the event for editing

Touch to add a note to the event

Respond to a Google Event Invitation

When you receive an invitation to an event, you can choose your response on your HTC One in the invitation email message itself. Alternatively, you can respond through the Calendar app.

Respond from the Email Message

The Google event invitation email message enables you to respond in the email message itself. When you're managing your email, this is the easiest way to take care of an invitation.

1. In your Inbox, touch to open the event invitation email message.

2. Touch Yes, Maybe, or No to indicate whether you will attend.

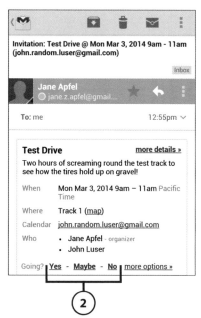

Respond from the Calendar App

When you receive an invite, your HTC One automatically inserts it in your Google calendar. It appears there as an event with no response selected.

1. Touch the new event.

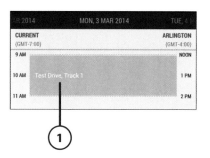

2. Touch the event location to have it mapped in Google Maps or in another mapping app that you have installed, such as Google Earth.

3. Touch to display the Response dialog.

4. Touch the appropriate button— Attending: Yes, Attending: Maybe, or Attending: No—to indicate whether you will attend.

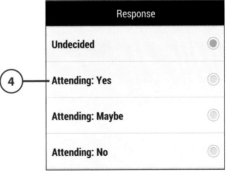

Respond to a Corporate Event Invitation

When you receive an invitation to an event on your corporate email account, you can either respond directly in the invitation email message itself or handle the invitation in the Calendar app.

Respond from the Email Message

Your HTC One makes it easy to respond to an event invitation in the email message itself. This is the quickest way to respond when you are working in the Mail app.

1. Touch to open the event invitation email message.

2. Touch if you want to check your calendar to see which events you already have scheduled.

3. Touch Maybe, Decline, or Accept to indicate whether you will attend. Alternatively, touch Propose to suggest a different event time. The Calendar app displays the Maybe dialog box, the Decline dialog box, or the Accept dialog box (shown here); each has the same controls, but a different title.

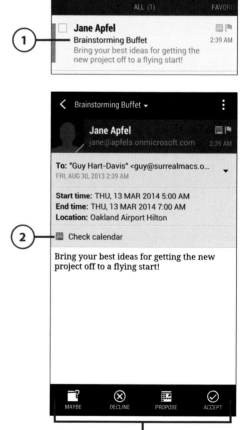

4. Touch Edit Response Before Sending, Respond Without a Comment, or Do Not Send a Response, as appropriate.

Should I Send a Response to an Invitation?

Normally, it is a good idea to send a response to an invitation so that the inviter can see that you have received the invitation and responded to it. If you accept or say "maybe" but touch Do Not Send a Response, Calendar adds the event to your calendar, but the inviter receives no indication of whether you have accepted, have declined, or are undecided.

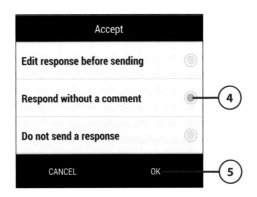

5. Touch OK. If you chose Respond Without a Comment, your HTC One now sends the response; skip the remaining steps in this list.

6. If you chose Edit Response Before Sending, type the text on the Compose screen.

7. Touch if you need to add an attachment to your response.

8. Touch to send the response.

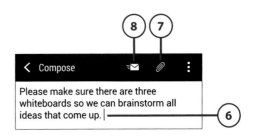

Respond from the Calendar App

When you receive an invitation on your corporate account, the Calendar app saves it to the Invites folder. You can then open the Invites folder and deal with all the invitations together.

1. In the Calendar app, touch the View pop-up menu.

2. Touch Invites to display the Invites folder.

3. Touch the invitation you want to view.

4. Touch Check Calendar to view any conflicts.

5. Touch Maybe, Decline, or Accept to indicate whether you will attend. Alternatively, touch Propose to suggest a different event time. The Calendar app displays the Maybe dialog box (shown here), the Decline dialog box, or the Accept dialog box; each has the same controls, but a different title.

6. Touch Edit Response Before Sending, Respond Without a Comment, or Do Not Send a Response, as appropriate.

7. Touch OK. If you chose Respond Without a Comment, your HTC One now sends the response. If you chose Edit Response Before Sending, type the text on the Compose screen, and then touch the Send button to send your response.

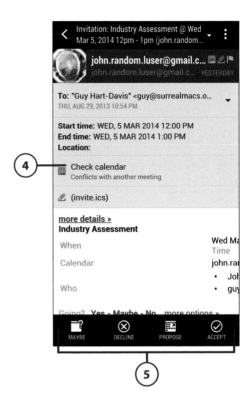

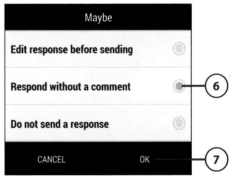

Propose a New Time for an Event

When you receive an invitation for a time or date that won't work for your schedule, you can propose a new time.

1. In the invitation, touch Propose.

2. Touch to change the start date if necessary.

3. Touch to change the start time if necessary.

4. Touch to change the end date if necessary.

5. Touch to change the end time if necessary.

6. Touch to change the location if necessary.

7. Touch to send the change proposal.

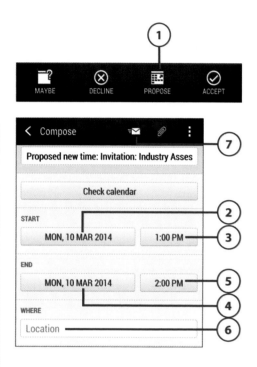

View Your Agenda

The Calendar app includes an Agenda view that shows a list of your events for the day. Agenda view is useful for getting an overview of your commitments. You can move easily from one day to another, as needed.

1. Touch the View pop-up menu.

2. Touch Agenda.

3. Swipe left to display the next day, or swipe right to display the previous day.

4. Touch an event to display the Event Details screen showing its full information.

Use Quick Responses

When your HTC One notifies you of an upcoming event, you can choose to Snooze or Email Guests. When you choose to Email Guests, you can choose a Quick Response to send them.

1. Pull down the Notification bar.

2. Pinch apart on the reminder to display the options for dealing with it.

3. Touch Send Mail to email a Quick Response to the meeting invitees.

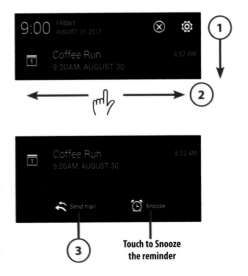

Touch to Snooze
the reminder

4. Touch the Quick Response you want to send. Alternatively, touch Custom Message and type a custom message.

5. Touch the email app you want to use for sending the message.

6. Touch Always if you want to always use this email app for your Quick Response messages, or touch Just Once if you want to use it only this time.

7. Complete the new message that your HTC One creates, and then send it.

Add, search, and manage your contacts

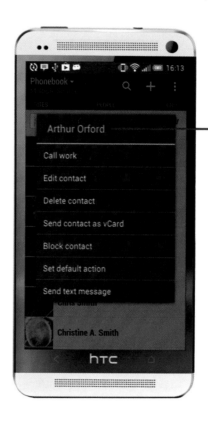

In this chapter, you become familiar with your HTC One's contact-management app, which is called People. You find out how to add contacts, synchronize contacts, link duplicate contacts, and create speed dial numbers. Topics include the following:

→ Importing contacts

→ Adding contacts

→ Synchronizing contacts

→ Creating favorite contacts

Contacts

On any smartphone, the app for managing contacts is essential because it is where you keep all your contacts' information. On the HTC One, this app is called People. It is the central hub for many activities, such as calling and sending text messages (SMS), multimedia messages (MMS), or email. You can also synchronize your contacts from many online sites, such as Facebook and Gmail, so as your friends change their Facebook profile pictures, their pictures on your HTC One change as well.

Adding Accounts

Before you look around the People app, add some accounts to synchronize contacts from. You already added your Google account when you set up your HTC One in the Prologue, "Getting to Know Your HTC One."

Open the Accounts & Sync Screen

To see the accounts you have already set up on your HTC One, or to start adding a new account, open the Accounts & Sync screen.

1. Touch the Settings icon on the Apps screen to open the Settings app.

2. Touch Accounts & Sync to display the Accounts & Sync screen.

3. Touch to start adding an account. The Add an Account screen appears.

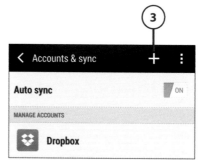

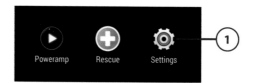

Adding Facebook, Twitter, and Other Accounts

Your HTC One comes with built-in account types for LinkedIn and Flickr. You can add your LinkedIn account to your HTC One by configuring the LinkedIn for HTC Sense account; similarly, you can set up Flickr by configuring the Flickr for HTC Sense account. Both options are covered later in this chapter.

To add accounts to your HTC One for your other online services, such as Facebook, Twitter, and so on, first check whether your HTC One has the apps for these services installed. If not, install the apps from Google Play. See Chapter 11, "Working with Android Apps," for instructions on installing Android apps. When you have installed the apps and signed in to them, you can find the accounts on the Accounts & Sync screen in the Settings app, as shown in the following sections.

Your accounts appear on the Accounts & Sync screen in the Settings app

Add an Exchange ActiveSync Account

If you have an Exchange ActiveSync account, you can add it to your HTC One by configuring the Exchange ActiveSync account in the Settings app.

1. Touch Exchange ActiveSync.

2. Type the email address for the account.

3. Touch Password and type the password.

4. Touch Show Password if you want to see the password rather than the dots the HTC One shows for security. Seeing the password can be helpful when entering complex passwords—as long as nobody's looking over your shoulder.

5. Touch Next to set up the account.

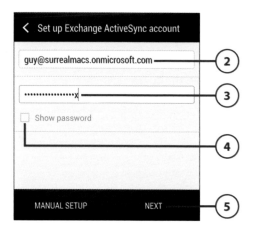

Providing ActiveSync Server and Domain Information

Your HTC One tries to work out some information about your company's ActiveSync setup, including the ActiveSync server name and the Exchange domain name. If your HTC One works out these details, it sets up the account; if not, it prompts you to enter them manually. Normally, you will get the ActiveSync server name and the Exchange domain name—and whether you need to enter the domain name—from your email administrator. But if your administrator isn't available, you can try guessing the server name. For example, if your email address is dsimons@allhitradio.com, the ActiveSync server is most probably webmail.allhitradio.com. The domain name is harder to guess, but you may not need it, so it's worth trying to set up the account without it.

You may need to enter the server name here.

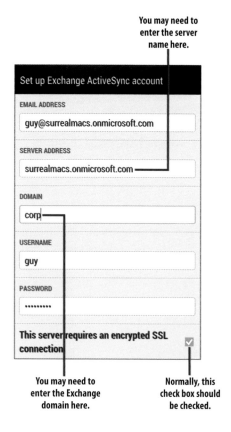

You may need to enter the Exchange domain here.

Normally, this check box should be checked.

6. Touch to enable or disable syncing Mail information.

7. Touch to enable or disable syncing Contacts information.

8. Touch to enable or disable syncing Calendar data.

9. Touch to enable to disable syncing Tasks data.

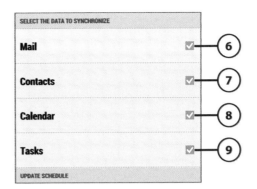

Which Update Schedule Should You Choose?

Your HTC One gives you four choices for updating your Exchange information: Smart Sync, Push Mail, Every 15 Minutes, or Manually. Smart Sync conserves battery power by increasing the length of time between mail checks the longer you leave the Mail app inactive. So if you keep looking at your email, Smart Sync checks for new mail frequently; if you go into a meeting and don't look at email for a couple of hours, Smart Sync checks only every now and then. Push Mail grabs your new mail as soon as it arrives at the server, but it uses more battery life. Every 15 Minutes checks every quarter-hour, as its name says. Manually lets you control when your HTC One checks for new mail.

10. Touch Smart Sync to have your HTC One decide how frequently to check for new mail based on how much you use the Mail app.

11. Touch Push Mail to have the mail server "push" the messages to your HTC One as soon as they arrive at the server.

12. Touch Every 15 Minutes to check once every 15 minutes.

13. Touch Manually to check manually whenever you want.

14. Touch Next.

15. Type a descriptive name for the account.

16. Touch Finish Setup to finish setting up the account.

The Accounts & Sync screen appears, with the Exchange ActiveSync account listed in the Manage Accounts section.

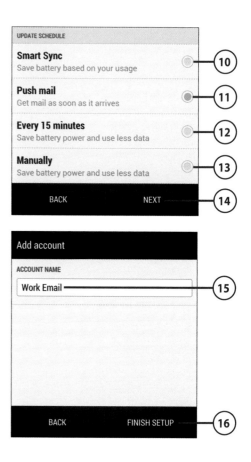

Add a LinkedIn for HTC Sense Account

If you have a LinkedIn account, you can add it to your HTC One by configuring the LinkedIn for HTC Sense account in the Settings app.

1. On the Add an Account screen, touch LinkedIn for HTC Sense.

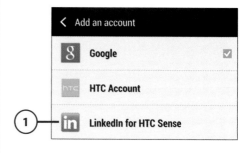

2. Type your LinkedIn email address.

3. Type your LinkedIn password.

4. By default, setting up your LinkedIn for HTC Sense account grants your HTC One access to your LinkedIn account until you revoke the permission. To limit the HTC One's access, touch Change.

5. Touch the pop-up menu that appears.

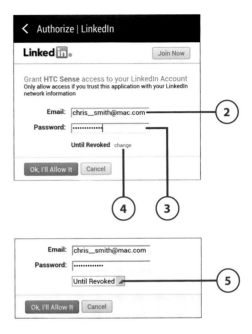

Why Limit Your HTC One's Access to Your LinkedIn Account?

If you use LinkedIn extensively, your account probably contains a great deal of sensitive information. Because of this, you may choose to limit your HTC One's access to your account to a specific period of time rather than granting access until you revoke it. You should also protect your HTC One with a PIN to prevent others accessing it.

6. Touch the time period in the dialog that opens. For example, touch Thirty Days.

7. Touch the OK, I'll Allow It button.

8. On the Security Verification screen, decipher the gibberish and type it into the box.

9. Touch Continue. Your HTC One sets up the account.

   The Accounts & Sync screen appears, with the LinkedIn for HTC Sense account listed in the Manage Accounts section.

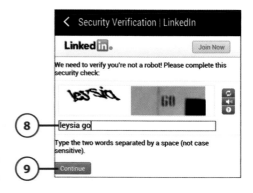

Add a Flickr for HTC Sense Account

If you have a Flickr account, you can add it to your HTC One by configuring the Flickr for HTC Sense account in the Settings app.

1. On the Add an Account screen, touch Flickr for HTC Sense.

2. Type your Flickr or Yahoo! email address.

3. Type your password.

4. Touch Sign In to sign in to the account.

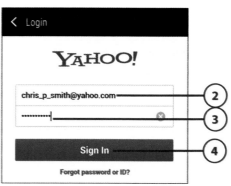

5. On the HTC Media Uploader Wants to Link to Your Flickr Account screen, read the authorizations required.

6. Touch the OK, I'll Authorize It button if you're okay with giving HTC Media Uploader permission to take these actions. Normally, you'll want to do this so that you can use Flickr fully on your HTC One.

The Accounts & Sync screen appears, with the Flickr for HTC Sense account listed in the Manage Accounts section.

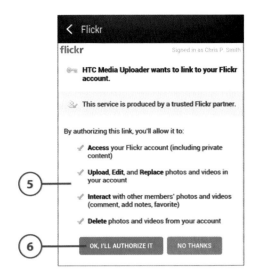

Navigating the People App

The People app consists of five tabs: Call History, Phone, Favorites, People, and Groups. Normally, the People app displays the People tab first, showing your list of contacts, but you can navigate to any of the other screens by swiping left or right.

1. From the Home screen, touch the Apps button to display the Apps screen.

2. Touch the People icon.

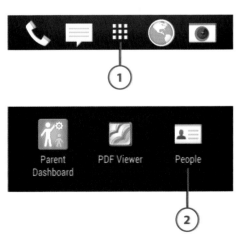

3. Swipe left or right to see the other tabs in the People app.

4. Touch to choose which contacts to display. See the section "Choose Which Contacts to Display," later in this chapter, for details.

5. Touch to search for contacts.

6. Touch to add a new contact. See the section "Add a Contact Manually," later in this chapter, for details.

7. Touch to display the menu, which contains various commands for working with your contacts.

8. Touch to review any suggestions the People app has for linking contacts to eliminate duplicate contact records.

9. Touch the contact record marked My Profile to edit your own profile.

10. Touch a contact to see all the available information about that contact.

11. Touch a contact picture (or picture placeholder) to see the available means of getting in touch with the contact.

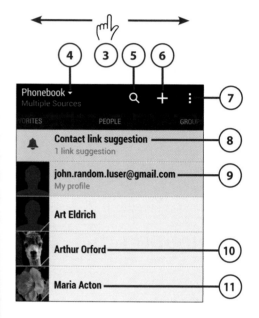

Getting in Touch with a Contact

When you touch a contact picture, the pop-up window displays the available means of getting in touch with the contact. This window enables you to quickly access different ways of communicating with the contact. Touch the icon for the means of contact you want to use, and then touch the phone number or address on the list that appears.

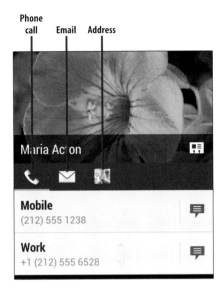

Browse a Contact's Data

The People app splits a contact's data onto four separate tabs:

- **Details**—This tab contains the contact's profile picture; buttons for contacting them via phone, email, and other means; and information such as their birthday and group membership.

- **Thread**—This tab shows lists of instant messages, email messages, and calls from the contact.

- **Updates**—This tab shows the latest information from the contact's social-networking accounts—for example, Facebook.

- **Gallery**—This tab shows the latest photos from the contact's social-networking accounts.

1. In the People app, touch the contact whose data you want to view. The contact record opens and displays the Details tab.

2. Touch to call the phone number shown.

3. Touch to start an instant message to the phone number shown.

4. Touch to start an email message to the email address shown.

5. Touch to display the contact's profile in the Facebook app.

6. Swipe left to display the Thread tab.

7. Touch to return a message.

8. Touch to return an email message. "No emails" appears if you have not received any email messages from this contact, or if People cannot identify any email messages (even though you have received some).

9. Touch to return a phone call.

10. Swipe left to display the Update tab.

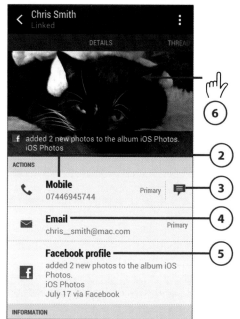

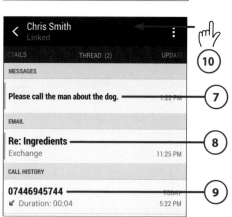

11. Touch to display the item shown in the Facebook app, where you can examine it in more detail, comment on it, or reply to it.

12. Swipe left to display the Gallery tab.

13. Touch a photo set to open it within the People app. You can then touch a photo to view it full screen.

14. Touch to return from the contact record to the list of contacts.

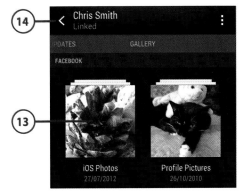

>>>Go Further

EDIT THE PEOPLE APP'S TABS TO SUIT YOU

You can rearrange the People app's five tabs—Call History, Phone, Favorites, People, and Groups—into the order you prefer. You can also turn off the display of the Call History tab, Favorites tab, or Group tab if you don't want to see them.

In the People app, touch the Menu button, and then touch Edit Tabs on the menu to display the Edit tabs screen.

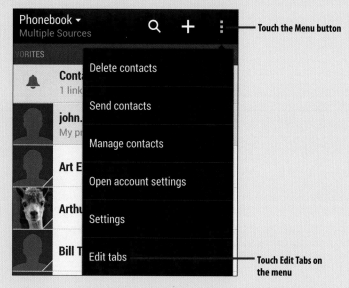

Phonebook ▾
Multiple Sources

Q   +   ⋮ ———— Touch the Menu button

/ORITES

🔔 Cont
1 link

Delete contacts

Send contacts

john.
My pr

Manage contacts

Art E

Open account settings

Arth

Settings

Bill T
Edit tabs ———— Touch Edit Tabs on the menu

Touch the Call History check box, the Favorites check box, or the Groups check box to display or hide its tab. You cannot enable or disable the Phone check box or the People check box, because having these tabs displayed is essential to the system.

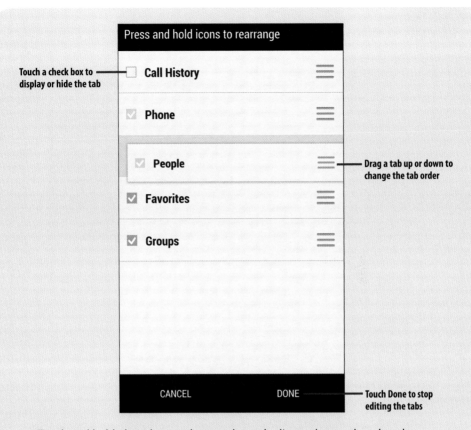

Touch a check box to display or hide the tab

Press and hold icons to rearrange

Call History

Phone

People — Drag a tab up or down to change the tab order

Favorites

Groups

CANCEL   DONE — Touch Done to stop editing the tabs

Touch and hold, then drag a tab up or down the list to change the tab order to the way you want it.

Touch Done when you finish editing the tabs. Your customized tabs then appear.

Check a Contact's Status

If you have added contacts that belong to social networks such as Facebook, you can check their status right from the Contacts app.

1. Touch a contact's picture.

2. Touch the icon for the social network. For example, touch Facebook.

3. Touch View Profile to view the contact's Facebook profile.

Edit a Contact

When you need to, you can easily change a contact's existing information or add further information to it. First, open the contact record for editing. Then you can make the changes needed.

Open the Contact Record for Editing

1. In the People app, touch the contact you want to edit.

2. Touch the Menu button.

3. Touch Edit Contact to open the contact record for editing.

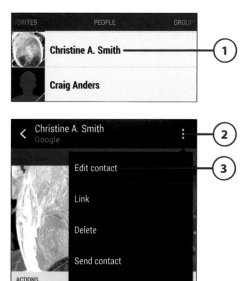

Add a Contact Photo

A contact record on your HTC One includes a contact photo when you link a social network account to the contact or when you import a contact record that includes a photo (for example, from a vCard file). You can manually add a picture as needed, either from an existing file or by taking a photo.

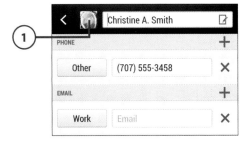

1. Touch the picture thumbnail or camera icon. The Select Photo dialog opens.

2. Touch Gallery to use an existing photo.

3. If necessary, touch to switch between albums and events.

4. Touch the album or event that contains the photo you want to use.

5. Touch the photo to display the Crop screen.

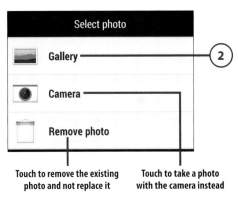

Touch to remove the existing photo and not replace it

Touch to take a photo with the camera instead

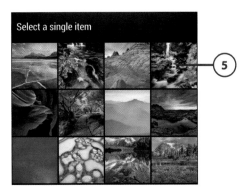

6. Drag the cropping box to select the area of the photo you want to use for the contact photo.

7. Drag the outside of the cropping box to expand or contract it as needed. You can drag either a corner handle or a side; either way, your HTC One keeps the cropping box as a square.

8. Touch Done to save the cropped photo as the contact photo.

Edit the Contact's Name

1. Touch to display the Edit Name screen.

2. Type the prefix for the contact's name.

3. Type the name suffix, if any.

4. Edit the contact's given name, if necessary.

5. Type the contact's middle name or initial.

6. Edit the contact's last name, if necessary.

7. Touch OK to close the Edit Name screen. Your changes appear in the contact record.

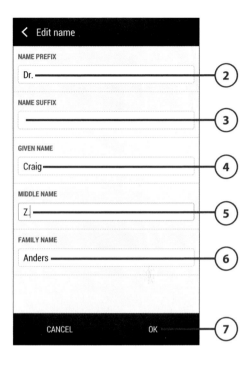

Edit the Contact's Other Information

1. Touch a + on the right side of an existing category to add another field of the same type. For example, touch + on the right of the Phone category to add a new phone number.

2. On the new field, touch the default button to display the Select Label dialog.

3. Touch the label you want to apply to the new item. For example, for a phone number, you might touch Mobile, Home, or Main.

4. Type the information for the new field. For example, type the phone number.

5. Touch an X to the right of an existing field to delete it.

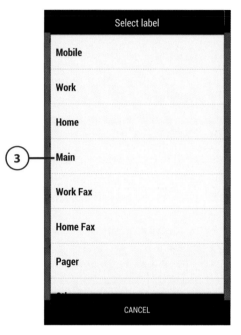

6. Touch to put the contact in a contact group. The HTC One comes with built-in groups, including Co-workers, Family, Favorites, Friends, Inner Circle, and VIP, but you can also create as many other groups as you need.

7. Touch to enter or edit the contact's company or organization name.

8. Touch to enter the contact's job title.

9. Touch to enter notes about the contact. Usually notes would be information that doesn't fit any of the other fields, but you can type anything you want to note about the contact.

10. Touch to enter a nickname for the contact.

11. Touch to add a new field to the contact record. The Select Field dialog opens. This dialog shows all the fields that are not currently used on the contact record, so its contents vary as you add and remove fields from the record.

12. Touch the field you want to add.

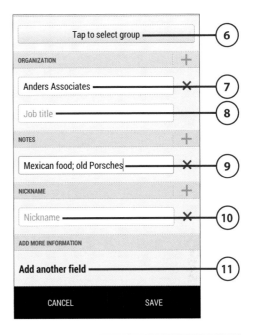

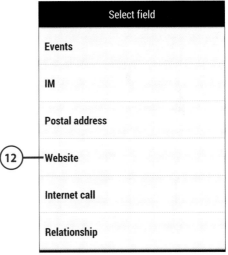

What Are the Events Field and Relationship Field For?

Touch the Events field in the Select Field dialog to add a birthday, anniversary, or other date to the contact record. After adding the field, touch its label button to display the Select Label dialog, and then touch Birthday, Anniversary, or Other. Touch the date button, choose the date in the Date dialog, and then touch OK.

Touch the Relationship field in the Select Field dialog to add a person's name and relationship to the contact—for example, Assistant, Spouse, or Manager. After adding the field, touch its label button to display the Select Label dialog, and then touch the relationship in the list. Touch the Relationship text box and type the name of the person.

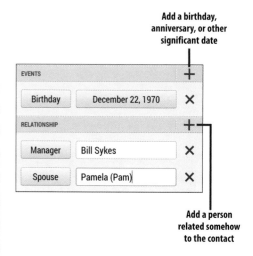

Add a birthday, anniversary, or other significant date

Add a person related somehow to the contact

13. Fill in the data for the field.

14. Touch Save to save the changes to the contact record.

Set the Ringtone and Default Communication Method for the Contact

To make calls from your contacts easier to identify, you can assign a specific ringtone to a contact. To enable you to get in touch with a contact more quickly, you can set the default communication method for that contact.

1. In the People app, touch the contact you want to change. The Details tab of the contact record opens.

2. Touch Ringtone.

3. Touch a ringtone to listen to it.

4. When you have selected the ring-tone you want, touch Apply.

5. Touch Set Default Action to choose your default method of communication with the contact. This is the method of contact your HTC One displays when you tap the contact's picture (not the other part of the contact listing) in the contacts list.

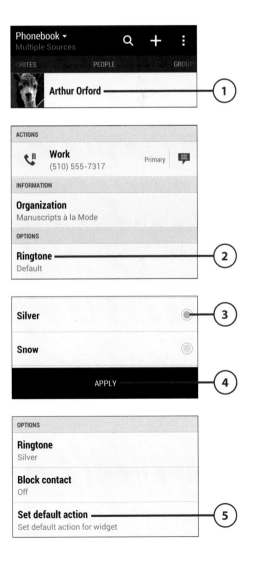

What Does the Block Contact Command Do?

Touch Block Contact when you want to avoid receiving calls, email messages, or instant messages from the contact. Touch OK in the Blocked Contacts dialog to implement the blocking. To remove the blocking, touch Block Contact again, and then touch OK in the Block Contact dialog.

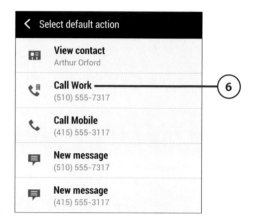

6. Touch the action you want to set as the default for the contact.

Adding and Managing Contacts

As you add contacts to your work email account or Google account, those contacts are synchronized to your HTC One automatically. When you reply to or forward emails on your HTC One to an email address that is not in your Contacts, those email addresses are automatically added to the contact list or merged into an existing contact with the same name. You can also add contacts to your HTC One directly.

Add a Contact from an Email

To manually add a contact from an email, first open your email client—either Email or Gmail—and then open a message. See Chapter 4, "Email," for more on how to work with email.

1. Touch the blank contact picture to the left of the sender's name.

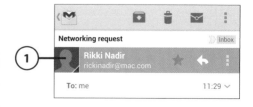

2. Touch Save to People to display the Save to People dialog.

3. Touch Create New Contact to create a new contact record for the person.

4. Type the contact's name.

5. Touch the Contact Type button and then touch the account to which you want to save the contact.

6. Touch the Email button and choose the email type—for example, Work or Home.

7. Touch Save to save the contact record.

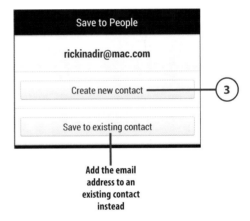

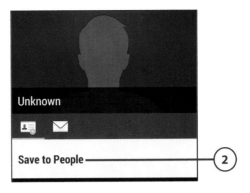

Add the email
address to an
existing contact
instead

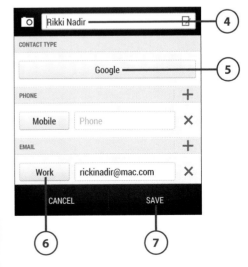

Add a Contact Manually

1. Touch the People icon on the Home screen.

2. Touch to add a new contact.

3. Type the contact's name. The People app parses most names into their components accurately, but if you want to specify which part is which, touch the button at the right end of the Name box to display the Edit Name dialog; then use it to enter the name.

4. Touch the Contact Type button to display the Create Contact Under Account dialog.

5. Touch the account in which to store the new contact. For example, you might want to add the new contact to your work email account instead of to your personal account.

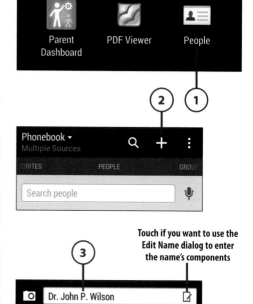

Touch if you want to use the Edit Name dialog to enter the name's components

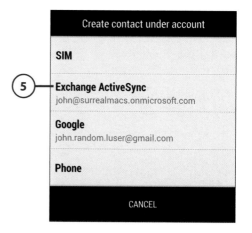

6. Touch a field that's already displayed and type in the data for it.

7. Touch the + to add another entry for a field that's already displayed.

8. Touch the Add Another Field button to add a field that's not displayed.

9. Touch to assign the contact to a contact group.

10. Touch to choose a contact picture or to take a photo with the camera.

11. Touch Save to save the new contact.

Dr. John P. Wilson — 10

CONTACT TYPE

Exchange ActiveSync

PHONE   **+** — 7

Mobile   (707) 965-0702 — **×** — 6

EMAIL   **+**

Email   **×**

GROUP

Tap to select group — 9

ADD MORE INFORMATION

Add another field — 8

CANCEL   SAVE — 11

Add a Contact from a vCard

A vCard is a file that contains a virtual business card—which can include a contact's name, job title, email address, physical address, phone numbers, and so on. You can easily exchange vCards with other people by attaching them to email messages or instant messages.

When you receive a vCard in a message, you can import it into the Contacts app as a new contact by using the following steps.

1. In the Attachments area of the message, touch the button for the vCard.

John,

Here's the contact information for you.

R.

ATTACHMENTS

Frank Ingen.vcf
238 B Text — 1

Choosing the App for vCard Files

If your HTC One displays the Complete Action Using dialog when you touch a vCard file to open it, touch People and then touch Always. This makes your HTC One always open vCard files in the People app, which is usually the best choice.

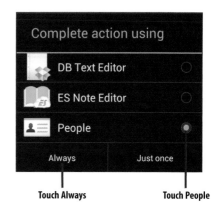

Touch Always   Touch People

2. Touch to select the account to add the new contact to. For example, you might want to add the new contact to your work email account instead of to your personal account.

3. In the new contact record that the People app creates, touch Save.

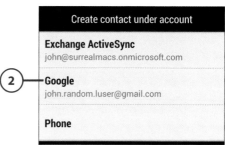

Add a Contact Using Near Field Communications

Your HTC One has Near Field Communications (NFC) functionality built in. This enables you to exchange contact cards and other data between NFC-enabled smartphones or to purchase items in a store by holding your HTC One near the NFC reader at the checkout counter.

If you encounter someone who has an NFC-enabled smartphone, or someone who has an NFC tag that contains her business card, follow these steps to import that information.

1. Hold the other person's smart-phone back to back with your HTC One and give the command for sharing via NFC, or hold the NFC tag close to the back cover of your HTC One. Your HTC One's screen dims and the phone plays a tone to indicate that it is reading the NFC information. The Create Contact Under Account dialog appears.

2. Touch the account you want to add the new contact to. For example, you may be able to choose between your Google account, your Exchange account, and the Phone account.

3. In the new contact record that the People app creates, touch Save.

Manage Contacts Settings

To make the Contacts app display contacts the way you prefer, you can customize it. For example, you can choose the contact list display order and whether to display contacts using their first names first or last names first.

1. Touch the People icon on the Home screen.

2. Touch the Menu button.

3. Touch Settings to display the Settings screen.

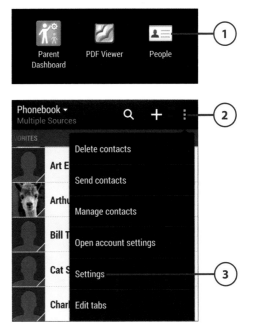

4. Touch to enable or disable showing only the contacts for whom you have phone numbers. You may find this setting useful if you use phone calls as your primary means of contact.

5. Touch to choose the sort order of the list of contacts in the Contacts app. You can sort the list by first name or last name.

6. Touch to choose how each contact is displayed. You can display contacts with the first name first or the last name first.

7. Touch to choose how to search your contacts. In the Search Contacts By dialog, select the check box for each field you want to search: Phone Number, Email Address, Company, Group Name, and Domain. Touch Done to close the dialog.

8. Touch to display the People You Know dialog, which enables you to search for friends on Facebook, Twitter, and other services.

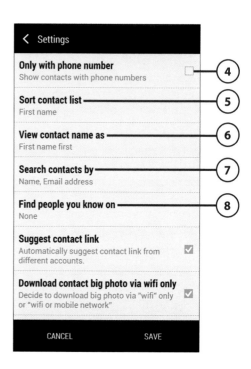

Think Before Using the Find People You Know On Feature

The Find People You Know On feature attempts to identify people on services such as Facebook and Twitter whose details match those of your contacts. This feature can be helpful, but you should be aware that, for the feature to work, your HTC One must upload your contacts to online servers. If allowing the People app to share your data like this is a concern, don't use the Find People You Know On feature.

Check this box to upload your contacts and search for matches on Facebook

9. Touch to enable or disabling the People app's feature for suggesting contacts you may want to link between different accounts. For example, if you have a Google contact called Bill Vasquez and an Exchange contact called Bill Vasquez, the People app will suggest you link the contact records.

10. Touch to select or deselect the check box. When the check box is selected, your HTC One downloads large contact photos only when connected to a Wi-Fi network. When the check box is deselected, the HTC One downloads the photos over the cellular network if Wi-Fi is not available.

11. Touch Save when you finish making your choices.

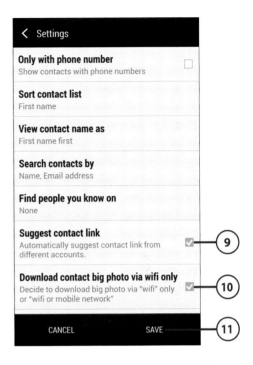

Create Contact Groups in the People App

You can use contact groups—such as Friends, Family, Inner Circle, or Co-workers—to separate your contacts into logical groups. This can be useful if you don't want to search through all your contacts. For example, to find a family member, you can touch the Family group and see only family members.

1. Touch the People icon on the Home screen.

2. Touch Groups in the tab bar to display the Groups tab. You can also swipe left to display this tab.

3. Touch the + to start creating a new group.

4. Type the name for your new group.

5. Touch the Menu button.

6. Touch Add Contact to Group to display the People tab. A check box appears to the right of each contact.

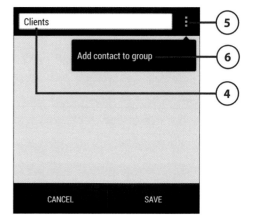

7. Touch to add a contact to the group.

8. Touch Save to save the contacts to the group.

9. Optionally, touch a handle and drag a contact to a different position on the list to change the order.

10. Touch the Save button. The People app saves the group, and it appears on the Groups tab.

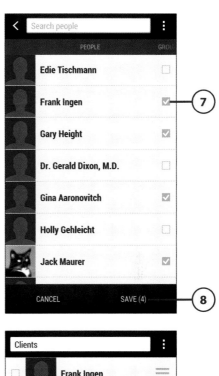

Change the Members of a Contact Group

1. Touch the People icon on the Home screen.

2. Touch Groups in the tab bar to display the Groups tab. You can also swipe left to display this tab.

3. Touch the group you want to edit.

4. Touch the Menu button.

5. Touch Edit Group to open the group for editing.

6. Touch a handle and drag a contact up or down to change the order of the group.

7. Touch to select the check box of a member you want to remove from the group.

8. Touch Save to apply your changes to the group. Saving the changes closes the group for editing, and the group's screen appears again.

Parent Dashboard   PDF Viewer   People

Phonebook ▾
Multiple Sources

ORITES   PEOPLE   GROUP

Maria Acton

Phonebook   +   ⋮

OPLE   GROUPS

Clients (4)

Clients (4)
Member view   +   ⋮

Edit group

Delete group

Frank Ingen   Gina Aaronovitch   Gary Height

Clients   ⋮

☐   Frank Ingen   ≡

☐   Gary Height   ≡

☐   Gina Aaronovitch   ≡

☒   Jack Maurer   ≡

CANCEL   SAVE

9. Touch the Menu button.

10. Touch Edit Group to open the group for editing again.

11. Touch the Menu button.

12. Touch Add Contact to Group to display the People screen, touch to select the check box for each contact you want to add, and then touch Save.

13. Touch Save to save the changes you've made to the group.

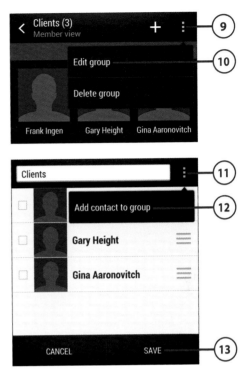

Choose Which Contacts to Display

You can choose between displaying all your contacts in the People app and displaying just some of them. Sometimes, it is more convenient to limit the display to only particular sources of contacts or groups of contacts—for example, just the contacts in your Google account, or only your business contacts.

1. In the People app, touch Phonebook to open the Phonebook menu.

2. Touch a check box to include or exclude that source's contacts from the list displayed.

3. To include only some groups from a source in the contacts list, touch the ... button.

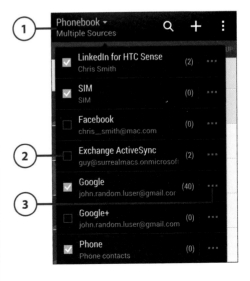

4. Touch a check box to include or exclude the group's contacts.

5. Touch OK to close the dialog.

6. Touch Phonebook to close the Phonebook menu.

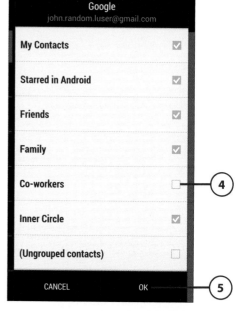

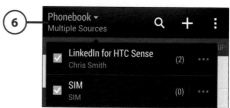

Link and Separate Contact Records

When you add contacts to your HTC One from several different accounts, and perhaps add other contact information from e-mail messages or vCard files, it is easy to get two or more contact records for the same contact. When this happens, you can link the contact records together so that the People app displays them as a single contact record, enabling you to see all the data you hold on the contact at a glance.

Other times, you may need to unlink linked contacts. You can perform both these operations easily in the People app.

Link Contact Records

1. On the People tab in the People app, touch the contact you want to link. The contact record opens.

2. Touch the Menu button.

3. Touch Link to display the linking screen.

4. Touch a contact in the Suggest Links section to link that contact. The People app bases this suggestion on the contact record containing similar information to the record from which you started.

5. Touch Clear Suggestion if this suggestion is not suitable.

6. Touch a contact in the Add Contact section to display the contact of the same name from that account (for example, in your LinkedIn account). You can then review the contact record and decide whether to link it.

7. Touch the Other Contacts button to display your full list of contacts. You can then touch the contact you want to link.

8. Touch Done to apply the links you have made.

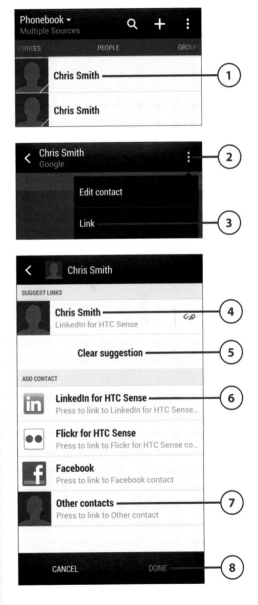

Unlink Linked Contacts

1. On the People tab in the People app, touch the contact from which you want to unlink one or more contacts. The contact record opens.

2. Touch the Menu button.

3. Touch Link to display the linking screen.

4. Touch a link symbol to break the link. The link symbol changes to a broken link symbol.

5. Touch Done to apply your changes.

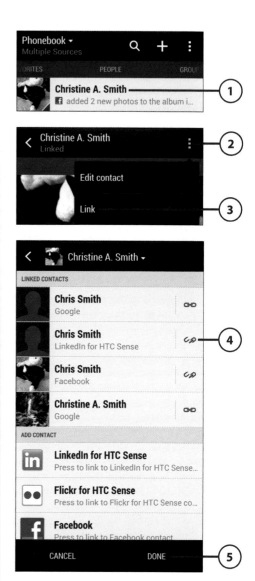

Set Up Speed Dial Numbers for Contacts

If you need to call a particular contact frequently, you can save time and effort by creating a speed dial number for that person.

1. On the People tab in the People app, touch the contact for whom you want to create a speed dial.

Call a Speed Dial Number

To call a speed dial number, touch Phone on the Home screen, then touch and hold the speed dial number until the app starts the call.

2. Touch the Menu button.

3. Touch Set Speed Dial.

4. Touch the Number button to display the Select Number dialog.

5. Touch the number you want to use for the speed dial.

6. Touch the Location button to display the Select Location dialog. Here, location means the number used for the speed dial.

7. Touch the number you want to assign to the speed dial.

8. Touch Save to save the speed dial assignment.

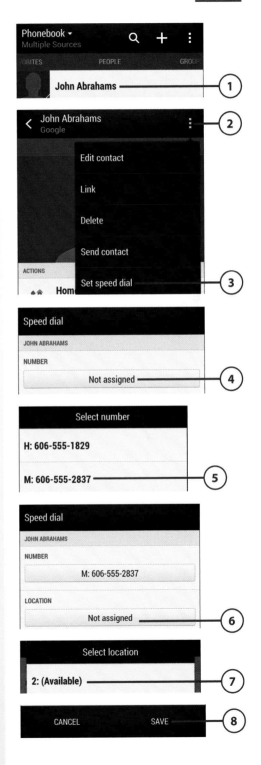

Turn your current call into a conference call

In this chapter, you find out how to make and take phone calls and send instant messages on your HTC One. Topics include the following:

→ Making phone calls
→ Making conference calls
→ Sending and receiving text messages
→ Sending and receiving multimedia messages

Phone and Instant Messaging

As a cellular phone, your HTC One includes powerful features that enable you to make phone calls swiftly and easily. Your HTC One can also send both text-only instant messages and multimedia instant messages by using the Messaging app.

Phone

With the Phone app, you can quickly make and receive calls across the cellular network. When you need to talk to more than one other person, you can easily turn your current call into a conference call.

Open and Navigate the Phone App

The Phone app contains four tabs that enable you to make calls in various ways and to track the calls you receive.

1. On the Home screen, touch Phone.

Opening the Phone App from the Lock Screen

You can open the Phone app directly from the Lock screen. Swipe the Phone icon up to unlock and go directly to the Phone app.

2. Use the dial pad to dial the number.

3. If the Phone app displays a suggested contact with a matching number, you can tap the contact if it is the one you want.

4. Touch to place the call.

Touch to use the full keyboard

Touch to use voice dialing

5. Touch Call History to see a list of the calls you have placed and received, including missed calls.

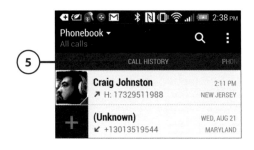

Making Your Logs Display the Information You Need

At first, the Phone app displays all your logs, but you can narrow down the view to specific logs so you can more easily find the calls and messages you need. You learn to do this later in this chapter.

6. Touch Favorites to see lists of Favorites and Frequently Contacted contacts.

7. Touch Contacts to display your full contacts list in the Contacts app.

8. Touch to see Contact Groups.

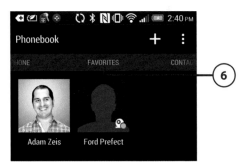

Touch to select the source(s) of the contact list

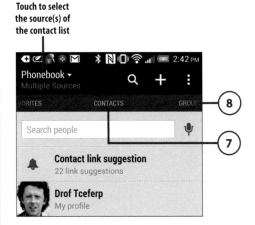

Receive a Call

When someone phones your HTC
One, you can accept the call, reject it,
or reject it and send a text message.

Accept a Call

1. When the phone rings, look at the
   contact name, if it is available, or
   the phone number if it is not, and
   decide whether to take the call.

2. Drag the green phone icon up to
   accept the call.

3. Touch to switch to the
   speakerphone.

4. Touch to mute the call. Touch
   again to turn off muting.

5. Touch to see a menu that allows
   you to put the call on hold and
   add a second line to the call
   (conference call).

6. Touch to end the call.

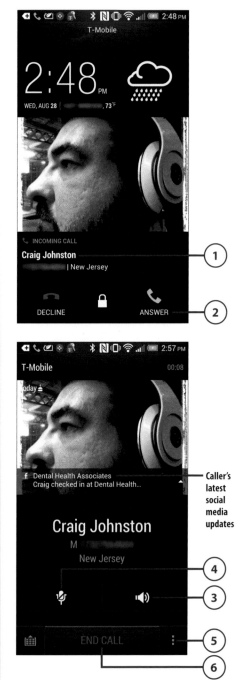

Caller's latest social media updates

Reject a Call

If you do not want to accept the call, you can reject it so that it goes to your voicemail, and you can choose to send a text message to the caller.

1. Drag the red phone icon up to reject the call.

2. Touch to send the caller a text message.

3. Touch to select one of the canned messages.

4. Touch to type a custom message.

5. Touch to send the message.

Creating Your Own Canned Reject Messages

To create and save your own canned reject messages, open the text messages app, open an existing text message thread, touch the Menu icon and touch Quick Text. On the Quick Text screen, you will be able to edit, add, and remove Quick Text responses.

Touch to create a task
to call the person
back in 20 minutes

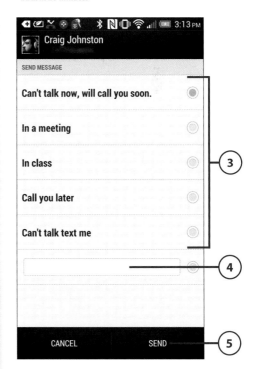

Handle Missed Calls

If you miss a phone call, you can quickly locate it in the Phone app's logs so that you can return it.

1. Swipe the Phone icon up to unlock your HTC One and go straight to the Phone app.

2. If the Call History tab is not displayed, touch to display it.

3. If you want to change the logs displayed, touch the Phonebook drop-down.

4. Select how you want to filter the Call History display.

Missed call notification

5. Touch a call log entry to dial the person back.

6. Touch and hold a call log entry to take some actions.

7. Touch to view this caller's entire history with you, including missed calls, text messages, and emails you have exchanged.

8. Touch to edit the caller's number and call that modified number.

9. Touch to view the caller's contact card if it is in your Contacts.

10. Touch to send a text message to the caller.

11. Touch to delete this single call history entry.

12. Touch to delete all calls from this contact.

13. Touch to block this person.

14. Touch to copy the caller's phone number into the clipboard so it can be pasted elsewhere, like in an email.

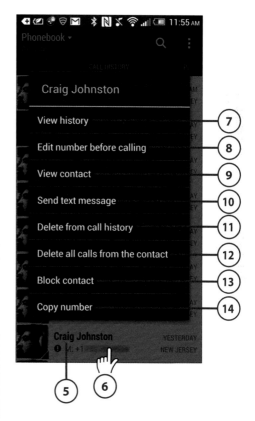

Place a Call

When you need to make a phone call, you can dial it manually using the keypad. But usually you can make a call more quickly by placing the call from a contact entry or by using your voice.

Dial with the Keypad

You can use the keypad to dial a call both when you need to call a number for which you do not have a contact and when you can remember part of the number for a contact.

1. Touch the Phone tab.

2. Start typing the phone number on the dial pad.

3. If Phone suggests the correct number, touch to dial it.

4. Alternatively, touch to display other matching numbers.

5. Touch the number you want to dial. If none of the suggestions are correct, touch Cancel and finish dialing the number manually.

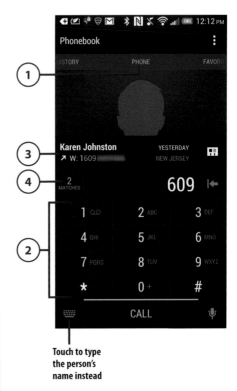

Touch to type the person's name instead

Dial from a Contact Entry

If you know you have a contact entry for the person you want to dial, you can start from that contact entry.

1. In the Phone app, touch the Contacts tab to bring it to the front. Android switches from the Phone app to the Contacts app.

2. Touch the contact to display the contact's details.

3. Touch the number you want to call.

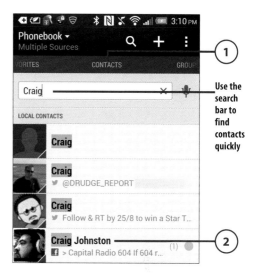

Use the search bar to find contacts quickly

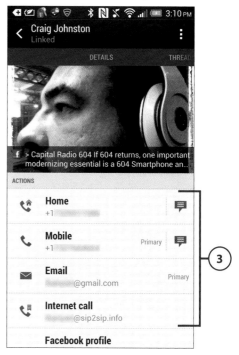

Choose the Sources for the List of Contacts

When you touch the Contacts tab, you have the ability to choose what sources the names are pulled from. For example, you may still have contacts stored on your SIM card and want them displayed here. Touch the Phonebook drop-down to choose where the contact names are pulled from.

Touch Phonebook

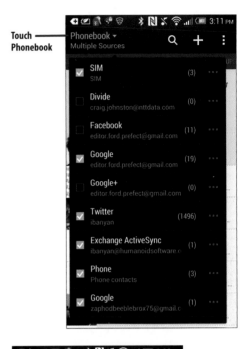

Control a Call

After accepting or establishing a phone call, you can control it from the Call screen.

1. Touch the Menu button.

2. Touch Hold to place the caller on hold.

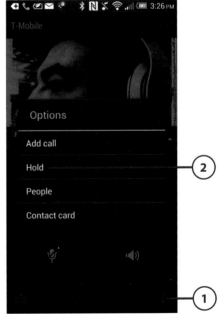

3. Touch the Menu button and touch Unhold to remove the hold.

4. Touch the Dial Pad icon to display the dial pad. Touch it again to hide the dial pad.

5. Touch Mute to mute the call. Touch again to remove muting.

6. Touch the speaker icon to enable the speakerphone.

7. Touch to end the call.

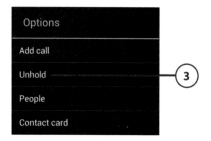

Using Other Apps During a Call

During a call, you can use most other apps freely, but you cannot play music or video. You can take photos with the Camera app, but you cannot shoot videos. To switch to another app, either use the Recent Apps list or press the Home button and use the Apps screen as usual. While you are using another app, your HTC One displays a green bar at the top of the screen to remind you that you are in a call. Swipe down the Notification bar, and touch the item in the list that shows your call in progress. It should indicate the caller's picture, the caller's name, and how long the call has been connected for. You can also touch the white phone icon to the right of the caller information to hang up.

Green bar indicates a call is in progress

Touch to return to your call

Make Conference Calls

You can quickly turn your current call
into a conference call by adding further participants.

1. Touch the Menu button.

2. Touch Add Call.

3. Dial the call in the most
   convenient way. For example,
   touch the Contacts tab, touch the
   contact in the list, and then touch
   the Call button on the contact's
   details screen.

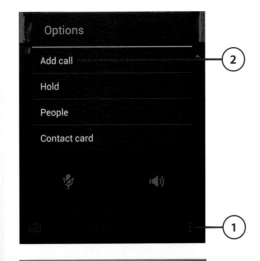

4. When your HTC One has established the new call, the original caller is on hold. Touch Merge to merge the calls.

5. Touch the ellipsis next to a person to perform actions specific to that call.

6. Touch to put the other call(s) on hold and have a private conversation with this person.

7. Touch to view the person's contact card.

8. Touch to hang up on just this person and return to the conference call.

9. Touch to add extra calls to the conference call. The exact number of people in a conference call depends on what your wireless carrier allows.

10. Touch to end the conference call.

Configure the Phone App

To make the Phone app work your way, you can configure its settings.

1. Touch the Menu button.

2. Touch Settings.

3. Touch to set up or manage Fixed Dialing Numbers.

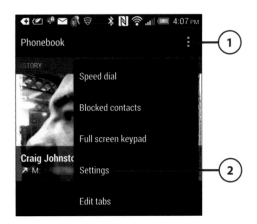

What Is Fixed Dialing Numbers?

Fixed Dialing Numbers (FDN) is a feature for when you want to lend your phone to someone and you want him or her to be able to dial only specific phone numbers. When you enable FDN, you have to provide a PIN that is used to disable FDN after it is enabled. After you have set up the list of allowed phone numbers, enable FDN and hand the phone to whomever you want to lend it to. The person will be able to dial only the numbers you entered until such time as you enter the PIN to disable FDN.

4. Touch to set up your voicemail service, or change it to use voicemail provided by a third party.

5. Touch to adjust voicemail settings.

6. Touch to enable support for hearing aids.

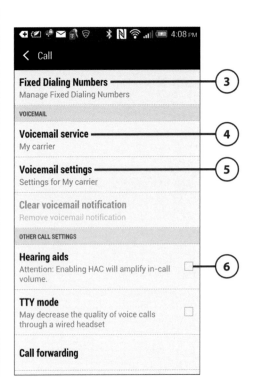

7. Touch to enable support for Teletype (TTY) mode that allows you to use Teletype equipment on a call.

8. Touch to choose when to forward calls. You can either forward all calls to a specific number or, more commonly, forward missed calls to your voicemail.

9. Scroll down for more settings.

10. Touch to choose whether you want to use Wi-Fi Calling.

What Is Wi-Fi Calling?

Wi-Fi Calling (or its technical name Universal Media Access [UMA]) is a technology that is provided by some carriers around the world, which allows your HTC One to roam between the cellular network and Wi-Fi networks. Typically when you are connected to a Wi-Fi network, any calls you make are free and of higher audio quality because of the faster speeds. As you move out of Wi-Fi coverage, your HTC One hands the call off to the cellular network, and vice versa, allowing your call to continue without interruption. If you want to read more about UMA or Wi-Fi calling, read this online article: http://crackberry.com/saving-call-charges-recession-your-blackberry. It may be on a BlackBerry blog, but the descriptions of the technology still apply.

11. Touch to change your Caller ID and Call Waiting settings.

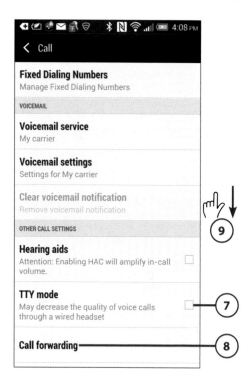

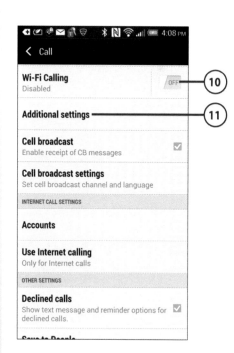

12. Touch to enable Cell Broadcast, which is a technology that allows broadcasting of emergency information.

13. Touch to change Cell Broadcast settings, including what channels you want to receive.

14. Touch to add Internet call (or SIP) accounts if you plan to use Internet calling.

15. Touch to choose when to use Internet calling. You can use it exclusively for all calls, only for Internet calls, or prompt each time a call is placed.

16. Touch to choose whether you want your HTC One to allow you to send text messages to people whose calls you decline or to set up reminders to call them back.

17. Scroll down for more settings.

18. Touch to choose whether you want to be prompted to save an unknown number to someone in your contact list.

19. Touch to choose whether to use home dialing assistance when roaming to other countries.

20. Touch to change your Home Dialing settings, which allows you to choose to leave a number as is that you are dialing from a foreign country or amend it to use the +<country code> annotation.

21. Touch to choose whether to preview missed call information on the Lock screen.

22. Touch to save your changes and return to the previous screen.

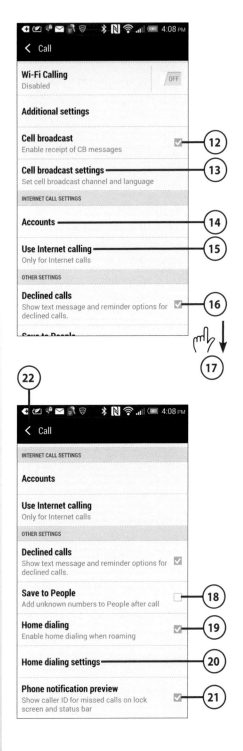

SMS and MMS

Short Message Service (SMS), also known as text messaging, has been around for a long time and is still used today as the primary form of communication for many younger phone users. Multimedia Message Service (MMS) is a newer form of text messaging that can contain pictures, audio, and video as well as text. Your HTC One can send and receive both SMS and MMS messages.

Get to Know the Messaging App

You use the Messaging app to send and receive text messages. This app has all the features you need to compose, send, receive, and manage these messages.

1. Touch the Messaging icon on the Home screen.

2. Touch to compose a new text message.

3. Touch the sender's picture to show the Quick Connect bar.

4. Touch a message thread to open it.

5. Touch the Menu button to change the Messaging app settings or to delete message threads.

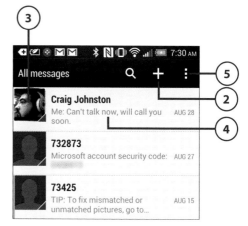

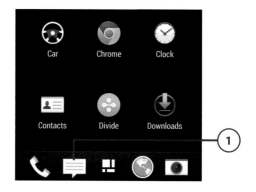

Manage Settings for the Messaging App

You use the settings of the Messaging app to manage how the app handles your SMS and MMS messages. Before you actually start working with SMS and MMS, let's take a look at the settings.

1. Touch the Menu button.

2. Touch to delete one or more message threads.

3. Touch to back up your message to a file and save it on your HTC One or email it to someone, and restore messages that are in an existing messages backup.

4. Touch to manage your messages block list.

5. Touch to choose threads and move them to a secure message Inbox.

6. Touch to choose contacts in message threads already in your message list to block.

7. Touch to mark all message threads as read.

8. Touch to change the way in which the message list is sorted. You can choose to sort by date or name.

9. Touch Settings to see more settings.

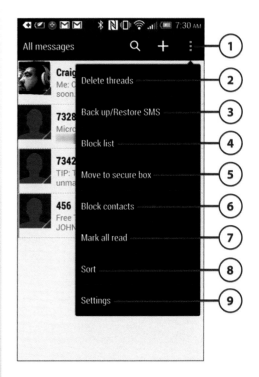

What Is a Secure Box?

A Secure Box is a special password protected Inbox where you can move messages to keep them from prying eyes. To access the Secure Box, touch the All Messages drop-down on the top left of the screen. The first time you access the Secure Box, you are asked to choose a password. Each time you access it in the future, you must type that password in to see the messages.

10. Touch to set how and when Notifications are sent for messages.

11. Touch to set SMS-specific settings.

12. Touch to set MMS-specific settings.

13. Touch to set general settings.

14. Touch to set emergency alert settings.

Notification Settings

1. Touch to choose whether to show a notification for messages you receive.

2. Touch to choose to also play a notification sound when a notification is displayed.

3. Touch to choose the notification sound to be played.

4. Touch to choose to also vibrate when a notification is received.

5. Touch to choose whether you want a preview of the message to be shown on the Lock screen.

6. Scroll down for more settings.

7. Touch to choose whether you want to be notified when a message you have sent has completed sending.

8. Touch to choose whether you want to be notified if a message you sent has failed.

9. Touch to play a notification sound when your message has been sent.

10. Touch to choose the notification sound to be played.

11. Touch to choose whether to also vibrate when playing the sent notification sound.

12. Touch to choose if any messages should be displayed on the screen when your messages successfully send or fail, both, or no message.

13. Touch the Back button to return to the main Settings screen.

Text Message (SMS) Settings

1. Touch to choose whether you want to receive a delivery report for each SMS you send.

2. Touch to change the SMS Service Center number if necessary.

3. Touch to manage any old SMS messages still on your SIM card.

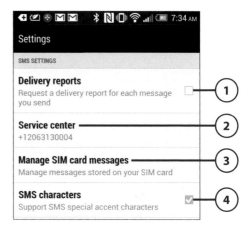

What Does the Manage SIM Card Messages Command Do?

Many old cell phones store text messages on the SIM card and not in the phone's memory. If you have just upgraded from an older phone, you might still have text messages on the SIM card that you would like to retrieve. Touch Manage SIM Card Messages on the Settings screen in the Messaging app to display the Manage SIM Card Messages screen. You can then copy the messages to your HTC One's memory and copy the senders to your contacts in the Contacts app.

4. Touch to choose whether to support accented characters in SMS messages.

5. Touch the Back button to save your changes and return to the main Settings screen.

Multimedia Message (MMS) Settings

1. Touch to choose whether you want to receive a delivery report for each MMS you send.

2. Touch to choose whether you want to receive a read report for each MMS you send.

3. Touch to automatically retrieve the MMS and its contents when you receive it.

4. Touch to automatically retrieve the MMS and its contents when you receive it while you are roaming.

5. Touch to set the priority level for MMS messages you send. You can choose Low, Medium, or High.

6. Touch to choose the maximum size of an MMS you send. Remember that the smaller the size, the more degraded pictures and video are.

7. Touch the Back button to save your changes and return to the main Settings screen.

General Settings

1. Touch to choose whether you want to include sent messages when you search.

2. Touch to choose whether you want to include call history when you search the Call History.

3. Touch to include the recipient's email address in search results.

4. Touch to choose how many lines of the message to show in the message preview.

5. Scroll down for more settings.

6. Touch to delete old messages when limits you set have been reached. These limits are set in step 7 and 8.

7. Touch to set the maximum number of text messages (SMS) to keep per conversation.

8. Touch to set the maximum number of multimedia messages (MMS) to keep per conversation.

9. Touch to set or change the password for the Secure Box where you store your private messages.

10. Touch to choose whether to save messages that you block in the Block Message box.

11. Touch to choose whether you want to append a signature to all outgoing messages.

12. Touch to enter the signature for all outgoing messages if you enabled it in step 11.

13. Scroll down for more settings.

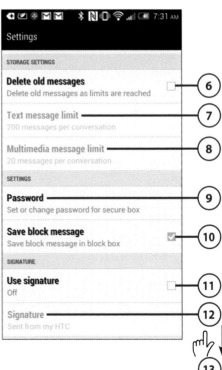

14. Touch to set a custom background for the messages app by selecting a picture.

15. Touch to change the color of the message bubble color and text.

16. Touch to restore your background and color changes to the default.

17. Touch to set the font size for the text used in the message thread display.

18. Touch the Back button to save your changes and return to the main Settings screen.

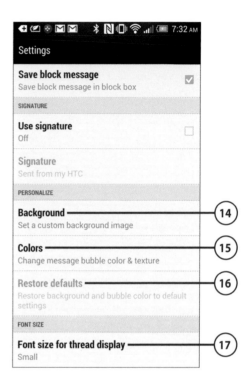

What's the Difference Between a Delivery Report and a Read Report?

A delivery report indicates that the message has reached the destination device. A read report indicates that the message has been opened for viewing. There is still no guarantee that whoever opened the message has actually read it, let alone understood it.

Don't Autoretrieve MMS While Roaming

Disable the automatic retrieval of multimedia messages when you travel to other countries because automatically retrieving these messages when you're roaming can result in a big bill from your provider. International carriers love to charge large amounts of money for people traveling to their countries and using their networks. The only time it is a good idea to leave this enabled is if your carrier offers an international SMS or MMS bundle where you pay a flat rate upfront before leaving. When you have autoretrieve disabled, you see a Download button next to a multimedia message. You have to touch it to manually download the message.

Compose Messages

When you compose a new message, you do not need to make a conscious decision about whether it is an SMS message or an MMS message. As soon as you add a subject line or attach a file to your message, your HTC One automatically treats the message as an MMS message.

Here is how to compose and send messages:

1. Touch to compose a new message.

2. Start typing the recipient's phone number, or if the person is in your contacts, type the name. If one or more matches are found, touch the mobile number you want to use.

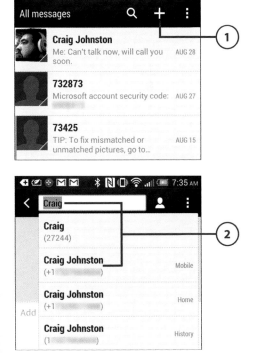

3. Touch and start typing your message.

4. Touch to send your message.

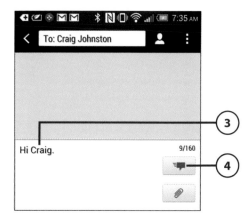

MESSAGE LIMITS AND MESSAGES

Text messages can be only 160 characters long. To get around this limit, most modern phones break up text messages you type into 160-character chunks. Your HTC One displays a readout showing the number of characters remaining and the number of messages it will send: The readout starts at 160/1 when you begin a new message and runs down to 1/1, then starts at 145/2 (because there is some overhead on linking the messages). The phone receiving the message combines them all together into one message. This is important to know if your wireless plan has a text message limit. When you create one text message, your HTC One might actually break the message into two or more.

Message count indicator

Attach Files to Messages

If you want to send a picture, audio file, or video along with your text message, all you need to do is attach the file. Attaching a file turns your SMS message into an MMS message.

1. Touch to attach a file.

2. Touch to choose the type of attachment.

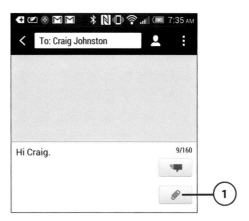

Touch to display Music Channel, which shows visualizations and lyrics as the music plays

Touch to shuffle the songs into a random order

Touch to repeat all songs, one song, or none

In this chapter, you discover your HTC One's audio and video capabilities, including how your phone plays video and music and how you can synchronize audio and video from your desktop or laptop computer or Google Music. This chapter also covers how to take pictures and videos. Topics include the following:

→ Using Music and Google Music to enjoy songs

→ Using the Gallery app for pictures and video

→ Taking photos, Zoe photos, and videos

→ Enjoying videos with the YouTube app

Audio, Video, Photos, and Movies

Your HTC One is a powerful multimedia smartphone with the capability to play many audio and video formats. The large screen enables you to turn your HTC One sideways to enjoy a video in its original 16:9 ratio. You can also use your HTC One to search YouTube, watch videos, and even upload videos to YouTube right from your phone. Android version 4 fully embraces the cloud, which enables you to store your music collection on Google's servers so you can access it anywhere.

Enjoying Music with the Music App

Your HTC One includes an app called, simply, Music for listening to music. The Music app is straightforward to use and automatically adds the songs you have copied to your HTC One from your computer using the Music pane in HTC Sync Manager.

Open and Navigate the Music App

1. Touch the Music icon on the Apps screen.

2. Touch to change the music category shown. Your choices are Artists, Albums, Songs, Playlists, Genres, Podcasts, and Folders.

3. Touch to search your music library for the search term you type.

4. Touch to display the menu, which includes commands such as Play All, Media Servers, Update Artist Photos, and Settings.

5. Touch to control playback of the current song or last song played.

6. Touch to display a dialog of options for the item.

7. Touch to play the artist, album, or song now.

8. Touch to add to a playlist. You then can choose which playlist—either an existing playlist or a new one you create at this point.

9. Touch to add the song to the playback queue.

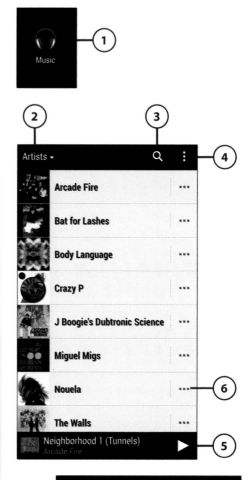

What Is the Queue?

In the Music app, the queue is the list of songs that is currently set to play. You can add a song—or a group of songs, such as an album or all the works your library contains by a particular artist—to the queue by touching the … button and then touching Add to Queue in the dialog that opens.

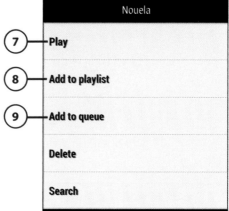

10. Touch to delete the item from your music library. The Music app prompts you to confirm the deletion in case you touched the button by mistake.

11. Touch to search for the current item. In the dialog that opens, touch the app you want to use for the search—for example, Chrome or Internet to search the Web, Play Music to search the Play Store, or YouTube to search for videos.

12. In the Artists list, touch an artist to display the albums and songs by that artist.

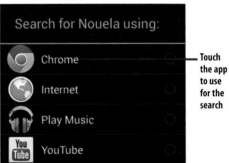

Touch the app to use for the search

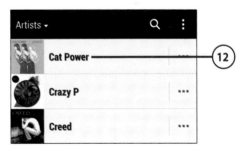

13. Touch Play All to play all the songs in order.

14. Touch an album to start playing that album from the start.

15. Touch a song to start playing that song.

Control Playback

After you open the song you want to play, you can easily control playback, skip to other tracks, or enjoy the Music Channel's visualizations and lyrics.

1. Touch to shuffle the songs into a random order. Touch again to restore the regular order.

2. Touch once to go back to the beginning of the current song. Touch again to go back to the beginning of the previous song. Touch and hold to rewind through the song; watch the time readout and lift your finger when you reach the appropriate point.

3. Touch to pause or resume playback.

4. Touch to go to the beginning of the next song. Touch and hold to fast-forward through the song; as with rewinding, watch the time readout and lift your finger when you want to resume playback.

5. Touch to turn on repeat. Touch again to repeat only the current song. Touch a third time to turn off repeat.

6. Drag the Playhead to scrub quickly through the song.

7. Touch the Menu button to display further commands.

8. Touch Get Info to display information for the song in the SoundHound app. This app listens to the song and displays a screen of information about it. The information typically includes the lyrics and details of where to buy the song.

9. Touch Queue to add the song to the playback queue.

10. Touch Add to add the song to a playlist, and then touch the playlist on the Select Playlist screen. Touch the + to start a new playlist.

11. Touch Update Album Art to download the latest album art available.

12. Touch Select Player to select a Wi-Fi player for playing the song back.

13. Touch Details to display the Details dialog, then touch Song Details, Album Details, or Artist Detail, depending on which information you want to see.

14. Touch Share to display the Share dialog, in which you touch Share Music Info to share the song's details or Share File to share the file itself.

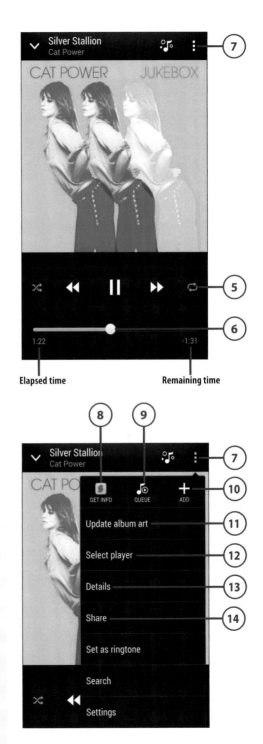

Elapsed time   Remaining time

15. Touch Search to search for the current item. In the dialog that opens, touch the app you want to use for the search—for example, Chrome.

16. Touch Set as Ringtone to display the Set as Ringtone dialog.

17. Touch Trim the Ringtone to trim the ringtone.

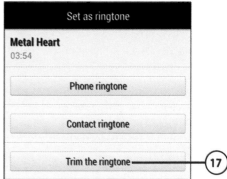

18. Drag the Start mark to the point at which you want the ringtone to start. The song starts playing back automatically so you can hear what you're doing.

19. Drag the End mark to the point at which you want the ringtone to end.

20. Touch Set As to use the portion of the song you have selected. The Set As ringtone dialog appears again, this time without the Trim the Ringtone button.

21. Touch Phone Ringtone or Contact Ringtone, as appropriate. If you touch Contact Ringtone, touch the contact on the People screen that appears.

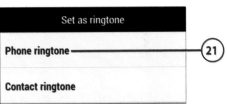

Create Playlists

Playlists enable you to group together related songs or those you want to hear in a particular sequence. You can easily create new playlists in the Music app or add songs to existing playlists.

You can either create a playlist starting from the music you're listening to or create a new, empty playlist and then add songs to it. Let's look at each method in turn.

Create a Playlist Starting from a Particular Song

Sometimes you may want to create a playlist starting from a particular song you're listening to. When you do this, you can either add more songs immediately or leave the playlist containing a single song and then add more songs later when you hear suitable songs.

1. With the song open or playing, touch the ... button to display the dialog of actions.

2. Touch Add to Playlist.

3. Touch the + to start creating a new playlist.

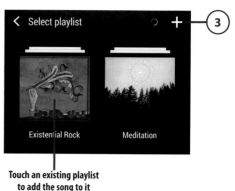

Touch an existing playlist
to add the song to it

4. Type the name for the new playlist.

5. Touch Save to save the new playlist.

At this point, the new playlist contains only the single song you added to it. But you can easily add other songs, as discussed a little later in this chapter.

Touch the + if you want to add more songs to the playlist now

Create a New, Empty Playlist

Other times, you may prefer to create a new, empty playlist so you can add songs to it later as needed. Or you can create an empty playlist and start adding songs to it immediately if you prefer.

1. From a screen such as the Artists screen, touch the pop-up menu in the upper-left corner to display the menu of sources.

2. Touch Playlists to display the Playlists screen.

3. Touch the + to start creating a new playlist.

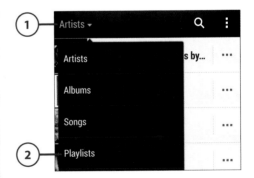

4. Type the name for the new playlist.

5. Touch Save to save the new playlist.

Touch the + if you want to add songs to the playlist now

Edit a Playlist

After creating a playlist in either of the ways explained earlier in this section, you can quickly add songs to it, remove songs from it, or change the play order of the songs.

1. From a screen such as the Albums screen, touch the pop-up menu in the upper-left corner to display the menu of sources.

2. Touch Playlists to display the Playlists screen.

3. Touch the playlist you want to edit. The playlist opens.

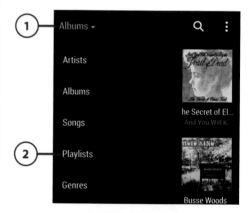

4. Touch the + to add songs.

5. Touch the pop-up menu, and then touch the category by which you want to browse: Artists, Albums, Songs, Genres, Podcasts, or Folders. This example uses Songs, which makes the Music app display the Select Music Track screen.

6. When you have located the songs you want to add, touch to select the check box for each one.

7. Touch the Add button to add the songs to the playlist. This button's name shows the number of songs you have selected—for example, Add (4).

8. Touch the Menu button.

9. Touch Edit Playlist to open the playlist for editing.

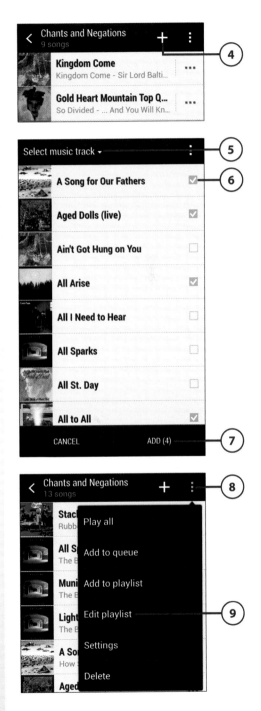

10. Edit the name or type a new name if you want.

11. Touch the + to add songs to the playlist.

12. Touch to place an x in a check box to mark a song for removal.

13. Touch the handle and drag a song up or down the list as needed.

14. Touch the Save button to save the changes to the playlist.

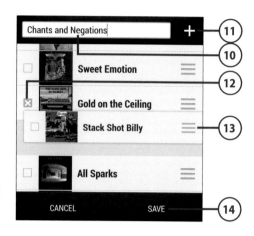

Add Songs to an Existing Playlist While Browsing

While browsing your music library, you can add a song to a playlist by touching its … button, touching Add to Playlist in the dialog of actions that appears, and then touching the destination playlist on the Select Playlist screen.

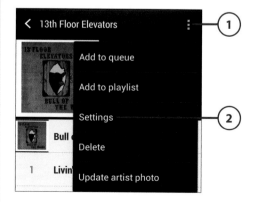

Touch to add this song to a playlist

Choose Settings for the Music App

To make the Music app work your way, you can choose settings for it. Your options include selecting which items to update automatically, whether to use only Wi-Fi to update them, and whether to start the Music Channel feature automatically.

1. Touch the Menu button.

2. Touch Settings to display the Settings screen.

3. Touch to enable or disable automatically downloading the album art.

4. Touch to enable or disable automatically downloading photos of the artist.

5. Touch to enable or disable automatically downloading lyrics to songs.

6. Touch to enable or disable restricting downloads to Wi-Fi. Restricting the downloads to Wi-Fi helps avoid consuming cellular data unnecessarily.

7. Touch to enable or disable starting the Music Channel feature automatically. Usually, you're better off starting the Music Channel manually when you want to see visualizations and lyrics—but you may feel otherwise.

8. Touch to see tips and help on getting the most out of the Music app.

9. Touch to return from the Settings screen to the music.

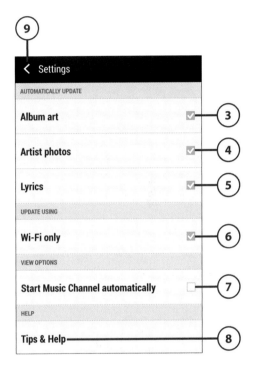

Enjoying Music with Google Music

If you find the HTC One's built-in Music app too limited, you will probably want to add Google's Play Music app to your phone. The Play Music app enables you to listen to music stored on your phone as well as from your collection in the Google Music cloud.

Install the Play Music App if Your HTC One Doesn't Have It

If your HTC One does not include the Play Music app, you'll need to install Play Music. Touch the Apps icon on the Home screen, then touch the Play Store icon to open the Play Store app. Touch Apps, touch the Search icon, and then type **play music**. Touch the Google Play Music search result, touch Install, and then touch Accept & Download. When the download finishes, touch Open to open the app.

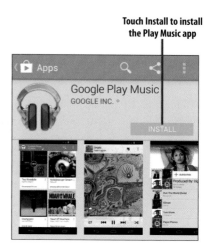

Touch Install to install the Play Music app

Load Music for the Play Music App to Play

Before using the Play Music app, you'll need to add some music to your Google account or your HTC One. You can add your existing music to Google Music or buy music from Google. We'll look at each method in turn.

Add Your Existing Music to Google Music

You can upload up to 20,000 songs from Apple iTunes, Microsoft Windows Media Player, or music stored in folders on your computer to your Google Music cloud account by using the Google Music Manager app on your desktop computer. If you haven't already installed Google Music Manager, follow the steps in the "Install Google Music Manager" section in the Prologue, "Getting to Know Your HTC One."

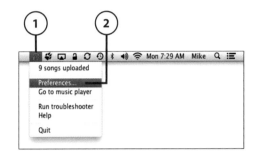

1. Click (right-click for Windows) the Google Music Manager icon. On the Mac, this icon appears in the menu bar at the top of the screen. On Windows, the icon appears in the taskbar at the bottom of the screen.

2. Click Preferences. (On Windows, choose Options.)

3. Click to upload new songs you have added to iTunes.

4. Click to upload the remainder of songs that have not yet uploaded.

5. Click to upload songs in certain playlists. This works only for iTunes or for Windows Media Player.

6. Choose the playlists to upload.

7. Click Upload after you have made your selections.

8. Click to allow Google Music Manager to automatically upload new songs added.

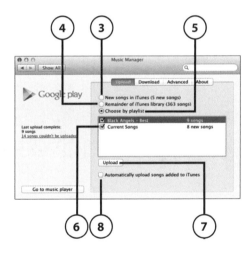

Automatic Upload

If you choose to have your music uploaded automatically in step 8, Google Music Manager continually monitors Apple iTunes, Microsoft Windows Media Player, or your Music folders to see if music has been added. If Google Music Manager finds new music, it automatically uploads the tracks. After you install Google Music Manager, the app runs continuously, enabling it to detect music you add to iTunes, Windows Media Player, or your Music folders.

What If I Don't Have iTunes or Windows Media Player?

If you don't have or don't use Apple iTunes or Microsoft Windows Media Player to store and play your music, Google Music Manager can use folders on your computer to upload music from. Click the Advanced tab and then click Change. Select Music Folder to use the folder on your computer called Music, or select Other Folders to let you choose folders where you store your music. Click Add Folder to add a new folder to the list.

Click Other Folders to choose a custom list of folders

Click Add Folder to add a folder to the list

Can I Download Music to My Computer?

You can download your entire music collection from Google Music to your computer, or just download music you have purchased on your HTC One. In Google Music Manager Preferences, click the Download tab, and then click the Download My Library button.

Click Download My Library to download all your songs

Find Songs on Google Play

Adding your own music to your Google account is the quickest way of building up your music library. After you have done that, you may want to add music from Google Play.

1. Touch the Play Music icon on the Apps screen.

2. Touch the icon in the upper-left corner to display the navigation panel.

3. Touch Shop to switch to the Music section of the Play Store.

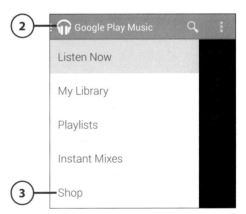

Navigating Among Tabs by Swiping or Touching

As you navigate the Play Store, you can move from screen to screen by either touching tabs on the tab bar or by swiping left and right.

4. Touch See More in the New Releases section to see more new releases.

5. Touch the Genres tab or swipe right to see a list of music genres.

6. Touch the Top Albums tab or swipe left to see the Top Albums list.

7. Touch Top Songs or swipe left again from the Top Albums list to see the Top Songs list.

8. Touch to search for music.

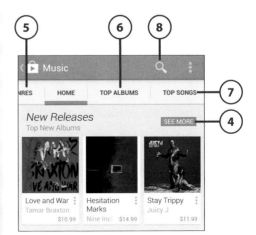

Purchase Music

After you find a song or album you want to purchase, use the following steps to make the purchase.

Free Music

Sometimes songs are offered for free. If a song is offered for free, you see the word Free instead of a price for the song. Even though the song is free, you still need to follow the steps outlined in this section; however, the price appears as 0.

1. Touch the price to the right of the song title or album.

2. Make sure the Purchase dialog shows the correct payment card.

3. Touch Buy. The Play Store app downloads the song, and you can then play it using the Play Music app.

Touch to play a preview of the song before purchasing it

Touch to change your payment method

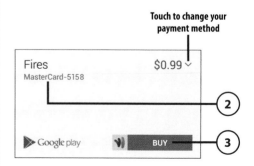

It's Not All Good

CLOUD AND DATA USAGE

Although cloud storage (where your music is stored on Google computers rather than on your HTC One) can be very beneficial, it does mean that anytime you listen to your music collection it is streamed over the network. If you are connected to Wi-Fi, this data streaming is free; but if you are not connected to Wi-Fi, the data is streamed over the cellular network and counts against your data package. If you don't have a large or unlimited data package, you could incur large overage fees, so do be careful.

Another disadvantage of streaming from the cloud is that when you have no cellular or Wi-Fi coverage, or you have very slow or spotty coverage, you are unable to access and listen to your music collection, or the songs stutter because of the poor connection. Be extra careful about this when traveling abroad because international data roaming charges are very high.

Use the Music Application

Now that you have some music synchronized to Google Music, it's time to take a look at how to use the Google Music app on your HTC One.

Open the Music App and Navigate to Its Different Areas

1. Touch the Play Music icon on the Apps screen.

2. Touch the icon in the upper-left corner to display the navigation panel. This panel enables you to switch among your different sources of music.

3. Touch Listen Now to display the Listen Now screen, which contains music you have added recently. Listen Now also recommends music to you based on the music you have and your recent listening habits.

4. Touch My Library to display your music library. Your library contains both the music on your HTC One and the music in your Google account.

5. Touch Playlists to display the Playlists screen. The Play Music app automatically creates some playlists for you, and you can manually create as many other playlists as you want. Read more about playlists later in this chapter.

6. Touch Instant Mixes to display the Instant Mixes screen, which contains both instant mixes you create yourself and ones that Google Play recommends to you. An *instant mix* is a selection of songs based on—and supposedly related to—a particular starting song. For example, you can create an instant mix based on "Berzerk" or "Blurred Lines."

7. Touch Shop to switch to the Play Store app and go to the Music section of Google Play, where you can browse and buy music as explained earlier in this chapter.

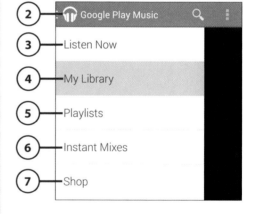

Listen to Music in Your Library

1. Touch the icon in the upper-left corner to display the navigation panel, then touch My Library to display your music library.

2. Touch to display a pop-up menu that enables you to switch between all your music (touch All Music) and only the music on your HTC One (touch On Device).

3. Touch to search for music using search terms.

4. Touch Genres to display the list of genres. You can then touch the genre by which you want to browse your library.

5. Touch Artists to display the list of artists so you can browse by artists.

6. Touch Albums to display the list of albums so you can browse by albums.

7. Touch Songs to display the list of songs. You can then easily locate a song by name in the alphabetical list.

8. Touch the Menu button on an item to display a pop-up menu of commands you can perform for that item. In this example, you can start an instant mix for this artist or shop the artist's music at the Play Store.

9. Touch the Play button or Pause button to control playback on the current song or most recent song played.

10. Touch an artist to display the albums and songs your library contains by that artist.

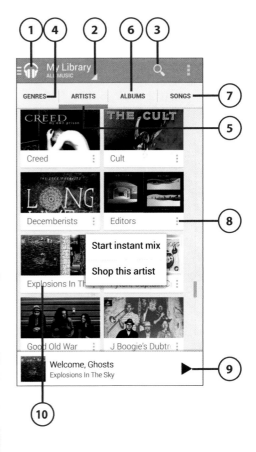

11. Touch the album you want to open. The album's songs appear.

12. Touch the song you want to start playing.

13. Touch Pause to pause playback. Touch the resulting Play button to start the music playing again.

14. Touch the album picture to display the Now Playing screen, which gives you full control of your music, as explained in the next section.

The My Library section shows the items in your music library

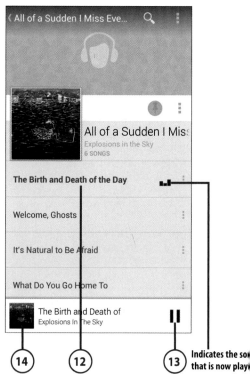

Indicates the so[ng] that is now play[ing]

Control Playback

While playing music, you can control both how the music plays and the selection of music that plays.

1. Touch to display the queue, which shows the songs that are lined up to play. You can then touch a song to start it playing.

2. Touch to return from the Now Playing screen to the previous screen.

3. Touch to indicate you like the song. The thumbs-up icon turns solid to indicate you have applied the rating. Touch again to remove the rating. The Google Music app also adds the song to the "Thumbs Up" playlist.

4. Touch to indicate you do not like the song. The thumbs-down icon turns solid to indicate you have applied the rating, and Play Music starts playing the next song.

5. Touch once to go back to the start of the current song. Touch again to skip back to the previous song in the album, playlist, or shuffle.

6. Touch to skip ahead to the next song in the album, playlist, or shuffle.

7. Touch to pause the song. The button turns into the Play button when a song is paused. Touch again to resume playing a paused song.

8. Touch and drag the Playhead to change the position in the song.

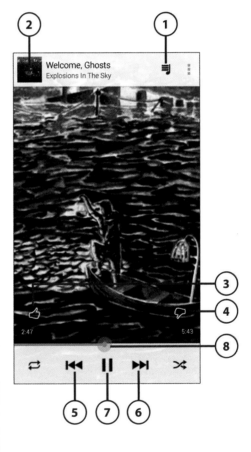

9. Touch to enable or disable song shuffling. When Shuffle is enabled, songs in the current playlist, album, or song list are randomly played.

10. Touch to enable repeating. Touch once to repeat all songs, touch again to repeat the current song only, and touch a third time to disable repeating.

11. Touch the Menu button to display the menu of actions you can take with the song.

12. Touch to start an instant mix based on the song.

13. Touch to add the song to a playlist. In the Add to Playlist dialog that opens, you can either touch New Playlist to start creating a new playlist or touch the name of an existing playlist to use that playlist.

14. Touch Go to Artist to display the artist the song is by.

15. Touch Go to Album to display the album the song is on.

16. Touch Clear Queue to clear the playback queue.

17. Touch Save Queue to save the playback queue. In the Add to Playlist dialog that opens, you can either touch New Playlist to create a new playlist containing the songs on the queue or touch the name of an existing playlist to add the songs to that playlist.

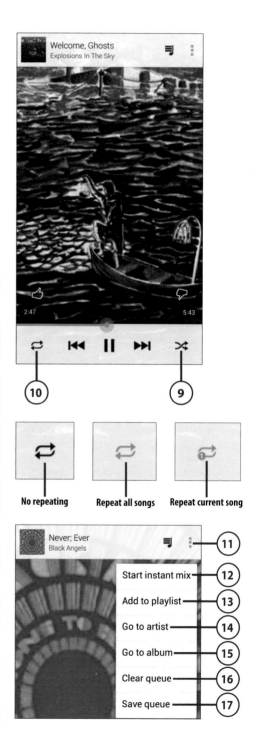

What Is an Instant Mix?

If you are playing a song and choose to create an instant mix as mentioned in step 12, the Google Music app creates a new playlist and adds songs to it that are similar to the one you are currently playing. The name of the playlist is the name of the current song plus the word *mix*. For example, if you are playing the song "Trail" and choose to create an instant mix, the playlist is called "Trail Mix."

Work and Listen to Music

You don't have to keep the Play Music app displayed while you are playing music. Instead, you can switch back to the Home screen and run any other app but still control the music easily.

1. Pull down the Notification bar.

2. Touch to pause the song.

3. Touch to skip ahead to the next song in the list, album, or playlist.

4. Touch the song title to open the Google Music app for more control.

5. Touch to stop playing the song and remove the playback control from the Notification bar.

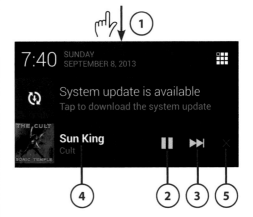

What If I Get a Call?

If someone calls you while you are listening to music, your HTC One pauses the music and displays the regular incoming call screen. After you hang up, the music continues playing.

Work with Playlists

Playlists can be a great way of listening to music, enabling you to group together related songs or those you want to hear in a particular sequence. On your HTC One, you can create new playlists, add songs to existing playlists, rename playlists, and change the order of the songs they contain.

Create a New Playlist on Your HTC One

1. Using the techniques described earlier in this chapter, navigate to a song you want to add to the new playlist.

2. Touch the song's menu button to open the dialog of actions.

3. Touch Add to Playlist. The Add to Playlist dialog opens.

4. Touch New Playlist. The Playlist Name opens.

5. Type the name for the new playlist.

6. Touch OK.

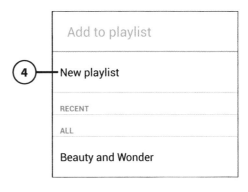

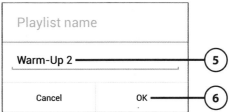

Add a Song to an Existing Playlist

1. Using the techniques described earlier in this chapter, navigate to a song you want to add to the existing playlist.

2. Touch the song's Menu button to open the menu of actions you can take with the song.

3. Touch Add to Playlist. The Add to Playlist dialog opens.

4. Touch the playlist you want to add the song to.

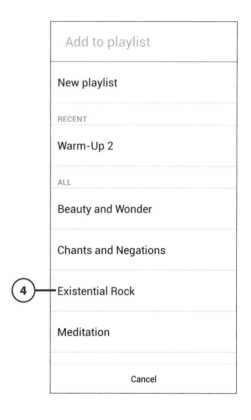

Delete a Playlist

1. Touch the icon in the upper-left corner of the screen to display the navigation panel, and then touch Playlists to display the Playlists screen.

2. Touch the Menu button for the playlist you want to delete.

3. Touch Delete. A confirmation dialog opens.

4. Touch OK.

Renaming a Playlist

At this writing, the Play Music app doesn't provide a command for renaming a playlist. To work around this, create a new, empty playlist with the new name. Then touch the Menu button for the playlist you want to rename, touch Add to Playlist to display the Add to Playlist dialog, and then touch your new playlist. You can now delete the old playlist after its contents are in the new playlist.

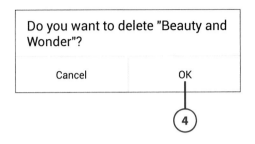

Listen to Music with No Wireless Coverage

If you use Google Music and store your music online, your HTC One streams the music over the cellular or Wi-Fi network when you play the music. If you know you are going to be without a signal but still want to listen to your music, you need to store it on your HTC One.

1. Using the techniques discussed earlier in this chapter, go to the music you want to store on your HTC One.

2. Touch the gray pushpin, which indicates that the music is not stored on your HTC One.

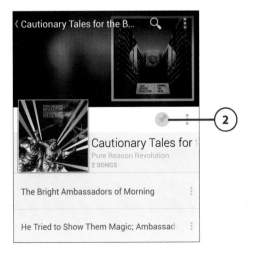

3. Your HTC One downloads and stores the music. As it does so, the pushpin displays a progress indicator. When the music is available, the pushpin appears on an orange background.

Remove Music from Your HTC One

If you need to remove music from your HTC One, navigate to the music in the Play Music app and then touch the white pushpin on the orange background. The Play Music app removes the music and then changes the pushpin's background to gray.

IMPROVE THE AUDIO OUTPUT WITH AN APP THAT HAS AN EQUALIZER

Your HTC One can produce an impressive volume of sound, so chances are you will enjoy listening to music on it. Neither the Music app nor the Play Music app provides a graphical equalizer for altering the sound balance, but you can add a third-party app that will give you precise control over how the music sounds. You can find various music apps with equalizers in the Play Store, but Poweramp is well worth checking out, especially because it has a 14-day free trial.

Playing and Sharing Videos

The Gallery app enables you to view pictures and video. You can also use the Gallery app to share pictures and video with people on Facebook, or via instant messaging, Bluetooth, YouTube, and email.

This section explains how to view and share videos. Later in this chapter, you learn how to take pictures and share them.

1. Touch the Gallery icon on the Apps screen to launch the Gallery app.

2. Touch the navigation pop-up menu in the upper-left corner.

3. Touch the category you want to see. Your choices are Albums, Events, Locations, and Friends. This example uses Albums.

4. Touch an album to open it, revealing the pictures and videos it contains.

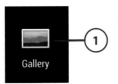

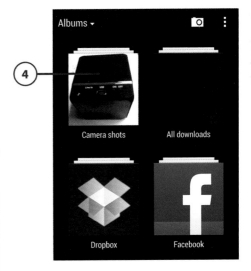

5. Touch a video to start it playing. Each video thumbnail has a little Play icon on it.

6. Touch the screen while the video is playing to reveal the video controls. If you do not use the controls, they disappear after a few seconds to make the video easier to view.

7. Touch to pause or unpause the video.

Changing the Orientation for a Video

When watching a video shot in landscape orientation, rotate your HTC One from portrait orientation to landscape orientation so you can enjoy the video full screen.

8. Drag the slider to scrub quickly forward and backward.

9. Touch to take a still picture of the current frame of the video.

10. Touch to display the Volume slider, which you can then drag to adjust the volume.

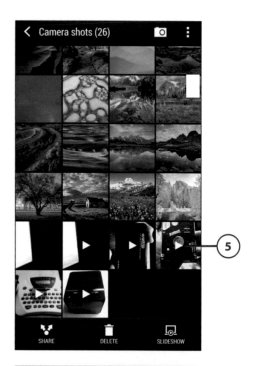

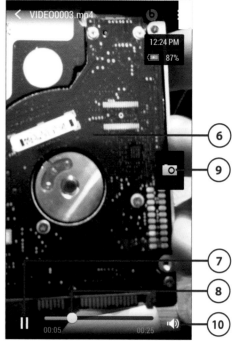

11. Touch to display the menu.

12. Touch Full Screen to switch to full-screen view. To return to best-fit view, touch the Menu button again, and then touch Best Fit.

13. Touch Edit to edit the video clip. See the following section for details.

14. Touch to play the video clip on a Wi-Fi player. On the Select Player screen that appears, touch the player you want to use.

15. Touch Share to share the video with other people. See the section "Share Videos," later in this chapter, for details.

16. Touch to return to the screen from which you opened the video.

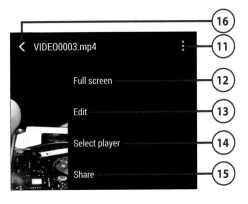

PLAY PHOTOS AND VIDEOS ON YOUR TV

Your HTC One can share what's displayed on its screen with a TV or monitor. This can be a great way of enjoying your videos, movies, photos, and other material with other people.

The easiest way to display your HTC One's screen on a TV (or a monitor) is by using DLNA, a standard set by the DLNA organization. If your TV has DLNA support built in, you're don't need any extra hardware. If not, you can get a device such as the HTC Media Link HD wireless adapter, which connects to the TV via HDMI; select the correct HDMI input on the TV to get the HTC Media Link HD input. (If your TV doesn't have HDMI, you can get a suitable converter box, such as an HDMI-to-Component Video converter—but you might also want to think about getting a new TV with HDMI and DLNA.)

Once your DLNA device is in place, your HTC One automatically detects the device when the HTC One is connected to a wireless network within range. All you then need to do is open the content you want to share, using an app such as Gallery or YouTube, and swipe three fingers up the screen to start sending the screen's content to the TV.

If you don't have DLNA, you can connect your HTC One to a TV or monitor by using a micro-USB–to-HDMI converter and an HDMI cable. The converter must be compliant with the Mobile High-Definition Link standard, MHL for short. Some converters need a power supply, typically via a micro-USB socket, and will not provide a signal without power.

Trim a Video

While playing a video, you can quickly trim it down to only the part you want to keep.

1. With the video open, touch the screen to display the controls.

2. Touch the Menu button to open the menu.

3. Touch Edit to switch to Edit mode. Your HTC One displays the editing controls and switches the video to landscape orientation if it was in portrait orientation.

4. Drag the Start marker to the point at which you want the cropped clip to start.

5. Drag the End marker to the point at which you want the cropped clip to end.

6. Touch the Play icon to play back the video clip and make sure you've selected the right part.

7. Touch Save. Gallery displays the Video Trimming screen while it trims the clip. The video then appears again.

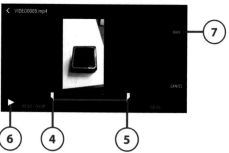

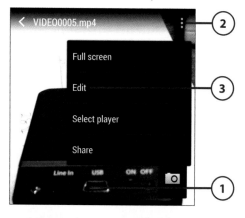

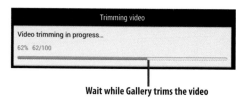

Wait while Gallery trims the video

Share Videos

From the Gallery app, you can share small videos with other people.

1. Touch and hold the video you want to share until the dialog of actions appears.

2. Touch Share to open the Share Via dialog.

Share a Video You're Watching

You can also start sharing a video you've opened for watching. Touch the screen to display the controls, touch the Menu button to display the menu, and then touch Share.

3. Touch the means of sharing you want to use. This example uses Mail.

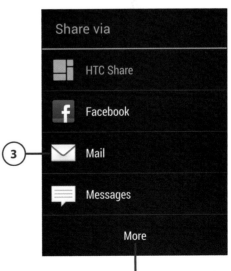

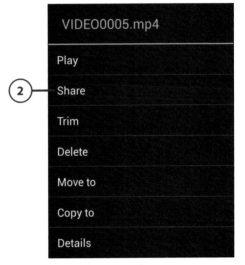

Touch More to see other ways of sharing the video

4. Provide the information needed to share the video. For example, address the message, give it a subject line and any text needed, and then send it.

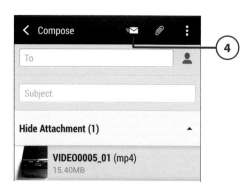

Share Several Videos at Once

If you want to share several videos at once using the same method of sharing, touch Share at the bottom of the screen in the Gallery app. On the pop-up menu, touch the means of sharing—for example, Facebook. If the menu doesn't show the means of sharing at first, touch More to expand the menu to its full list, then touch the means of sharing.

Gallery displays the Select One or More Items screen. Touch to check the box for each item you want to share, and then touch Next.

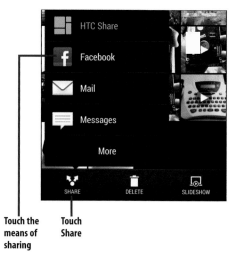

Touch the means of sharing
Touch Share

Sharing Only Small Videos

It is best to share only small videos from your HTC One. Even when using email, try to share videos no larger than 10MB, which is only two or three minutes of high-quality video. Otherwise, your videos will be too large to transfer successfully.

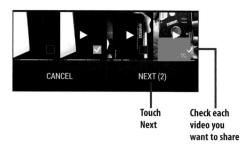

Touch Next
Check each video you want to share

Bluetooth Sharing Might Fail

Many phones do not accept incoming Bluetooth files, but devices such as computers do.

Even on computers, recipients must configure their Bluetooth configuration to accept incoming files. After you have set up Bluetooth sharing, it normally works well, so it is usually best for regular use rather than one-time use.

Share a Video on YouTube

1. Enter the title of your video.

2. Enter a description of your video.

3. Touch the Privacy pop-up menu and choose whether to make your video public for everyone to see, keep it private so only you can view it, or mark it as Unlisted.

Sharing a YouTube Video Only with Specific People

As well as the Public setting and the Private setting, the Privacy pop-up list provides an Unlisted setting. Choose Unlisted when you need to share the video with some people but not with everyone. The video then does not appear in the public view of your YouTube account, but you can send the URL for the video to anyone you want to view it.

4. Enter any tags for your video. Tags are keywords that help people find videos by searching.

5. Touch to upload the video to YouTube.

Share Video on Facebook

If you have not previously set up a Facebook account on your HTC One, you are prompted to do so before you can upload your video.

1. Enter a description of your video.

2. Touch if you want to add the location to the video.

3. Touch to set the audience for the video.

4. Touch Public, Friends, Only Me, or Acquaintances, as needed.

5. Touch Post to post the video.

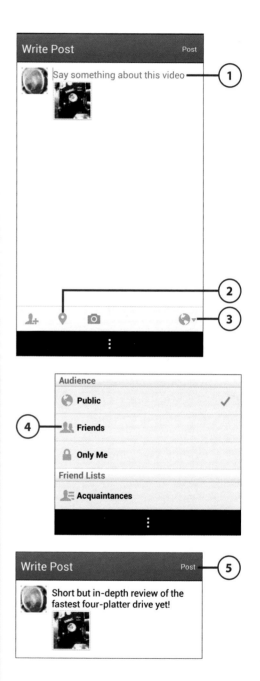

Delete Videos

1. Touch Delete at the bottom of the Gallery screen. Gallery displays the Choose Items to Delete screen.

2. Touch each video you want to delete, placing a red x on it.

3. Touch Delete. Gallery deletes the videos without confirmation.

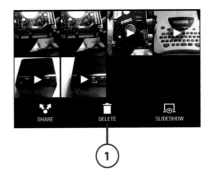

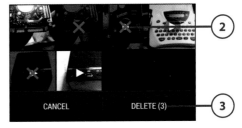

Taking Photos and Videos with the Camera App

The Camera app enables you to take still photos and record videos. You can also record what HTC calls *Zoe photos*, a series of photos combined with a three-second video. Zoe photos are designed to capture a moment more fully than regular photos do.

The Camera app provides a wide range of settings to help you get high-quality photos. We'll start with the basics and move along to the advanced features.

Take Photos

The Camera app is great for taking quick photos with the main camera, the one on the rear of the HTC One. You can also take photos with the front camera, the one on the screen side; this is great for self-portraits. The HTC One also offers settings for taking photos in different conditions, such as backlight shots; a Night mode for taking photos in dark conditions; and a High Dynamic Range (HDR) feature, which takes several photos in sequence and uses them to create a single photo with a better color and light balance.

Open the Camera App

1. Touch the Camera icon to launch the Camera app. You can touch the Camera icon either on the Launch bar or on the Apps screen.

2. Make sure the Camera app is set to take still photos. If not, touch the Camera button at the bottom of the screen.

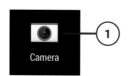

Camera

Indicates the camera is set to take still photos. Touch to switch to Zoe photo mode.

Take Photos with the Main Camera

1. Aim the lens at your subject so that the screen shows what you want to see.

2. Drag the slider right to zoom in or left to zoom out.

3. Touch to zoom all the way out.

4. Touch to zoom all the way in.

5. Touch to cycle the flash among its three settings: Auto, On, and Off.

Making the Most of the Flash

Choose the Off setting for the flash when you need to take photos where the flash would be disruptive. Choose the On setting when you need to light the foreground of a shot even though the rest of the scene is amply lit—for example, to light your subject's face in front of a bright background. Choose the Auto setting for general use.

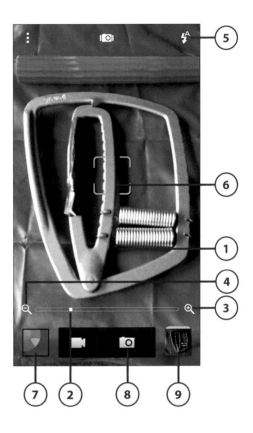

6. Touch where you want to focus. By default, the Camera app focuses on the center of the screen, where the subject is most likely to be.

7. Touch to apply an effect to the photo. See the next section for details.

8. Touch to take the photo.

9. Touch the thumbnail to open the last photo you took.

Auto   On   Off

Apply an Effect to a Photo

The Camera app includes a series of special effects you can apply to make your photos look different—for example, applying a monochrome filter or a sepia tint, or reversing the colors. By applying an effect, you can alter a photo's look completely, but you can also make relatively subtle changes.

1. Touch Effects to open the panel of effects.

2. Scroll the effects panel left to find the effect you want.

3. Touch the effect you want to apply. The Camera app shows how the effect will look.

4. When you have chosen the effect, touch Effects again to close the Effects panel.

5. Touch to take the photo as usual.

   To remove the effect you have currently applied, touch the leftmost icon in the Effects panel.

Touch the leftmost thumbnail to remove the current effect

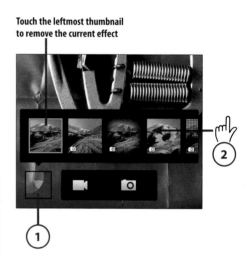

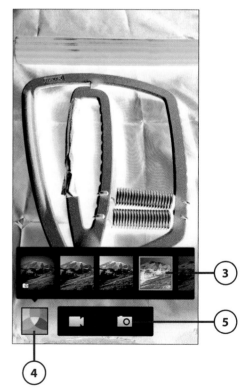

Take a Burst of Shots

The rear camera can take up to 20 consecutive photos in a burst. Touch and hold the shutter button to take a burst. After you release the shutter button, the Camera app automatically displays the burst shots for your review. You can choose to identify a single shot to keep, or you can manually delete all the photos you don't want and keep the remaining photos.

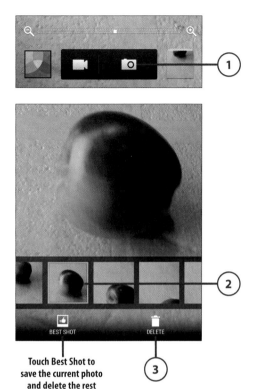

1. Touch and hold the shutter button for as long as you want to keep shooting, or until the Camera app reaches its limit of 20 photos and stops automatically.

2. In the panel of thumbnails that appears, touch the photo you want to see.

Touch Best Shot to
save the current photo
and delete the rest

3. Either touch Best Shot to keep the current photo and delete all the rest, or touch Delete to choose which photos to keep and which to delete.

4. On the Choose Items to Delete screen, touch each photo you want to delete, putting a red x on it.

5. Touch Delete to delete those photos. Camera keeps the other photos.

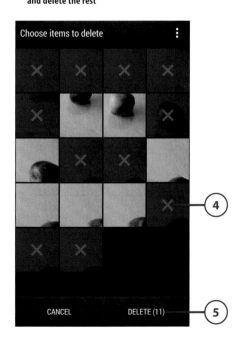

Take Photos with the Front Camera

When you need to take a self-portrait of yourself or a small group of people, switch to the front camera, the one on the screen side of the HTC One. This camera has lower resolution and no zoom or flash, so it's suitable only for light use.

1. Touch the Menu button to display the menu panel.

2. Touch Front to switch to the front camera. The menu panel closes.

3. Touch anywhere on the screen to start the two-second countdown timer. Camera then takes the photo.

4. To switch back to the main camera, touch the Menu button and then touch Main in the menu panel.

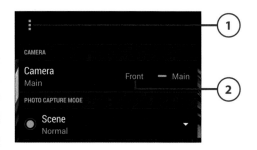

Switch Quickly Between the Main Camera and Front Camera

To switch quickly between the main camera and the front camera, swipe either left or right in the Camera app.

Use the Photo Capture Modes

To help you shoot good-looking pictures in different lighting conditions, your HTC One includes 10 photo capture modes. There are four main modes, one of which has six submodes, as explained in the following list:

- **Scene**—Use this mode for shooting regular photos: all those that are not night photos, High Dynamic Range (HDR) photos, or panoramas. Choose the Normal submode for standard photos. Choose the Portrait submode for photos featuring people in which you want to smooth the look of the skin, giving a more flattering look. Choose the Landscape submode for pictures of landscapes and scenery. Choose the Backlight submode when your subject is backlit and you want to avoid the subject being too dark; with this setting, Camera balances the light metering on the assumption the middle of the screen is backlit. Choose the Text submode to maximize the contrast and definition when you are taking a photo of a text document. Choose the Macro submode for close-up shots.

- **Night**—Use this mode for shooting photos in low light.

- **HDR**—Use this mode when you need to increase the dynamic range of a photo. If you notice the sky looking too white or the rest of the frame too dark when you're lining up the photo, try switching to HDR. HDR takes multiple photos and combines them to improve the dynamic range; it's slower than taking regular photos, so use it for stationary subjects, not for moving subjects.

- **Sweep Panorama**—Use this mode for shooting panorama photos.

To use a photo capture mode, you turn on the appropriate mode, and then take the photo.

1. Touch the Menu button to display the menu panel.

2. Touch Night to turn on Night mode.

3. Touch HDR to turn on HDR mode.

4. Touch Scene to use the current submode set for Scene mode.

5. Touch the pop-up menu to display the submodes.

6. Touch the submode you want to use.

   When you touch the mode or submode, the menu panel closes automatically. You can then take the photo as usual by touching the shutter button.

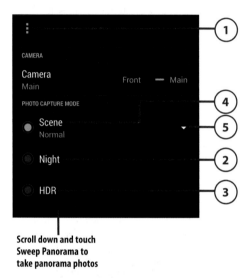

Scroll down and touch Sweep Panorama to take panorama photos

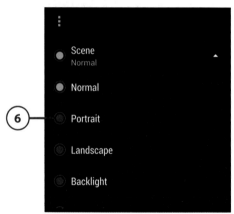

Take Zoe Photos

One of your HTC One's standout features is its capability to take *Zoe photos*, a series of photos combined with a three-second video. Zoe photos are intended for capturing moments so you can share them with others or savor them yourself later.

Zoe photos include audio, so start any audio accompaniment needed before taking a Zoe photo.

1. Touch the Zoe icon at the top of the screen to switch to Zoe mode.

2. Touch the shutter button to start taking a Zoe photo.

3. Move your HTC One as needed to capture the visual content you want in the Zoe.

4. After Camera finishes capturing the Zoe photo, you can touch the thumbnail to view it.

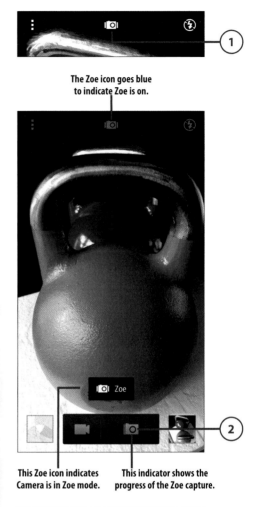

The Zoe icon goes blue to indicate Zoe is on.

This Zoe icon indicates Camera is in Zoe mode.   **This indicator shows the progress of the Zoe capture.**

Change Camera Settings

You can get good photos by using your HTC One with its default settings, as described earlier in this chapter, and using the flash, zoom, and photo capture modes. But you can get better photos by changing settings to harness the full power of the Camera app.

1. Touch the Menu button to display the menu panel.

2. Scroll down until you see the Settings section.

3. Touch Self-Timer and then touch + or – to adjust the number of seconds.

4. Touch Crop and then touch the cropping you want: Wide, Regular, or Square.

5. Touch Video Quality and then touch the video quality you want: Full HD (1920×1080), HD (1280×720), or MMS (176×44). Normally, you'll want to use Full HD unless you need to conserve space.

6. Touch Review Duration and then touch the review duration for photos. Your choices are No Review, 5 Seconds, 10 Seconds, or No Limit. Choose No Review if you want to keep shooting without interruption.

7. Touch Image Adjustments and then touch + or – to adjust the Exposure, Contrast, Saturation, and Sharpness settings.

8. Scroll down to reach the next few settings.

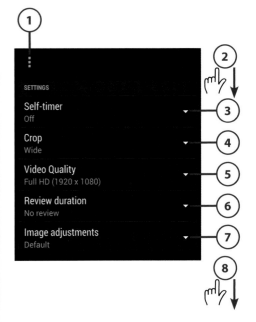

SETTINGS

Self-timer
Off

Crop
Wide

Video Quality
Full HD (1920 x 1080)

Review duration
No review

Image adjustments
Default

9. Touch ISO and then touch the ISO sensitivity rating you want to use. Your choices are Auto (the best choice unless you need to set the ISO manually), 100, 200, 400, 800, or 1600.

10. Touch White Balance and then touch the white balance setting to use: Auto (best for general use), Incandescent (old-style electric bulbs), Fluorescent, Daylight (for bright daylight, such as sunny conditions), or Cloudy.

11. Touch Continuous Shooting and then select or deselect the check boxes in that section, as needed. The Continuous Shooting check box controls whether you can take bursts of photos, which is usually helpful unless you find yourself taking bursts when trying to take a single photo. The Limit to 20 Frames check box sets a 20-frame limit for bursts; deselect this check box if you want to take more. The Auto Review check box controls whether Camera prompts you to review each burst immediately after taking it.

12. Touch Camera Options and then select or deselect the check boxes in that section as needed. The Face Detection check box controls whether Camera tries to detect faces in the photos. The Auto Smile Capture check box controls whether, when shooting photos of faces, Camera waits for a flash of teeth—be it smile or snarl—before capturing the photo. The Geo-Tag Photos check box controls whether Camera adds GPS location data to the photos.

Pros and Cons of Geo-Tagging Your Photos

If you select the Geo-Tag Photos check box, Camera automatically adds GPS location data to each photo. This location data can be helpful if you want to be able to sort your photos by locations or see exactly where each photo was taken. But if you share your photos with others, the location data may be a threat to your privacy.

13. Touch Shutter Option and then select or deselect the check boxes in that section, as needed. The Touch to Capture check box controls whether you can take a photo by touching the screen rather than touching the shutter button. The Shutter Sound check box controls whether the HTC One plays a shutter sound when you take a picture. Deselect this check box if you need to take photos discreetly.

14. Scroll down to reach the remaining settings.

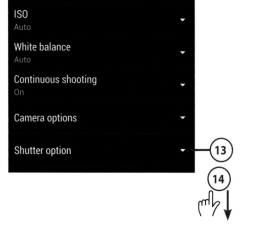

15. Touch to enable or disable locking the focus while taking video.

16. Touch to enable or disable the display of the grid, which can help you to compose your shots.

17. Touch to turn Auto Upload on or off. The first time you touch this button to turn Auto Upload on, you must specify which account to use.

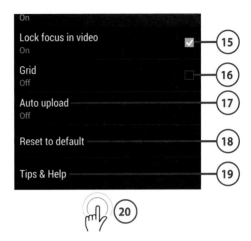

Be Careful with Auto Upload

Unless you take photos with extreme care and consideration, it is usually best not to use the Auto Upload feature. Normally, it is better to take photos freely, review them on your HTC One, delete the duds, and then upload only the best of the rest.

18. Touch to reset all the Camera settings to their defaults. Doing this can be useful if you have been experimenting with the settings and have messed up something, but can't identify what. Touch Yes in the Reset to Default dialog that opens.

19. Touch to display tips and help on using the Camera app.

20. Touch outside the menu panel to close it.

View Your Photos and Zoe Photos

After taking photos and Zoe photos, you can quickly view the photos you have taken, highlight them, edit them, share them with other people, or delete them.

1. In the Camera app, touch the thumbnail to view the last photo you took. The photo appears. If it is a Zoe photo, the video plays, and you hear the audio.

2. Swipe left or right to display other photos.

3. Touch to display the onscreen controls. They disappear after a few seconds of not being used.

4. Touch Highlight to highlight the photo.

5. Touch Share to share the photo. On the pop-up menu, touch the means of sharing, and then provide any information needed—for example, the recipient for a photo you share via email.

6. If you want to delete the photo, touch Delete, and then touch OK in the Delete dialog that opens.

7. Touch Edit to edit the photo. The Photo Editor screen appears.

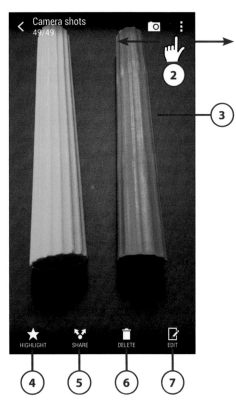

Zooming In and Out on Your Photos

When viewing a photo, you can zoom in by placing two fingers on the screen and pinching outward or by double-tapping on the area you want to expand. Pinch inward or double-tap again to zoom back out.

8. Touch Effects to apply an effect to the photo—for example, apply the Auto Enhance effect to automatically enhance the color balance.

9. Touch Frames to apply a decorative frame to the photo.

10. Touch Retouch to display the Retouching tools, which include Skin Smoothing, Lighting, Face Contour, and Red Eye Remover. By using these tools carefully, you can greatly improve a photo.

11. Touch Transform to display the Transform tools, which consist of the Rotate tool, the Crop tool, the Flip tool, and the Straighten tool. Use these tools to deal with issues with the photo's composition.

12. Touch to return from the Photo Editor to the Camera Shots screen.

13. Touch to return to the Camera app.

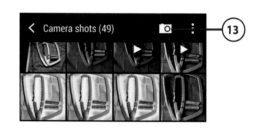

Record Videos with the Camera App

Recording videos with the Camera app is even easier than taking still photos because there are fewer options to choose.

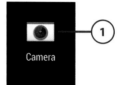

1. Touch the Camera icon to launch the Camera app.

2. Touch the Video icon to switch to video mode. The Camera app starts recording video automatically.

3. Drag the slider to zoom in or out.

4. Touch to zoom all the way in.

5. Touch to zoom all the way out.

6. Touch to focus on a particular spot. Otherwise, the Camera app automatically adjusts the focus for the middle of the screen.

7. Touch to turn the flash on or off.

8. Touch to take a still photo as the video records.

9. Touch to stop recording.

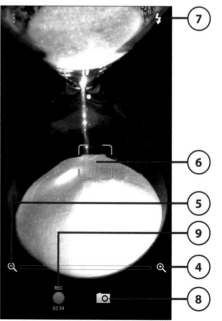

SHOOT SLOW-MOTION VIDEO

Your HTC One's Camera app can shoot slow-motion video as well as regular-speed video. To set up Camera to shoot slow-motion video, touch the Menu button, scroll down the Video Capture Mode section, and then touch the Scene button. In the section of the menu panel that appears, touch Slow Motion Video to select it. You can now start shooting the footage.

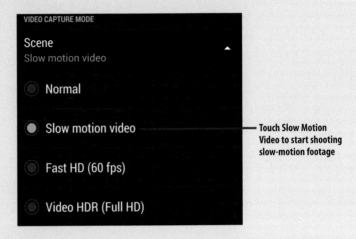

Touch Slow Motion Video to start shooting slow-motion footage

Enjoying Videos with the YouTube App

Your HTC One comes with a YouTube app that enables you to find and watch videos, rate them, add them to your favorites, and share links with other people. The app even enables you to upload your own videos to YouTube.

Meet the YouTube Main Screen

1. Touch the YouTube icon to launch the YouTube app.

2. Touch to search YouTube using keywords.

3. Touch your account name to see your account details.

4. Touch Browse Channels to display the Browse Channels screen, which contains channels such as Recommended for You, Most Subscribed, Most Viewed, and Local.

5. Touch to browse the What to Watch screen.

6. Touch to view and manage your subscriptions.

7. Touch a category in the From YouTube list to browse videos by category.

8. Swipe left to close the Account pane and browse the videos in your chosen category full screen.

9. Touch a video to see more information about it and play it.

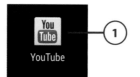

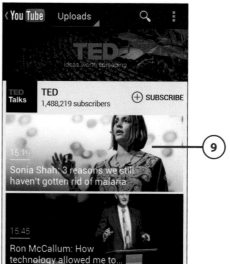

Play a Video

While playing a YouTube video, you can rate the video, read comments about it, or share it with other people.

1. Touch the video to display the onscreen controls for a few seconds.

2. Touch to start or pause the video.

Viewing a Video Full Screen

Rotate your HTC One into Landscape mode to view the video full screen. Return your HTC One to Portrait mode to restore the previous view.

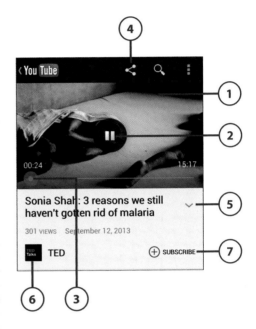

3. Drag to scrub forward or backward through the video.

4. Touch to share the video's link (its URL) via apps such as Gmail, Facebook, or Twitter.

5. Touch to see more information about the video, including the video title, description, and how many times it has been viewed.

6. Touch to see the YouTube channel of the person or group who uploaded the video.

7. Touch to subscribe to the person's or group's YouTube channel.

8. Touch the Menu button to display the menu, which contains further options.

9. Touch to add the video to your Watch Later list, your YouTube Favorites list, or another playlist.

10. Touch to like the video.

11. Touch to dislike the video.

12. Touch to copy the YouTube video link to the HTC One's clipboard. You can then paste it into text in any app—for example, email.

13. Touch to flag the video as inappropriate—for example, for hateful or abusive content, or because it infringes your rights.

14. Touch to check or change your YouTube settings. See the next section for details.

15. Touch to send feedback to YouTube, either about this video or in general.

16. Touch to open your browser to help screens on using YouTube.

Change YouTube Settings

To get more out of YouTube, you might want to change your settings. Your options include choosing whether to watch high-quality videos on cellular connections, setting up connected TVs to play back video, clearing your YouTube search history, and enabling the preloading of items on your subscriptions list or your Watch Later list.

1. From within the YouTube app, touch the Menu button.

2. Touch Settings.

3. Touch General.

4. Touch to enable or disable always starting videos in High Quality mode. The video might take longer to start playing, and it uses more data in High Quality mode.

5. Touch to set the size of the font used when a video has captions.

6. Touch to choose when your HTC One uploads videos to YouTube. Your choices are Only When on Wi-Fi or On Any Network.

7. Touch to choose a specify country or region that you want to prioritize—for example, the country you live in.

8. Touch to enable or disable sending anonymous usage data to YouTube to help improve the service.

9. Touch to return to the main Settings screen.

10. Touch Connected TVs.

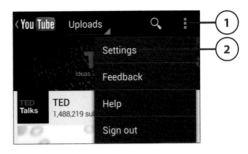

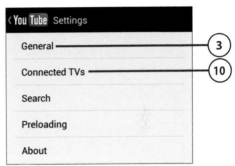

11. Touch to pair your HTC One with a TV so you can broadcast to the TV.

12. Touch to edit your list of paired TVs. You can rename a TV for clarity or remove a TV you no longer want to use.

13. Touch to return to the main Settings screen.

14. Touch Search.

15. Touch to clear your YouTube search history. Touch OK in the Clear Search History? dialog that opens.

16. Touch to enable the Never Remember History feature, which prevents YouTube from ever storing your search history.

17. Touch to set the types of videos that are displayed when you search. Your choices are Don't Filter, Moderate, and Strict. If you set this setting to Don't Filter, no videos are filtered out based on content.

18. Touch to return to the main Settings screen.

19. Touch Preloading.

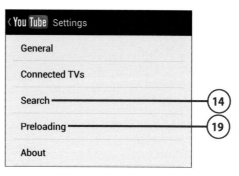

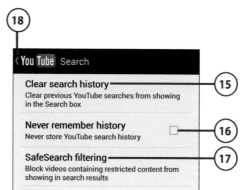

20. Touch to enable or disable preloading of videos to which you have subscribed. Preloading videos enables you to start watching them sooner on slow networks, but storing the files takes up space on your HTC One.

21. Touch to enable or disable preloading of videos you have added to your Watch Later list.

22. Touch to return to the main Settings screen.

23. Touch the YouTube button to return to the YouTube app.

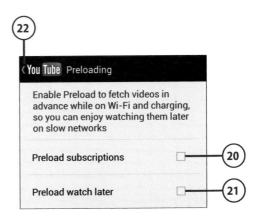

Upload a Video to YouTube from the YouTube App

After you create your own channel, you can easily upload your videos to YouTube straight from the YouTube app.

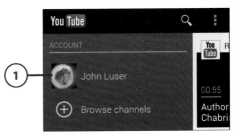

1. In the navigation panel, touch your account name to display the screen for your account.

2. Touch the Upload icon to start uploading a video.

3. In the Choose Video to Upload dialog, touch the source of the video. For example, touch Gallery.

4. Touch the video you want to upload.

5. On the Upload Video screen, enter the information for the video, as discussed earlier in this chapter, and then touch the Upload icon.

Browse quickly
through thumbnails
of magazine pages

In this chapter, you discover your HTC One's capabilities for carrying and displaying books and magazines. Topics include the following:

→ Reading books with the Play Books app

→ Installing and using Amazon's Kindle app

→ Finding free e-books online

→ Reading magazines with Google Play Magazines

Books and Magazines

With its large, bright screen, your HTC One is great for reading books and magazines. You can load an entire library and newsstand onto your HTC One, take the phone with you anywhere, and read to your heart's content.

Reading Books with Play Books and Kindle

Books are perfect media for your HTC One because their file sizes are mostly small, but they deliver long-lasting entertainment. Your HTC One likely comes with one or more apps for reading books, but you will probably want to supplement them with other apps, such as the free Kindle app from Amazon.

Open the Play Books App and Meet Your Library

Google's Play Books app provides straightforward reading capabilities and ties in to the Books area of Google's Play Store, from which you can buy many books and download others free of charge.

1. On the Apps screen, touch Play Books.

2. Touch My Library in the navigation panel to display the books in your library. Normally, this panel opens automatically, but you can also open it manually by touching the button in the upper-left corner of the Play Books screen.

Where to Get Books

Depending on where you bought your HTC One, your library might include several public-domain books as samples—plus any books you have already added to your library on your HTC One or another Android device. If your library is empty, you can get books from the Play Store.

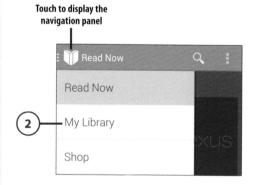

Play Books

Touch to display the navigation panel

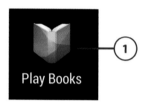

3. Touch to open the pop-up menu.

4. Touch to choose which list of books to view. Your choices are All Books, Uploads, Purchases, and Samples. Uploads are books you have uploaded to your Google account. You learn how to upload books later in this chapter.

5. A blue dot indicates the book is stored on your HTC One, so you can read it offline. You can touch a book to download it to your HTC One so you can read it anytime.

6. Touch to search your library for books by keyword. Searching is useful when you have built up a large library. When your library contains only a few books, it is usually easier to browse through them.

7. Touch the Menu button.

8. Touch Sort to display the Sort By dialog.

9. Touch the way you want to sort: Recently Read, Title, or Author. The Play Books app displays the books in that sort order.

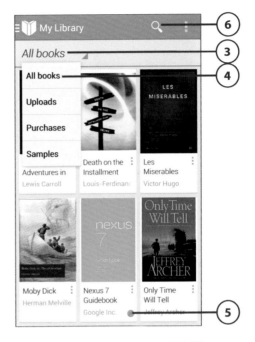

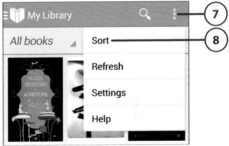

10. Touch a book to open it. If the book is not stored on your HTC One, Play Books downloads the book and then opens it.

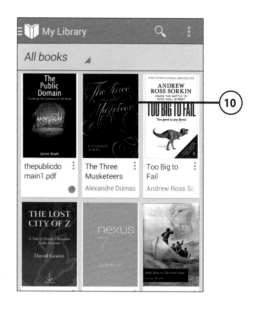

Get Books from the Play Store

The Books area of the Play Store offers a fair number of e-books for free and a much larger number of e-books for sale. You can access the Books area of the Play Store easily from the Play Books app.

1. Touch the button in the upper-left corner of the Play Books app to display the navigation panel.

2. Touch Shop to display the Books area of the Play Store. The Featured list appears first.

3. Touch to search for books.

4. Touch to see the list of top-selling books.

5. Touch to see the new arrivals in the Fiction category.

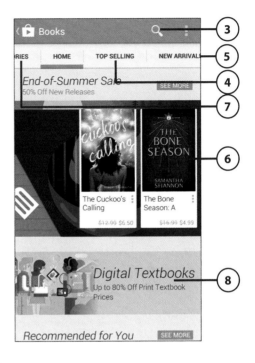

Navigate Quickly Among Tabs by Swiping

The Books area of the Play Store contains various tabs, including Categories, Home, Top Selling, New Arrivals in Fiction, New Arrivals in Nonfiction, and Top Free. You can navigate among these tabs by tapping their names on the tab bar, but it is usually quicker to swipe left or right one or more times to change tabs.

6. Touch a featured book or a recommended book to see its details.

7. Touch a featured category to see the list of books it contains.

8. Touch to display the list of categories. You can also swipe right once from the Home screen to display the list of categories.

9. Touch the category you want to display. The Featured list for the category appears first.

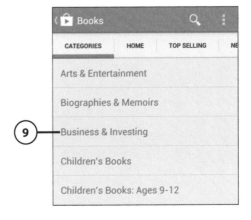

10. Swipe up to see more of the list.

11. Touch the New Arrivals tab or swipe left to see the New Arrivals list for the category.

12. Touch a book to display its details.

13. Touch to add the book to your wish list.

14. Touch Rate & Review to rate or review the book. You would normally do this after reading the book, but many raters and reviewers skip the reading step.

15. Touch to expand the description.

16. Swipe up to read the reviews, to see the Users Also Viewed list of books that may interest you if this one does, and to read the About the Author blurb.

17. Touch Free Sample to download a free sample of the book. Reading the sample can be a great way to decide whether to spend the money on the book. Android downloads the book and displays its first page in the Google Books app.

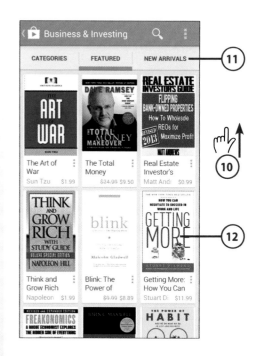

Buying Books from the Play Store

To buy a book from the Play Store, you must either add a credit card to your Google account or redeem a voucher. When you go to buy a book, the Play Store app prompts you to add a credit card and walks you through the steps for adding it.

18. Touch the price button to buy the book, and then follow through the payment process on the next screen. If the book is free,

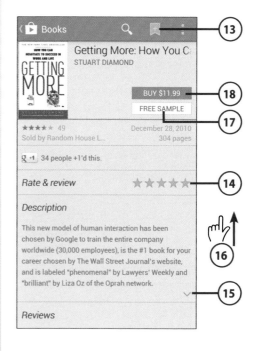

touch the Open button. Android downloads the book and displays its first page in Google Books.

Share a Book with Other People

When you find a book you simply must tell someone about, you can do so easily from the Play Store app. Touch the Menu button to open the menu, then touch Share. In the Share dialog, touch the means of sharing you want to use, and then complete the sharing in the app that Android opens.

Touch the means of sharing you want to use

Finding Free E-Books Online

Apart from buying e-books online at Google's Play Store or other stores such as Amazon (www.amazon.com) and Barnes & Noble (www.barnesandnoble. com), you can find many books for free. Most online stores offer some free e-books, especially out-of-copyright classics, so it is worth browsing the Free lists. Other good sources of free e-books include ManyBooks.net (www.manybooks.net) and Project Gutenberg (www.gutenberg.org).

Read Books with the Play Books App

1. In the navigation panel of the Play Books app, touch Read Now to display your Read Now screen. This screen shows the books you have been reading recently plus books you have recently bought (or downloaded for free) or uploaded to your Google account. Further down the screen is a Recommended for You section that suggests books you may be interested in based on the books you have.

2. Touch the book you want to open. The cover or default page appears if this is the first time you have opened the book. Otherwise, the page at which you last left the book appears.

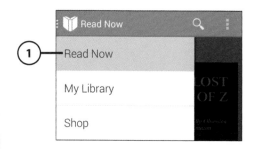

A blue pin means your HTC One has downloaded the book.

A gray pin means the book has not been downloaded yet.

3. Touch the middle of the screen to display the navigation controls at the top and bottom of the screen. The controls remain onscreen for a few seconds and then disappear if you do not use them. You can make them disappear more quickly by touching the screen again.

4. Touch to search within the book for specific text.

5. Drag to move quickly through the book.

6. Touch the right side of the screen or drag left to turn the page forward. Dragging lets you turn the page partway to peek ahead.

7. Touch the left side of the screen or drag right to turn the page back.

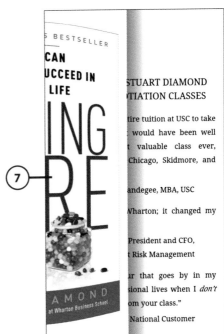

Choose Options for the Play Books App

You can configure the Play Books app to make it work your way. Options include changing the font, the text alignment, the brightness, and the theme.

1. In the Play Books app, touch the Menu button.

2. Touch to display the book's table of contents. From here, you can touch the section to which you want to jump.

3. Touch to buy the book in the Play Store. This command appears only when you are reading a sample of a book.

4. Touch to display the book's page in the Play Store.

5. Touch to share the book's URL on the Play Store via Facebook, Gmail, Twitter, or another means of sharing.

6. Touch to add a bookmark to the current page. To remove the bookmark, go to the page, touch the Menu button, and then touch Remove Bookmark.

7. Touch to get help on the Play Books app.

8. Touch to open the Display Options panel.

9. Touch to choose among the Day theme, the Night theme, and the Sepia theme. The Day theme uses black text on a white background; the Night theme uses white text on a black background; and the Sepia theme uses black text on a sepia background.

10. Touch to change the typeface used.

11. Touch to change the text alignment. The choices are Default, Left, and Justify.

12. Touch to enable or disable automatic brightness.

13. Drag to adjust the brightness manually.

14. Touch to decrease the font size.

15. Touch to increase the font size.

16. Touch to decrease the spacing between lines.

17. Touch to increase the spacing between lines.

18. Touch the book page to close the Display Options panel.

19. Touch the Menu button.

20. Touch Settings to display the Settings screen.

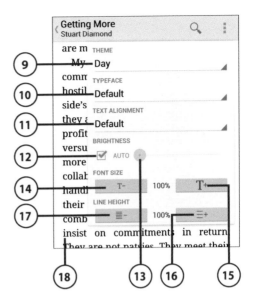

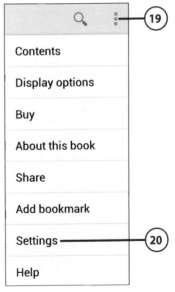

21. Touch Account if you need to change the Google account you are using for the Play Books app.

22. Touch Auto-Rotate Screen if you want to specify how to control rotation. In the Auto-Rotate Screen dialog that opens, touch Use System Setting, Lock in Portrait, or Lock in Landscape, as appropriate.

23. Touch to enable or disable restricting the Play Books app to downloading over Wi-Fi. Enable this restriction if your cellular plan gives you only a miserly data allowance.

24. Touch to enable using the volume key on the side of the HTC One to turn the pages in the Play Books app. This setting can be helpful if you normally hold your phone with your fingers over the volume key.

25. Touch to enable or disable the 3D effect for turning pages. Disable this effect if you don't like it.

26. Touch to enable or disable the HTC One's capability to read text aloud for you. You need to turn on the TalkBack feature in Accessibility settings to get reading aloud to work.

27. Touch to enable or disable using a higher-quality, more natural-sounding voice for reading aloud. This feature needs an Internet connection and may need to transfer a considerable amount of data, so you should use it only when your HTC One is connected to wireless networks, not via a cellular connection.

28. Touch to leave the Settings screen and return to the screen you were previously using in the Play Books app.

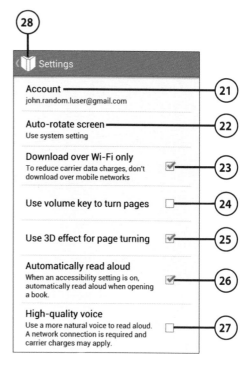

Delete a Book from Your Play Books Library

When you no longer want a particular book in your library, you can delete it directly using the Play Books app. Note that deleting the book removes it from your Google Play library entirely, not just from your HTC One (or whichever other device you're using).

1. In the Play Books app, touch the Menu button that appears on the book's listing.

2. Touch Delete from Library. The Delete from Library? confirmation dialog opens.

3. Touch Delete.

>>>Go Further

UPLOAD YOUR DOCUMENTS TO GOOGLE PLAY BOOKS

The Play Books app is great for reading books you buy or get for free from the Play Store, but you can also use it to read your own PDF files and e-books in formats such as the widely used ePub format. To do so, you use your computer to upload the files to your Google account, from which the Play Books app can then access them.

To upload the files, open your computer's web browser and go to play.google.com. Click the Sign In button, and then sign in with your Google account. Click Books in the navigation panel on the left, and then click My Books to display the screen containing your books. Now click the Upload Files button, and then follow the instructions onscreen to select the file or files.

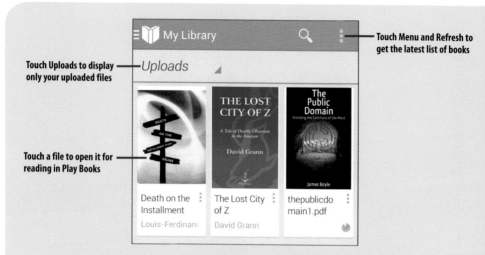

Touch Uploads to display only your uploaded files

Touch a file to open it for reading in Play Books

Touch Menu and Refresh to get the latest list of books

After you upload a file, Google processes it to make it compatible with the Play Books app. The books appear in your library, but you might find it easier to access them on the Uploads screen; to display this screen, touch the pop-up menu in the upper-left corner of the My Library screen, and then touch Uploads. If the books do not appear, touch the Menu button and then touch Refresh to force Play Books to refresh the list. You can then touch a book to download it and read it.

Install the Kindle App

Google's Play Store has a good selection of books, but if you want to buy or download books from Amazon's vast bookstore, you need to use the Kindle app instead.

Installing the Kindle App

If the Kindle app is not already installed on your HTC One, you need to install it from the Play Store. Touch Play Store on the Apps screen, touch Apps on the Google Play screen, touch the Search icon, and type **kindle**. Touch the Kindle result and then touch Install. Touch Accept in the App Permissions dialog, and then wait for the installation to finish.

Touch to search   Touch to install

Sign In and Navigate the Kindle App

1. On the Apps screen, touch the Amazon Kindle icon. The first time you run the Kindle app, it displays the Start Reading screen.

2. Touch the Sign In button to sign in to your existing account.

Creating an Amazon Account

To buy books or download free books from Amazon, you must have an Amazon account. If you do not have one, touch the Create an Account button on the Start Reading screen and then follow through the screens to create an account.

3. Type your email address.

4. Touch and type your Amazon password.

5. Touch Sign In. The Kindle app signs you into your account and then displays its Home screen. The books in your Kindle library appear on a carousel, with a Recommended list of purportedly related books below it.

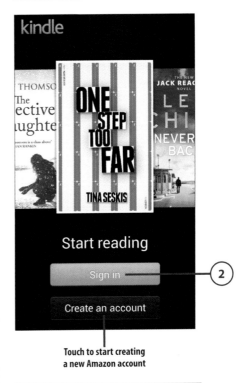

Touch to start creating
a new Amazon account

6. Touch to refresh the display of books. You would do this if you have just bought a book using your computer or a different device and the book hasn't yet appeared on the Kindle app on your HTC One.

7. Touch to go to the Kindle Store to browse or buy books.

8. Touch to display the navigation panel.

9. Touch Search Kindle to search your Kindle library for the terms you type.

10. Touch Home to display the Kindle Home screen.

11. Touch All Items to display the All Items screen. This screen shows all the items in your Kindle library, whether they are on your HTC One or not.

12. Touch On Device to see the list of books and other items stored on your HTC One.

13. Touch Books to see the list of books, rather than documents, newspapers, and magazines.

14. Touch Docs to display the documents stored in your Kindle account. These are documents you have sent via email to your Send to Kindle email address, a Kindle-only address that Amazon provides with Kindle accounts.

15. Touch Newsstand to display your Newsstand items.

16. Touch Kindle Store to go to the Kindle Store.

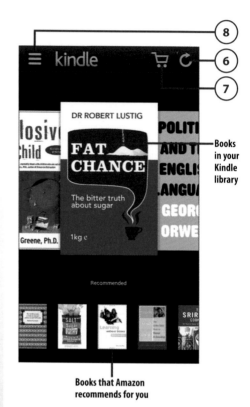

Books in your Kindle library

Books that Amazon recommends for you

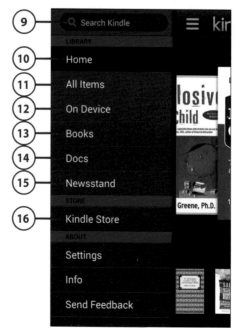

17. Touch Settings to display the Settings screen for configuring the Kindle app.

18. Touch Info to display information about Kindle and the Kindle app.

19. Touch Send Feedback to send feedback to Amazon.

Read a Book with the Kindle App

1. In the Kindle app, touch the book you want to open. This example uses the On Device screen, but you can also start from another screen, such as the Home screen or the All Items screen.

Reaching the On Device Screen from a Book

If you currently have a book open in the Kindle app, touch the Back button to go back to the main screens. Alternatively, touch the screen to display the controls, and then touch the Kindle button to return from the book to the screen from which you opened the book.

Touch Kindle to return to the main screens

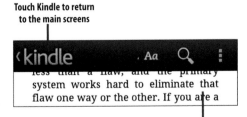

Touch the screen to display the controls

2. Touch the middle of the screen to display the title and location bar. Touch again to hide these items.

3. Drag the slider to change the location in the book.

4. Touch the right side of the screen to display the next page. You can also display the next page by dragging or swiping left.

5. Touch the left side of the screen, or drag or swipe right, to move back a page.

6. Touch the Menu button to display the menu.

7. Touch Shop in Kindle Store to display the Kindle Store, where you can shop for books and other items.

8. Touch Go To to display the Go To panel.

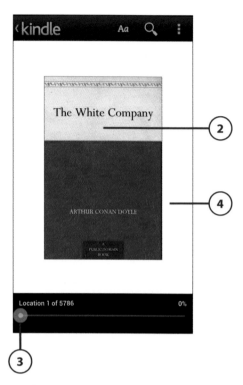

9. Touch to display the cover.

10. Touch to display the table of contents. This command is unavailable if the book has no table of contents.

11. Touch to go to the beginning of the text, after the cover.

12. Touch to go to a page by number. If the book does not have page numbers, this command is unavailable.

13. Touch to go to a location. The locations are numbered divisions of the text. You can see the number of the current location by touching the middle of the screen and looking at the Location slider. But unless you know the number of the location to which you want to go, this command is of little use.

14. On the main menu, touch View My Notes & Marks to view the list of notes and bookmarks you have added to the current book. From there, you can touch one of your bookmarks or notes to go to its page.

15. Touch Sync to Furthest Page Read to go to the furthest point you've reached in this book on any of your Kindle devices.

16. Touch Add a Bookmark to add a bookmark to the current page. The bookmark appears as a small gray triangle across the upper-right corner of the page. To remove the bookmark, touch it on the page, or touch the Menu button and then touch Remove Bookmark.

17. Touch Share Progress to display the Share Progress dialog, in which you can share your reading progress via Facebook, Gmail, or other means.

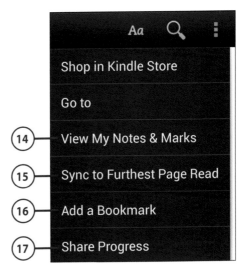

Choose View Options for the Kindle App

To make your books easy to read, you can choose view options for them.

1. With a book open in the Kindle app, touch the screen to display the controls.

2. Touch View Options to display the View Options panel.

3. Touch to decrease the font size.

4. Touch to increase the font size.

5. Touch to adjust the space between lines.

6. Touch to adjust the margin width.

7. Touch to choose the color scheme: White, Sepia, or Black.

8. Drag to adjust the brightness.

9. Touch the document to close the View Options panel.

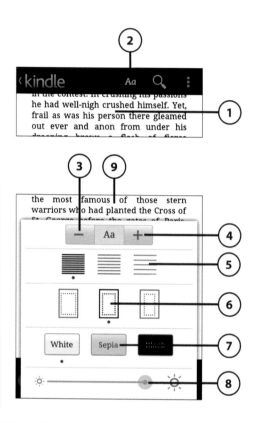

EXPLORE OTHER BOOK READERS

Between them, the Play Books app and the Kindle app give you access to a phenomenal range of books. But there are many other book readers you might want to explore to give yourself access to other bookstores and other books. In particular, the Aldiko app, the Kobo app, and the Nook app are worth trying. You can get each of these apps from the Play Store for free. The Nook app ties into Barnes & Noble's online bookstore.

>>>Go Further

Reading Magazines with Play Magazines

Your HTC One includes Google's Play Magazines app, which gives you access to a wide range of magazines.

EXPLORING OTHER MAGAZINE APPS

>>>Go Further

If the Play Magazines app does not deliver the content you need, or does not otherwise suit you, explore other magazine apps such as PressReader and Zinio. You can download both these apps for free from the Apps section of the Play Store.

Open the Play Magazines App and Choose Your Magazines

1. On the Apps screen, touch Play Magazines. The app may open in either Read Now view, showing magazines you have read and ones you have added recently, or in My Library view, showing your entire magazine library.

2. Touch the button in the upper-left corner to open the navigation panel.

3. Touch Shop to display the Magazines section of the Play Store.

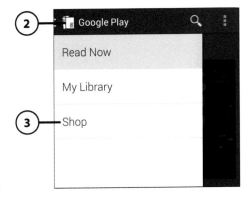

4. Touch to see the list of top-selling magazines. You can also swipe left once from the Home screen.

5. Touch to see the list of newly released magazines. You can also swipe left twice from the Home screen or once from the Top Selling screen.

6. Touch a featured magazine or a recommended magazine to see its details.

7. Touch a featured category to see the list of magazines it contains.

8. Touch to display the list of categories. You can also swipe right to display the list of categories.

9. Touch the category you want to display.

10. Swipe up to see more of the list.

11. Touch New Arrivals or swipe left to see the New Arrivals list for the category.

12. Touch a magazine to display its details.

13. Touch to add the magazine to your wish list.

14. Touch Rate & Review to rate or review the magazine.

15. Swipe up to read the reviews and to see the Similar Magazines list, which might contain magazines that interest you. At the bottom of the screen, you also find the Back Issues list.

16. Touch Subscribe to start a 14-day trial subscription to the magazine, followed by a paid subscription if you do not cancel it. You can choose between a yearly subscription and a monthly subscription. Android downloads the magazine and displays its first page in the Google Magazines app.

17. Touch the price button to buy the magazine, and then follow through the payment process on the next screen. If the magazine is free, touch the Open button. Android downloads the magazine and displays its first page in Google Magazines.

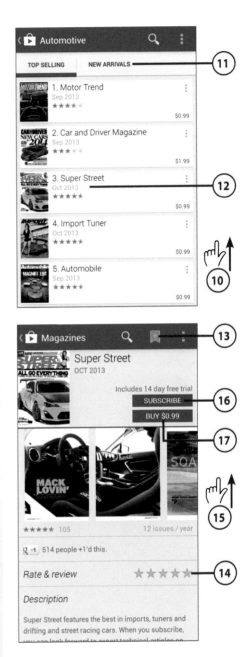

Read a Magazine with the Play Magazines App

1. On either the Read Now screen or the My Library screen in the Play Magazines app, touch the magazine you want to open. The cover appears if this is the first time you have opened the magazine. Otherwise, the page at which you last left the magazine appears.

2. Touch the middle of the screen to display the navigation controls at the top and bottom of the screen. The controls remain onscreen for a few seconds and then disappear if you do not use them. You can make them disappear more quickly by touching the screen again.

3. Touch to display a text-only version of the magazine. The text-only version can be much easier to read on your HTC One's screen, but only some magazines have a text-only version.

4. Drag to scroll through the pages.

5. Touch to display the next page.

6. Touch a page's thumbnail to display that page.

7. Touch to display a table of contents.

8. Touch an article to display the page that contains it.

9. Double-tap or pinch outward with two fingers to zoom the page as needed.

10. Swipe left to display the next page or swipe right to display the previous page.

Choose Options for the Play Magazines App

1. From the Read Now screen or the My Library screen in the Play Magazines app, touch the Menu button.

2. Touch Settings.

3. Touch to change the account used for Play Magazines.

4. Touch to enable or disable automatic downloading of all your magazine purchases and subscriptions.

5. Touch to enable or disable limiting magazine downloads to when your HTC One has a Wi-Fi connection. Because magazine files can be relatively large, checking this box is a good idea if your cellular data plan is limited.

6. Touch to allow Play Magazines to show you notifications about new issues or to prevent it from doing so.

7. Touch to return to the previous screen.

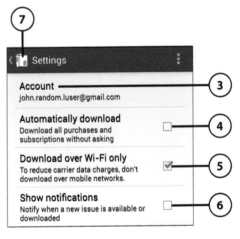

Search for apps

Browse for apps

In this chapter, you find out how to purchase and use Android apps on your HTC One. Topics include the following:

→ Finding apps with Google Play
→ Purchasing apps
→ Keeping apps up to date

Working with Android Apps

Your HTC One comes with enough apps to browse the Web, read and send email, enjoy music and video, and perform various other activities. But if you want to play games, track your commitments, or keep a hi-tech grocery list, you'll likely need to add apps.

Google Play is the main source for Android apps, offering hundreds of thousands of apps in a variety of categories. To access Google Play, you use the Play Store app. Read on to learn how to find, purchase, and buy apps for your HTC One.

Configuring Google Wallet

Before you start buying apps in the Play Store, you must first sign up for a Google Wallet account. If you plan to download only free apps, you do not need a Google Wallet account.

1. From a desktop computer or your HTC One, open the web browser and go to http://wallet.google.com.

2. Sign in using the Google account that you will be using to synchronize email to your HTC One. See Chapter 4, "Email," or Chapter 7, "Contacts," for information about adding a Google account to your HTC One.

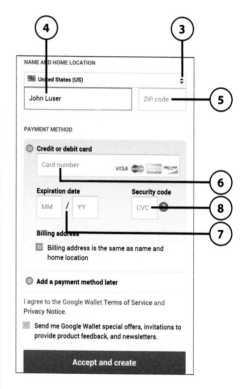

3. Choose your location. If your country is not listed, you have to use free apps until it's added to the list.

4. Enter your name.

5. Enter your ZIP code.

6. Enter your credit card number. This can also be a debit card that includes a Visa or MasterCard logo, also known as a check card, so that the funds are withdrawn from your checking account.

7. Select the month and year of the card's expiration date.

8. Enter the card's Card Verification Code (CVC) number, which is also known as the security code. This is a three- or four-digit number that's printed on the back of your card.

9. Check this box if your billing address is the same as your name and home location. Otherwise, uncheck this box and enter your billing address and phone number when prompted.

10. Click Accept and Create when you finish filling in the form.

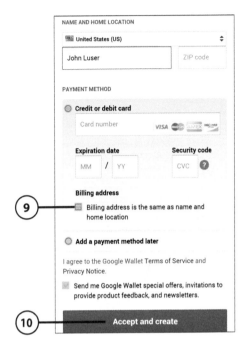

Navigating Google Play

Android is the operating system that runs your HTC One, so any apps that are made for your HTC One need to run on Android. Google Play is Google's vast online store, which includes a section where you can search for and buy Android apps.

1. On the Home screen, touch Apps.

2. Touch the Play Store app icon.

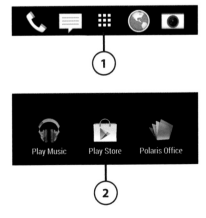

3. Touch the Menu button to see Google Play actions.

4. Touch My Apps to see the apps you have already purchased or downloaded.

5. Touch My Wishlist to see the items you have added to your wish list. The wish list is a storage area for keeping the items you would like to buy or you would like others to buy for you.

6. Touch Redeem to redeem a coupon you have acquired. You also use Redeem to add funds to your Google Play account from Google Play cards.

7. Touch Accounts to select which Google account you want to use when you use the Google Play store. If you have multiple accounts, such as a business account and a personal account, use this command to switch between them. If you have only one account, Google Play will already be using that account.

8. Touch Settings to change the settings for Google Play. See the "Manage Google Play Settings" section later in this chapter for more information.

9. Touch Help to get help on using Google Play.

10. Touch Apps to browse all Android apps.

11. Touch Games to browse all Android games.

12. Touch to search Google Play. If you know the name of the app you're looking for, searching is usually the quickest way to locate it.

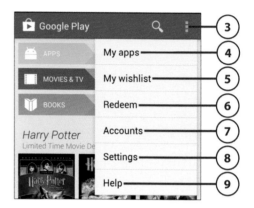

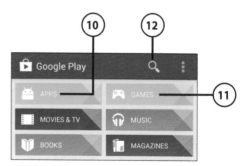

Download Free Apps

You don't have to spend money to
get quality apps. Some of the best
apps are free.

1. In the Play Store app, touch the
   app you want to download.

2. Scroll down to read the app's
   features, reviews by other people
   who installed it, and information
   on the person or company who
   created the app.

3. Scroll left and right to see the app
   videos and screenshots.

4. Touch Install to download and
   install the app.

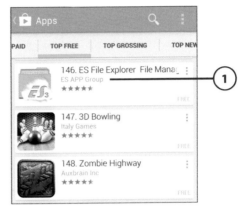

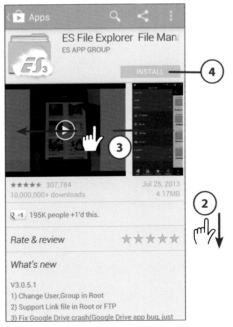

5. Touch to accept the app permissions and proceed with the download.

Read the Permissions Before Accepting Them

Each time you download a free app or purchase an app from Google Play, you are prompted to accept the app permissions. App permissions are permissions the app wants to have to use features and functions on your HTC One, such as access to the wireless network or access to your phone log.

Pay close attention to the kinds of permissions each app is requesting and make sure they are appropriate for the type of functionality that the app provides. For example, an app that tests network speed will likely ask for permission to access your wireless network, but if it also asks to access your list of contacts, it might mean that the app is malware and just wants to steal your contacts.

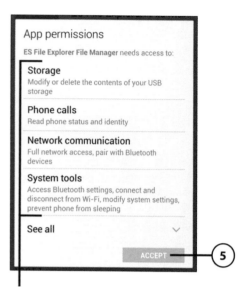

App permissions

ES File Explorer File Manager needs access to:

Storage
Modify or delete the contents of your USB storage

Phone calls
Read phone status and identity

Network communication
Full network access, pair with Bluetooth devices

System tools
Access Bluetooth settings, connect and disconnect from Wi-Fi, modify system settings, prevent phone from sleeping

See all

ACCEPT ———— 5

Permissions the app is requesting to read data and use features on your HTC One

Choose Whether to Update Apps Automatically on Wi-Fi

If the Update Apps Automatically When on Wi-Fi? dialog appears when you download an app, touch OK if you want to update your apps automatically when your HTC One is connected to a wireless network. Touch Not Now if you want to postpone this decision. Even if you set an app to update automatically, Android doesn't update it if the update contains a change to the permissions. This is because you need to approve the permission change.

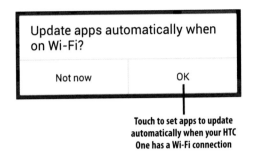

Touch to set apps to update automatically when your HTC One has a Wi-Fi connection

Buy Apps

If an app is not free, the price appears next to the app icon. If you want to buy the app, remember that you need to already have a Google Wallet account. See the "Configuring Google Wallet" section earlier in the chapter for more information.

1. Touch the app you want to buy.

What If the Currency Is Different?

When you browse apps in Google Play, you might see apps that have prices in foreign currencies, such as in euros. When you purchase an app, the currency is converted into your local currency using the exchange rate at the time of purchase.

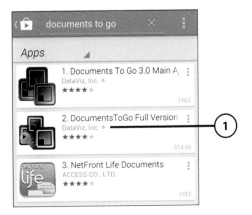

2. Scroll down to read the app's features, reviews by other people who have used it, and information on the person or company who created the app.

3. Scroll left and right to see the app screenshots.

4. Touch the price button to begin the process of purchasing the app.

5. In the App Permissions dialog, review any permissions the app needs. Some apps, such as the app shown here, do not need any special permissions.

6. Touch Continue to accept the app permissions and proceed with the purchase.

7. Touch Buy to purchase the app. You will receive an email from Google Play after you purchase an app. The email serves as your invoice.

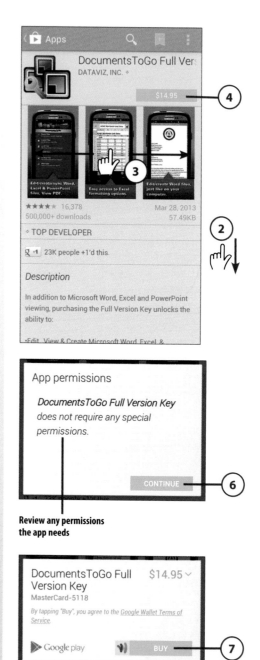

Review any permissions the app needs

Pay with a Different Means of Payment

If you need to pay using a different means of payment than the card shown in the payment dialog, touch the price button to expand the dialog. Touch the Payment Options button to display the Payment Options dialog, in which you can choose another card you've set up, add a new card, redeem a voucher, or buy Google Play credit.

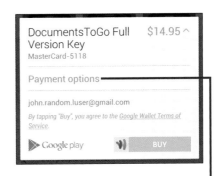

Touch Payment Options to choose a different means of payment

Manage Apps

Use the My Apps section of Google Play to update apps, delete them, or install apps that you have previously purchased.

1. Touch the Menu button.

2. Touch My Apps.

3. Touch All to see all apps that you have purchased or downloaded from the Play Store.

4. Look for the Installed readout to see whether the app is currently installed.

5. Touch an app marked with Free to install a free app again. The Free readout shows a free app that you previously installed, but that is no longer installed.

6. Touch to remove an app from the list of apps, then touch OK in the Remove dialog that opens.

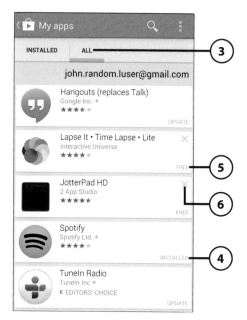

Install an App You Have Previously Purchased

On the My Apps screen, you can touch an app marked with Purchased to install again an app that you previously purchased and installed, but that is no longer installed. Because you have already purchased the app, you do not need to pay for it again.

Allowing an App to Be Automatically Updated

When the developer of an app you have installed updates it to fix bugs or add new functionality, you are normally notified in the Notification bar and Notification pane so that you can manually update the app. Google Play enables you to choose to have the app automatically updated without your intervention. To do this, open the My Apps screen and touch the app you want to update automatically. Touch the Menu button, and then touch Auto-update; after you do this, a check mark appears to the right of Auto-update on the menu. Be aware that if these updates occur while you are on a cellular data connection, your data usage for the month will be affected.

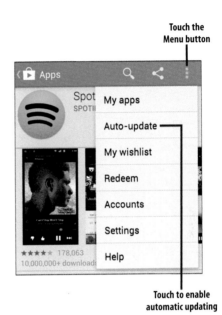

Touch the Menu button

Touch to enable automatic updating

Uninstalling an App

When you uninstall an app, you remove the app and its data from your HTC One. Although the app no longer resides on your phone, you can reinstall it as described earlier in this section because the app remains available in your Google account.

Manage Google Play Settings

1. Touch the Menu button.

2. Touch Settings.

3. Touch to enable or disable notifications of app or game updates.

4. Touch Auto-Update Apps to display the Auto-Update Apps dialog.

5. Touch to turn off automatic updating of apps.

6. Touch to allow apps to update automatically at any time over whichever connection is available. Because this option may use a lot of cellular data, it is not usually a good choice unless you have a very generous plan or someone else is paying for it.

7. Touch to allow apps to update automatically only over Wi-Fi connections. This is usually the best choice if you allow automatic updating.

8. Touch to allow or prevent an app icon from appearing on your Home screen for each app that you install.

9. Touch to clear the Google Play search history. Your HTC One clears the search history without prompting for confirmation or telling you that it has done so.

10. Touch to adjust or set your content filtering. The Allow Apps Rated For dialog appears.

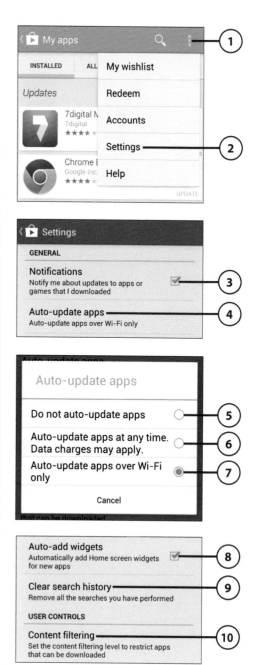

11. Touch to select the check box for each category you want to allow. Touch to deselect the check box for each category you want to disallow.

12. Touch OK to close the Allow Apps Rated For dialog. The Content PIN dialog appears.

13. Type a personal identification number (PIN) to restrict access to the content-filtering settings you have applied.

14. Touch OK to close the Content PIN dialog. In the Confirm content PIN dialog that appears, type the PIN again and touch OK.

15. Touch Password to set a password for restricting purchases on your account.

16. Touch to return to the main Google Play screen.

Why Lock the User Settings?

Imagine if you buy a HTC One for your child but want to make sure that he doesn't get to any undesirable content. First, you set the content filtering to restrict the content visible in Google Play. Next, you set the PIN so he can't change that setting. A similar idea goes for limiting purchases.

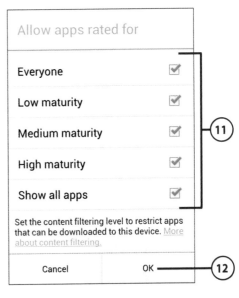

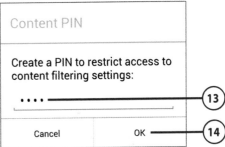

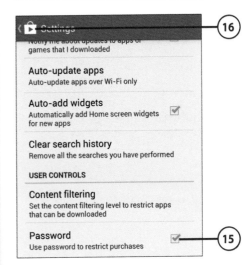

Accidentally Uninstall an App?

What if you accidentally uninstall an app or you uninstalled an app in the past but now decide you'd like to use it again? To get the app back, go to the My Apps view in Google Play. Scroll to that app and touch it. Touch Install to reinstall it.

Keeping Apps Up to Date

Developers who write Android apps often update their apps to fix bugs or to add new features. With a few quick touches, it is easy for you to update the apps you have installed.

1. If an app you have installed has an update, you see the update notification in the Notification bar.

2. Pull down the Notification bar.

3. Touch the update notification.

4. Touch one of the apps that has an update available.

5. Touch Update.

Update All Your Apps at Once

If updates are available for multiple apps, you can update them all in one move by touching Update All on the My Apps screen.

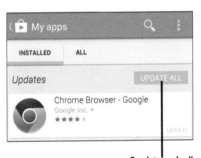

Touch to apply all available updates at once

Choose power-saving options to keep your HTC One running longer

In this chapter, you learn how to maintain your HTC One and solve problems. Topics include the following:

- → Updating Android
- → Optimizing battery life
- → Identifying battery-hungry applications
- → Caring for your HTC One

12

Maintaining and Troubleshooting Your HTC One

Every so often Google releases new versions of Android that have bug fixes and new features. In this chapter, you find out how to upgrade your HTC One to a new version of Android and how to tackle common problem-solving issues and general maintenance of your HTC One.

Updating Android

New releases of Android are always exciting because they add new features, fix bugs, and tweak the user interface. You can either check manually for an update or wait until your HTC One alerts you to an update. Here is how to update your phone.

Install an Update from a Notification

Your HTC One checks automatically for updates to its software. When it finds an update, the HTC One displays a notification telling you that an update is available. Touch the notification to jump straight to the installation screen, then touch Install.

Update Information

Updates to Android are not on a set schedule and may depend on your phone's carrier as well as on HTC. The update messages appear as you turn on your HTC, and they remain in the Notification bar until you install the update. If you touch Install Later, your HTC One reminds you every 30 minutes that there's an update. When to install the update is up to you. You may prefer to wait to see if each new update contains any bugs that need to be worked out rather than applying each update immediately.

1. Touch Settings on the Apps screen to open the Settings app.

2. Touch About.

3. Touch Software Updates. Your HTC One checks for updates and displays what it finds. You may see a System Update dialog, as in this example, or a Software Updates screen.

4. Touch to enable or disable down-loading the update only over Wi-Fi instead of using cellular if Wi-Fi is not available. You can look at the readout to see how large the update is.

5. Touch Download to start down-loading the update. Depending on the file size and the speed of the HTC One's Internet connec-tion, the download may take a while. When the download fin-ishes, the System Update dialog opens automatically.

6. Touch Install Now.

7. Touch OK. Your HTC One restarts, installs the update, and displays the lock screen. You can then unlock it and get back to work or play.

The readout shows the size of the update

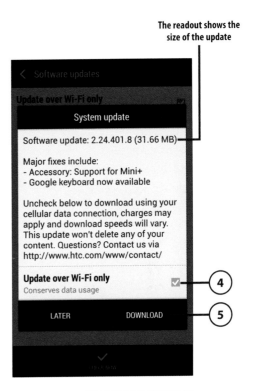

Download and Install the Updates Later

Sometimes you may prefer to install the updates later rather than immediately. For example, you may be using other apps and not want to restart your HTC One yet. In this case, touch Later on the Software Updates screen.

On the Software Updates screen that appears, touch Check Now to check again for the update when you are ready to install it.

If you touch the Install Later option button in the System Update dialog and then touch OK, your HTC One displays another System Update dialog prompting you to choose when to receive a reminder about the update.

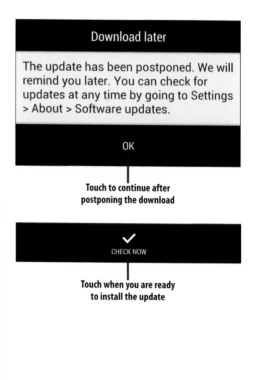

Download later

The update has been postponed. We will remind you later. You can check for updates at any time by going to Settings > About > Software updates.

OK

Touch to continue after postponing the download

CHECK NOW

Touch when you are ready to install the update

Optimizing the Battery

The battery in your HTC One is a lithium-polymer unit that provides good battery life as long as you take care of it. You can change the way you use your HTC One to prolong the battery life so that the battery lasts long enough for you to use the phone all day.

Looking After the Battery

You can take specific steps to look after the battery in your HTC One and make it last longer.

Follow these steps to care for your HTC One battery:

1. Try to avoid discharging the battery completely. Fully discharging the battery too frequently harms the battery. Instead, try to keep it partially charged at all times (except as described in the next step).

2. To avoid a false battery level indication on your HTC One, let the battery fully discharge about every 30 charges. Lithium-polymer batteries do not have "memory" like older battery technologies, but fully discharging the battery once in a while helps keep the battery meter working correctly.

3. Avoid letting your HTC One get overheated, because this can damage the battery and make it lose charge quickly. Do not leave your HTC One in a hot car or out in the sun anywhere, including on the beach.

4. Charge the battery whenever it needs charging. A lithium-polymer battery's life is typically rated as a minimum number (for example, 500) of charge cycles, each of which is a full charge from empty to full rather than a charging session. So if you charge the battery once from 25% full and once from 75% full, you've used one charge cycle, just as you would by charging twice from 50% full. Charging the battery more frequently doesn't shorten its life.

5. Unplug your HTC One from the charger when the battery is charged. Leaving the HTC One connected doesn't overcharge the battery or reduce its life directly, but it can cause the battery to overheat, which can damage the battery.

6. Consider having multiple chargers. For example, you could have one at home, one at work, and one in your car. This enables you to always keep your phone charged.

KEEPING YOUR HTC ONE POWERED ALL DAY

Unlike some other phones that give you easy access to the battery compartment so you can easily switch batteries when one runs out, your HTC One has a sealed case that provides no access to the battery without technician-level tools and skills. So to keep your HTC One powered all day, you need to manage the amount of power you choose or recharge it when needed.

Using multiple chargers is one solution for recharging, but if you use your HTC One extensively while on the go, you may do better with an external battery. If you prize convenience, you can get a case with a built-in battery, such as the i-Blason PowerGlider or the Mophie Juice Pack. If you need general compatibility, get a separate external battery that can power USB devices, and simply plug in your HTC One when it needs charging.

Seeing What Is Using the Battery

Android enables you to see exactly what apps and system processes are using the battery on your HTC One. Armed with this information, you can alter your usage patterns to extend the phone's runtime on the battery.

1. On the Apps screen, touch Settings.

2. Touch Power.

3. Look at the Battery readout if you want to see exactly how much power the battery contains.

4. Touch Usage.

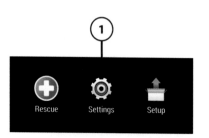

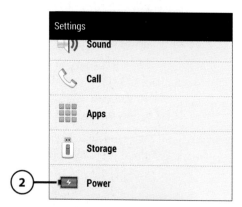

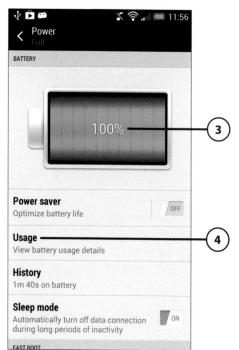

5. View the App Usage list. This list lets you see which apps have been using battery power, in descending order of greed.

6. Touch an app or Android service to see more details about it. The details depend on the app or the service, but they may include the percentage of battery power it has used; how much processor (CPU) time it has used, and how much of that was in the foreground (with the app active) rather than in the background (with another app active); and how much data it has sent and received.

7. Touch to return to the Usage screen. You can also touch the Back button.

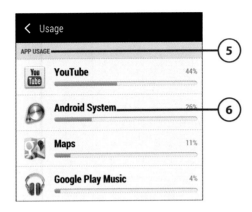

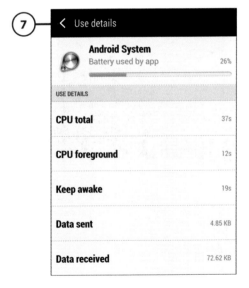

Choosing Power-Saving Options

Your HTC One includes a feature called Power Saver that enables you to reduce the amount of power it consumes. After choosing which of four power-saving options to use, you can turn Power Saver on and off by using its switch on the Power screen. There is also a Power Saver switch on the Power Saver screen itself, but normally the switch on the Power screen is more convenient.

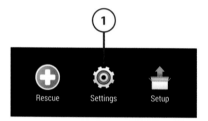

1. Touch Settings on the Apps screen.

2. Touch the main part of the Power Saver button, anywhere away from the switch at the right side.

3. Make sure the Power Saver switch is set to Off to make the settings available.

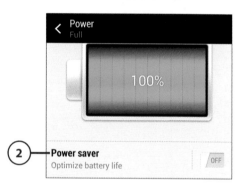

4. Check CPU Power to throttle back the processor when the HTC One is running on battery power.

5. Check Display to reduce the screen's brightness on the battery.

6. Check Vibration to turn off vibration feedback when you touch the screen.

7. Check Data connection to put the HTC One's data connections to sleep when the screen is off.

8. Touch to return to the Power screen, where you can turn the power-saver mode on and off by moving the Power Saver switch.

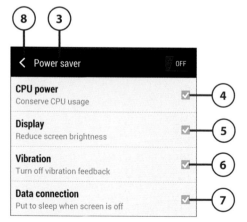

Applications and Memory

Each app you run on your HTC One has to share the phone's memory.
Although Android usually does a good job of managing this memory, sometimes you have to step in and close an app that has grown too large.

1. On the Apps screen, touch
   Settings.

2. Touch Apps.

3. Touch Downloaded.

4. Touch Running to see only apps
   that are currently running. You
   can also swipe left or touch
   Running on the tab bar.

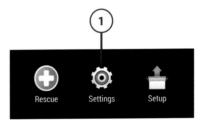

5. The RAM bar chart shows how much memory is being used by running apps, services, and cached processes, and how much is free.

6. Touch an app to see more information about it.

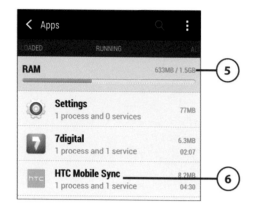

View Your HTC One's Cached Processes as Well

The Running tab on the Apps screen shows you the processes that are currently running but not those that are cached, held in memory but not active at the moment. Android caches inactive processes so as to make more space for the active processes but also to be able to resume the processes quickly as needed—for example, when you switch from one app to another.

To see the cached processes as well, touch the Menu button and then touch Show Cached Processes. To switch back to viewing the running processes only, touch the Menu button and then touch Show Running Services.

Touch the Menu button

Touch to see processes that Android has cached

7. On the Running App screen, touch Stop if you believe the app is not responding correctly.

8. Touch to report an app to Google. You may want to do this if it is misbehaving, using up too many resources, or you suspect it of stealing data.

9. Look here to see which processes the app is using.

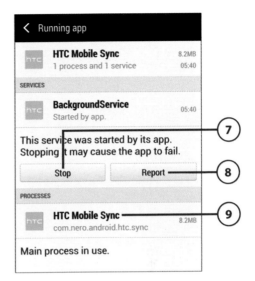

When Should You Manually Stop an App?

After you have been using your HTC One for a while, you'll become familiar with how long it takes to do certain tasks, such as typing, navigating menus, and so on. If you notice your phone becoming slow or not behaving the way you think it should, the culprit could be a new application you recently installed. Because Android never quits applications on its own, that new application continues running in the background, which may cause your HTC One to slow down. When this happens, it is useful to manually stop an app.

Reining In Your Data Usage

If you are worried that you may exceed your data plan in a month, you can set a usage limit on your HTC One. You can even prevent apps from using data while they are running in the background.

1. On the Apps screen, touch Settings.

2. Make sure the Mobile Data switch is set to On to enable data transfer over your HTC One's cellular connection.

3. Touch More to display the Wireless & Networks screen.

4. Touch Usage to display the Usage screen.

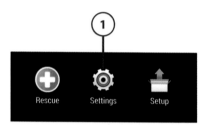

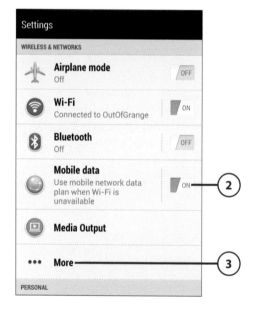

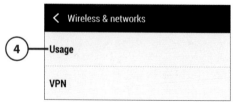

5. Check the Limit Mobile Data Usage check box to enable mobile data limits. When you enable this feature, your HTC One will automatically cut off all mobile data usage when you reach the limit you set in step 9. Android displays the Data Usage Limit dialog to make sure you know this will happen.

6. Touch OK to close the Data Usage Limit dialog.

7. Touch to enable or disable your phone giving you a warning when you reach the data usage limit. When you enable this feature, the Data Usage Alert dialog opens; touch OK to close it.

8. Touch Reset Data Usage to choose the day on which to reset your mobile data usage.

9. Touch Data Usage Cycle if you need to change the data usage cycle. Normally, you will want to make the dates shown match your carrier's billing dates; that way, you can track your data usage against your plan.

10. Touch the diagram to display the adjustment handles, then drag the red handle to set the data limit. Usually, it's easiest to set the limit to your cellular data plan limit, but you can set a different limit that you find more helpful.

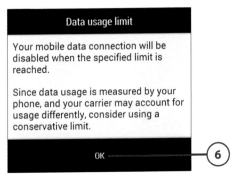

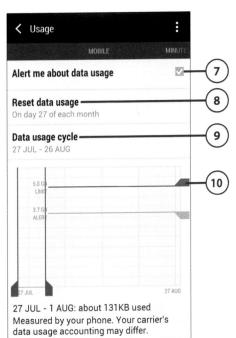

11. Drag the blue handle to set the alert limit. Normally, it's best to set the alert limit far enough below the data limit to warn you that your allowance is running out, but with enough data left to let you continue to use data—perhaps more sparingly—for the rest of the billing cycle.

12. If necessary, drag the gray handles to change the dates for the data-usage readout below the diagram.

13. Touch the app or service for which you want to see the data-usage statistics.

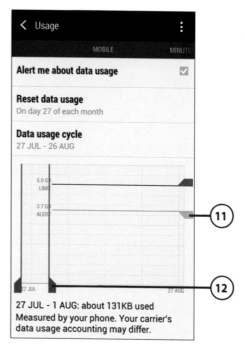

14. Look at the diagram and readout to see how much data the app or service has consumed in the period shown. You can drag the adjustment handles to change the period.

What Is Background Data?

An app is in the background when you have launched the app but you are not currently using it. An app in the background will still be taking up memory and may still be transferring data—for example, Gmail and Email can download your new messages in the background. In addition, many services transfer data in the background to keep your HTC One up to date and running smoothly.

15. Scroll down to display the lower part of the screen.

16. Check the Restrict Background Data check box to restrict the app from transferring data while it is in the background.

17. Touch OK to close the Restrict Background Data dialog.

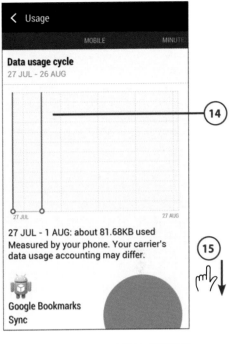

‹ Usage

MOBILE   MINUTE

Data usage cycle
27 JUL - 26 AUG

27 JUL   27 AUG

27 JUL - 1 AUG: about 81.68KB used
Measured by your phone. Your carrier's data usage accounting may differ.

Google Bookmarks
Sync

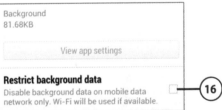

Background
81.68KB

View app settings

Restrict background data
Disable background data on mobile data network only. Wi-Fi will be used if available.

Restrict background data?

This feature may cause an app that depends on background data to stop working when Wi-Fi isn't available.

You can find more appropriate data usage controls in the settings available within the app.

CANCEL   OK

Caring for the Exterior of Your HTC One

Because you need to touch your HTC One's screen to use it, it picks up oils and other residue from your hands. You also might get dirt on other parts of the phone. Here is how to clean your HTC One:

1. Wipe the screen with a microfiber cloth. You can purchase these in most electronic stores, or you can use the one that came with your sunglasses.

2. To clean dirt off other parts of your phone, wipe it with a damp cloth. Never use soap or chemicals on your HTC One because they can damage it.

3. When inserting the Micro-USB connector, try not to force it in the wrong way. If you damage the pins inside your HTC One, you will need to get it repaired before you can recharge it. If your cable's connector does not have an easy-to-see mark on the front, add a piece of tape or a dab of nail varnish so you can easily tell which way the connector goes.

Protecting Your HTC One's Exterior

Another way to care for your HTC One's exterior is to protect it with a case. Many types are available from both bricks-and-mortar stores and online stores. To protect the screen, you can apply a screen protector. When choosing a screen protector, make sure it is thin enough for your touches to register properly but thick enough to give the screen some protection against falls and scratchy objects.

Getting Help with Your HTC One

You can get help with your HTC One through many resources on the Internet:

1. Visit HTC's official HTC One site at www.htc.com/www/smartphones/htc-one/.

2. Visit Google's official Android website at www.android.com.

3. Check out Android blogs such as these:

   - Android Central at www.androidcentral.com/

   - Android Guys at www.androidguys.com/

   - Androinica at androinica.com/

Index

QUEPUBLISHING.COM
Your Publisher for Home & Office Computing

Quepublishing.com includes all your favorite—and some new—Que series and authors to help you learn about computers and technology for the home, office, and business.

Looking for tips and tricks, video tutorials, articles and interviews, podcasts, and resources to make your life easier? Visit **quepublishing.com**.

- **Read the latest articles and sample chapters** by Que's expert authors

- **Free podcasts** provide information on the hottest tech topics

- **Register your Que products** and receive updates, supplemental content, and a coupon to be used on your next purchase

- **Check out promotions and special offers** available from Que and our retail partners

- **Join the site** and receive members-only offers and benefits

QUE NEWSLETTER
quepublishing.com/newslett

 twitter.com/
quepublishing

 facebook.com/
quepublishing

 youtube.com/
quepublishing

 quepublishing.com/
rss

MAKE THE MOST OF YOUR SMARTPHONE, TABLET, COMPUTER, AND MORE!

ISBN 13: 9780789751027

ISBN 13: 9780789752703

ISBN 13: 9780789751669

ISBN 13: 9780789752222

Full-Color, Step-by-Step Guides

The "My..." series is a visually rich, task-based series to help you get up and running with your new device and technology and tap into some of the hidden, or less obvious features. The organized, task-based format allows you to quickly and easily find exactly the task you want to accomplish, and then shows you how to achieve it with minimal text and plenty of visual cues.

Visit quepublishing.com/mybooks to learn more about the My... book series from Que.

quepublishing.com

My HTC One

Craig James Johnston
Guy Hart-Davis

FREE
Online Edition

Your purchase of **My HTC One** includes access to a free online edition for 45 days through the **Safari Books Online** subscription service. Nearly every Que book is available online through **Safari Books Online**, along with thousands of books and videos from publishers such as Addison-Wesley Professional, Cisco Press, Exam Cram, IBM Press, O'Reilly Media, Prentice Hall, Sams, and VMware Press.

Safari Books Online is a digital library providing searchable, on-demand access to thousands of technology, digital media, and professional development books and videos from leading publishers. With one monthly or yearly subscription price, you get unlimited access to learning tools and information on topics including mobile app and software development, tips and tricks on using your favorite gadgets, networking, project management, graphic design, and much more.

Activate your FREE Online Edition at
informit.com/safarifree

STEP 1: Enter the coupon code: GGKBOVH.

STEP 2: New Safari users, complete the brief registration form. Safari subscribers, just log in.

If you have difficulty registering on Safari or accessing the online edition, please e-mail customer-service@safaribooksonline.com